WITH MALICE TOWARD NONE

A War Diary

By the same author

STRICTLY PERSONAL

Cecil Harmsworth King

WITH MALICE TOWARD NONE

a War Diary by
CECIL H. KING

edited by William Armstrong

FAIRLEIGH DICKINSON UNIVERSITY PRESS

Madison · Rutherford · Teaneck

First American Edition 1971

Associated University Presses
Cranbury, N.J. 08512

Copyright © *Times Newspapers Limited 1970*

Library of Congress Catalogue Card Number: 70-175619
ISBN: 0—8386—1067—6

Printed in Great Britain

Contents

CONTENTS

Afterword
page 303

Notes to Text
page 308

Government Changes 1940–1945
page 316

Biographical Notes
page 318

Index
page 329

List of Illustrations

Frontispiece
CECIL HARMSWORTH KING

Between pages 160 and 161
CECIL KING IN AMERICA, 1945
NEVILLE CHAMBERLAIN. 'The old menace' (*Central Press*)
WINSTON CHURCHILL. 'To him war is a vast pageant' (*Popperfoto*)
DAVID LLOYD GEORGE. 'A man head and shoulders over any other politician I have met' (*Black Star*)
THE CITY OF LONDON ON THE NIGHT OF SUNDAY DECEMBER 29, 1940 (*Syndication International*)
CLEMENT ATTLEE. 'He's really not as bad as all that' (*Keystone*)
SIR STAFFORD CRIPPS. 'Embryo premier' (*Central Press*)
LORD BEAVERBROOK. 'Explosive qualities' and 'demoniac energy' (*Radio Times Hulton Picture Library*)
FLEET STREET ON FRIDAY JUNE 30, 1944 (*Syndication International*)

Editor's Note

Cecil King kept his diary regularly over the period 1940 to 1945, and after that spasmodically until 1949. He made it his practice never to reread what he had written in it, and thus the diary is, to use his own words, 'a statement of my news and views at the time, uncoloured by any attempt at consistency'. The original manuscript contains about 400,000 words. I have reduced it to about a quarter of this length.

A large proportion of the original diary is taken up with straightforward recording of the news. Most of this has been removed, together with conversations with the less important figures. What remain are the highlights: a record of great moments of the war, and the great events in Britain in which Cecil King was himself involved; Cecil King's encounters with the leading figures of the day; his personal reactions and experiences during this period; and much else that I thought interesting or amusing.

The diaries have been edited with the general reader in mind. I have added an introduction and a number of explanatory linking passages; footnotes on subjects with which the general reader might not be familiar; short biographical notes on most of the people mentioned in the text; and a chart showing the main Government changes between 1940 and 1945.

I am most grateful to the International Publishing Corporation for their permission to use various headlines from the *Sunday Pictorial* and *Daily Mirror* as illustrations, and also to quote two extracts from Cassandra's column. I am also grateful to C. and T. Publications Limited for permission to publish the letters from Winston Churchill to Cecil King.

Introduction

by WILLIAM ARMSTRONG

Cecil King's war diaries begin in January 1940, in the middle of the Phoney War. For the British public this was a period of anti-climax after the heightened emotions at the outbreak of war; a period of speculation and frustration, and no action; a time of triviality compared with the momentous events of the spring and summer of the coming year.

So far, all large-scale fighting had been confined to the eastern half of Europe. In September 1939 the Wehrmacht destroyed the much overrated Polish army. In November, Russia, in her second act of unprovoked aggression in three months (on September 17 she joined Germany in the invasion of Poland), attacked Finland. The Red Army encountered a more determined and intelligent resistance than it had bargained for, suffered much humiliation, and only in March 1940 managed to break down the Finnish defences.

Meanwhile the British Government did little, and the public yearned almost masochistically for the smack of firm government. The existing administration, which has been described by A.J.P. Taylor as a 'Government of National pretence', inspired few people. It was headed by an undynamic cabal of men who, before the war, had attempted unsuccessfully to appease Hitler and were now trying, unconvincingly, to project themselves as worthy opponents of him.

At the beginning of the war the Prime Minister, Neville Chamberlain, as a warlike gesture brought Winston Churchill into the Government to be First Lord of the Admiralty. This appointment was also a tribute to Churchill's abilities and to the moral authority he had acquired in the pre-war years by constantly denouncing the folly of appeasement. To many people he seemed the only person who could win the war, or at least save the situation.

But even with Churchill in the Government the War Cabinet preferred discussion to action. Many plans were debated – and rejected: floating mines down the Rhine; setting the Black Forest on fire; bombing Russian oil wells in Baku (to stop Hitler getting the oil); even sending an expeditionary force to aid the embattled Finns.

For in the final analysis there was little the Government could do. The initiative rested with Adolf Hitler. And throughout 1940 it was Hitler and Hitler alone who dominated events. It was his attack on Norway in April that brought Churchill to power, and his air offensive against Britain in the late summer that brought the civilian population into the front line.

At the beginning of the war Cecil King was a director of the *Daily Mirror* and the *Sunday Pictorial*. He was aged thirty-eight, and thus unlikely to be called upon for military service. It later transpired that he was also medically unfit, being classed D4 by his examining board.

Debarred from active service, he attempted to find a job in the newly formed Ministry of Information, where he felt that his knowledge of popular psychology, already amply proved by the leading role he had played in resuscitating the *Daily Mirror* and the *Sunday Pictorial*, could be put to good use in the Ministry's propaganda effort. He was interviewed but heard no more about it. He offered himself again on a number of occasions, again without success. It was a surprising rejection, but in keeping with the Ministry's curious preference for amateur propagandists.

Thus, rejected by the Ministry of Information, Cecil King spent his war years in Fleet Street, closely involved in the affairs of two popular newspapers whose combined circulation rose steadily from about 3,750,000 at the beginning of the war to close on 7,500,000 in 1946. During all this time he kept a detailed diary. It was a record of the war, of his reactions to it, and of his meetings and conversations with many of the country's leading politicians and administrators.

Cecil King had begun his newspaper career by working in vacations from Oxford for the *Daily Mail* and *The Times*, which were both owned by his uncle Alfred Harmsworth, Lord Northcliffe. After leaving Oxford he began work in 1922 for the *Glasgow Record*, owned by another Harmsworth uncle, Lord Rothermere.

The brothers Northcliffe and Rothermere were, to say the least, remarkable men. Northcliffe, 'the Napoleon of Fleet Street', was a journalistic genius, a man with an almost infallible instinct for what interested his working-class and middle-class readers. Apart from his *Daily Mail*, which under his direction in the years before the First World War achieved the world's greatest newspaper sale, he at one time owned *The Times*, the *Daily Mirror*, the *Evening News*, and a number of popular magazines. In 1914 he sold the *Mirror* to Rothermere, who also bought the *Daily Mail* and the *Evening News* after Northcliffe's death in 1922, *The Times* being bought by John Astor.

Rothermere was no journalist, but an able financier. One example of his business acumen was his launch of the *Sunday Pictorial* in 1915. This he brought out at very short notice, two weeks before the Sunday version of the *Daily Sketch*. By thus taking advantage of its rival's pre-publication publicity, the *Pictorial* achieved an immediate sale of 1,000,000. In 1926 Lord Rothermere's fortune was said to have been worth about £26,000,000. He lost a good deal of it in the Wall Street crash of 1929, and it was further diminished at that time by an expensive and losing battle with the Berry family for control of the provincial press. When he died in 1940 he left £300,000 before death duties.

Rothermere lacked Northcliffe's editorial flair. He involved his papers in bizarre campaigns, for instance against 'squandermania'. Another of his press campaigns ('Hats off to Hungary') was for the revision of the post-war Treaty of Trianon, which had drastically reduced Hungary's boundaries: his energetic championship of the Hungarians, a nation about which the British knew little and cared nothing, resulted in his being offered the crown of Hungary (which he refused). More sinister, he developed Fascist sympathies which were clearly reflected in the *Daily Mail*, though not in the *Mirror* or the *Pictorial*, in both of which he sold his interest in 1931.

Cecil King spent his first nine months of regular employment with Rothermere's profitable but uninspired *Glasgow Record*. Then he joined the *Daily Mail* and worked there for three years until 1926, when he was made assistant advertising manager of the *Mirror*. In 1929 he became its advertising director.

Both the *Daily Mirror* and the *Sunday Pictorial* had fallen on evil days. In 1933 the *Mirror*'s circulation – during the First World War larger than any other daily in the world – was 800,000 and falling at the rate of about 70,000 copies a year. Cecil King came to the conclusion that the only way to sell advertising was to increase the sale. 'Drifting around the office,' he wrote, 'a director of long standing but with no real job, was Guy Bartholomew. He had ideas, I had good judgment, so we put our heads together.' Thus began the famous journalistic revolution which resulted eventually in the *Mirror* achieving for the second time the world's largest daily sale.

Bartholomew (known generally as 'Bart') was nearly illiterate. But his wayward editorial genius was to be an essential element in the *Mirror*'s formula for success. He had strong visual sense – he had at one time been the *Mirror*'s picture editor – and it was to him that the revolutionized *Mirror* owed its challenging, dramatic appearance. He had also a natural sympathy for the underdog and the underprivileged, to whom the new *Mirror* made its strongest appeal.

Cecil King provided the paper with firm political guidance. The *Mirror* became a paper of the Left. It was now aimed at a working-class readership and not at the middle classes as hitherto. It began to cater for women in a way it had never done before, with special features and more human-interest stories. Cecil King's criterion for judging any story was: Would it interest a bus driver's wife in Sheffield? It was the first British paper to exploit strip cartoons, as Jane, Garth, and others – fantastic,

potent, and lovable – began their famous careers. About sex, the
Mirror became increasingly frank, disregarding the hackneyed
euphemisms of other papers and providing pictures of lovely
girls, perhaps now merely picturesque but then with undoubted
sex-appeal. The *Mirror* recruited a talented staff, including the
famous columnist William Connor ('Cassandra'), and Hugh
Cudlipp, one of the great popular journalists of the century, who
at the age of twenty-one became its features editor.

By the outbreak of war in 1939 the *Mirror*'s circulation had
risen by a million to 1,750,000. By 1943 it had passed 2,000,000,
by 1946 3,000,000, and by 1948 4,000,000.

The decline of the *Pictorial* continued unaffected by the early
successes of the new *Mirror* regime. Its circulation of 2,500,000
in 1927 had dropped to 1,300,000 by 1937. In that year Cecil
King became its editorial director, taking Hugh Cudlipp with
him from the *Mirror* as editor. Bartholomew, who remained editorial director of the *Mirror*, reacted malevolently to this move.
He respected but did not like Cecil King. Nor did he like the
Sunday Pictorial, having played an important part in its successful
launch without ever having been given what he considered his
due reward. Bartholomew told Cudlipp to expect no help from
him on the *Pictorial*, a promise which he faithfully kept.

The attentions of King and Cudlipp transformed the *Pictorial*.
By the outbreak of war it was selling nearly 2,000,000, and by
1946 nearly 4,000,000.

The *Pictorial* was given the same shock treatment as the *Mirror*.
Before the King–Cudlipp take-over, the first issue of 1937 had
proclaimed on its front page: 'BRASS BANDS PLAY TO
CATERPILLARS'. The front page of the first issue of 1938
symbolizes the change of emphasis: 'MONA TINSLEY'S
SPIRIT LED HER SLAYER TO THE GALLOWS'.

From being a nondescript amalgam of news and views with
vaguely right-wing politics, the *Pictorial* became a sensational
organ of the Left. It talked directly to its readers: 'SHHH . . .
THIS IS BABY'S PAGE'. It was packed with human interest:
'MANIAC KILLER SLAIN IN HIS FLOATING SOUTH
SEAS HAREM', 'TRYST IN LOVE TOMB DENIED'. There
were true confessions, advice to the love-lorn, lots about babies,

and more of those long-legged 1930s girls with their permed hair
and inviting simpers.

From the moment King and Cudlipp took it over, however,
the *Pictorial* had a serious and consistent purpose: to make the
British public realize that what was happening in Europe really
affected them, that it was folly to try to appease the dictators,
that the only talk to which these untrustworthy men would listen
was from a position of strength. And so the *Pictorial* urged Britain:
'ARM! ARM! ARM!' adding: 'Our Army is only playing at
soldiers ... 1918 weapons ... 1918 brains,' and: 'No more boot-
licking is nation's verdict.'

Cecil King and Hugh Cudlipp, under the pseudonym of
Charles Wilberforce (other directors objected to them using their
own names for political articles), wrote often and powerfully on
this theme. 'We have seen, during the past years,' wrote Wilberforce in 1938, 'the prestige of Britain steadily waning. We have
seen our counsels scouted. We have heard dictators' braggarts
insult us ...' 'Only a great modern army, a mighty navy,
and an invincible air fleet can guarantee the safety of our
hearths.'

The *Pictorial*'s views on the international and military situation
were those of Cecil King. His opinions were more prominent in
the *Pictorial* under his direct control than they had been in the
Mirror. They were very similar to those of Winston Churchill,
and it should be pointed out that in the years before the war,
Churchill's was not the only 'voice in the wilderness'. There was
Cecil King's *Sunday Pictorial* crying alarm to its rapidly growing
readership. No other newspaper was so consistent – or so right –
in its views on the international situation.

In 1939 Churchill was asked to contribute political articles to
the *Mirror*, and Cecil King was deputed to be the link between
him and that paper. Churchill wrote regularly until the outbreak
of war in September, when he became First Lord of the Admiralty.
After that, both papers continued to give him all possible support.
On October 1, 1939 the *Pictorial* prophesied: 'Churchill will be
our next premier.' Both papers attacked Chamberlain and his
ministers, 'the dynasty of yes-men', and urged their replacement

by a younger team. 'There are many enfeebled trees to fell before
we plant sturdy saplings,' wrote Cudlipp.

Nothing surpassed the vigorous patriotism of the *Mirror* and the
Pictorial. The *Pictorial* proclaimed: 'THE ENEMIES OF THIS
NEWSPAPER ARE THE ENEMIES OF BRITAIN'. Lloyd
George, who had led Britain to victory in 1918, provoked the
Pictorial's ire by suggesting in the early months of the Second
World War a negotiated peace. He received brutal treatment on
the front page: 'WE ACCUSE LLOYD GEORGE!... the
Marshal of the weak and the terrorized.' But he soon afterwards
became a regular contributor. Whatever differences he and the
Pictorial might have over the terms for ending the war, they were
at one in their denunciation of the Government's conduct of it.

At the beginning of January 1940 Hugh Cudlipp travelled
down to Lloyd George's farm to discuss future articles with the
old man, then seventy-six, still with a 'mind like a scorpion', and
now conscious that one day he might again be called upon to lead
his country. The first entry of Cecil King's diary for 1940 concerns
Cudlipp's report on his visit.

1940

N.B. At the end of the book there are brief biographical notes on most of the people mentioned in Cecil King's war diaries. With a few exceptions these notes deal only with the period covered by the diaries. There is also a chart showing the main Government changes between 1940 and 1945.

January 3, 1940
Cudlipp had lunch with Lloyd George in the country and spent about four hours with him. Lloyd George very active and communicative, though very pessimistic. Considered that we had been completely outwitted and outmanoeuvred in the last five years. Though he did not actually say so, he left Cudlipp with the impression that to seize a peace move in 1942 or '43 was the only alternative to military defeat. He considered the Russo–German Pact [August 1939] had nullified our naval blockade. He referred to the *Daily Express*' 'No war this year – or next' campaign, and said that Beaverbrook really believed there would be no war. Chamberlain told him so! (This campaign was run in the *Express* both before and after Munich.[1])

Discussing the events of the past ten years, Lloyd George sneered at Baldwin and at Chamberlain, whom he called 'a second-rater'. Cudlipp asked him why, then, he did not attack Chamberlain in public. 'Oh, I wouldn't like to make a personal attack upon him.' He meant this, Cudlipp said. Cudlipp also asked him how long it would take to shift Chamberlain. 'It will take longer to get rid of Chamberlain than you think. It took two years for Asquith to go in the last war. He was an abler man, but there were more alternatives at hand.'

He went on to speak of Churchill. 'I told Churchill three weeks ago that he was unwise to take the job at the Admiralty. If he succeeds in sinking all the German U-boats, he'll be very popular. But what if they launch 400 new ones? What if there are serious reverses? Winston will get it in the neck.' Cudlipp asked what was Churchill's reply. 'Oh,' said Lloyd George, 'Winston's enjoying the job and, of course, the Admiralty places him among the first three [ministers in the Government]. But mind you,' he added quickly, 'that's not what Winston said himself – that's what I think he meant.' If Churchill were to become Prime Minister, Lloyd George thought he would fail as a picker of men, that he was far too apt to choose people he liked regardless of their capacity.

On Daladier [*the French premier*] he was very bitter. Said he was an insignificant little fool sodden with Pernod. That he got up and made absurdly optimistic speeches to the Chamber when drunk and, when it had passed off, was merely a stupid and weak little man, his face blotched with alcohol.

On Hore-Belisha Lloyd George said: 'Lazy. I am told that officials at the War Office don't like him. But, of course, the generals didn't like me.'

On Haig: 'Haig was a very small man. When I discussed Haig's war diaries with Duff Cooper (who wrote the biography), Duff Cooper said that the whole of the material he had to work on was very trivial. He would plough through Haig's diary dealing with the events on the eve of a big battle and would find a long ver-batim account of the sermon he had heard in a French church the day before!'

Lloyd George thought Italy would remain neutral throughout the war; didn't believe finance would prove a vital factor in war economy; was not worried about Russian aggression in Scandi-navia; was much more bothered about a Russian thrust to India through Persia.

Talking of Churchill and Poland he said: 'Churchill telephoned me three weeks before the war and told me Hitler's latest terms for a Danzig settlement.[2] Winston said: "I think they are not unreasonable," and I agreed with him.

'The people who say Hitler is a fool are mad themselves. He is not epileptic. He has a fine head.

'This is a damn crazy war. For years the menace of Germany has been rising, but what did Baldwin do? He was too lazy to make a great decision. He thought it would shock the people of this country too much. He didn't have the courage that was necessary in a Prime Minister at that moment. We let Manchuria go to Japan; we allowed an interference in Spain, in spite of the peril to our Mediterranean sea routes which a Franco Spain would cause. We did nothing about Austria, nothing about the Rhine, nothing about Czechoslovakia. And then, when it was strategically and emotionally impossible for us to do a damn thing, we cried a halt at Poland.

'People call me a defeatist,' he said, 'but what I say to them is this: Tell me how we can win! Can we win in the air? Can we win at sea, when the effect of our naval blockade is wiped out by Germany's connections with Russia? How can we win on the land? The Germans cannot get through the Maginot Line: when do you think we can get through the Siegfried Line? Not until the trumpet blows, my friend. Even if Hitler marches into Holland and Belgium it will be to get nearer England, to build submarine bases and aerodromes; not, in my view, to invade France. In what field can action be decisive, for either side? In none. Hitler cannot win any more than we can – and he has the brains to see it. The war will drag wearily on. There will be no spectacular appeals to the emotions. The people will become bored and dreary, and in the end they won't stand for it. There is no excitement in a war like this. In the end they will demand peace.'

Discussing possible contributions to the Sunday Pic, Lloyd George said: 'I cannot write what I believe to be untrue. I cannot tell the public that we shall win, when I think that a victory is impossible for either side. This view has been forming in my mind for many months and I wanted to do all I could to hold Europe back from this horrible mess. Then – what did I find? I found that Liddell Hart had come to the same conclusion. Liddell Hart is a great man. He is the greatest military writer of our time. And he is a philosopher and a man of courage, too. I admire him more than I can tell you. Writing about war is his livelihood, and he has had the courage to give it up. He was military correspondent of *The Times*, and he refused to carry on because they wanted him to write a lot of optimistic slush.'

Cudlipp asked him what he would do if forced to be Prime Minister now. He walked up and down and dodged the question. When it was brought up again he said: 'That's all very well. It's all very well for the country to get in a devil of a mess and then to ask somebody to pull it out, when it is too late. Nothing can be done – nothing at all.' Cudlipp's final impression was that Lloyd George thinks we shall lose the war.

Sensational news in a dull period: the dismissal of Britain's War Minister, Leslie Hore-Belisha. It was not a straightforward dismissal. Chamberlain offered him the Board of Trade instead of the War Office. But Hore-Belisha refused it and resigned.

Hore-Belisha, a reforming War Minister who introduced conscription and promoted Harold Alexander to be the youngest major-general in the British Army, had fallen foul of the generals. The immediate cause of his dismissal was his criticism of the defences erected by the British Expeditionary Force on the frontier of France and Belgium. The generals, resenting this interference, brought pressure to bear on Chamberlain to get rid of him. Churchill was not, as Hore-Belisha suspected, in the plot; but he certainly gave Hore-Belisha no support.

The Government managed to keep Hore-Belisha quiet after his resignation by suggesting that if he behaved himself he would be back in office soon. In the event, he was out of office for the rest of the war.

January 5, 1940
Was rung up about 9.30 by Cudlipp to say Belisha had resigned from the War Office. Letters exchanged between him and Chamberlain make it evident that he was offered the Board of Trade, but preferred to take dismissal.

January 6, 1940
To the office at 3.0, where I find Cudlipp had had breakfast with Belisha. Sitting on Belisha's bed, Cudlipp heard the whole story.

Apparently Belisha had no suspicion whatever that any trouble was brewing, and was as surprised as anyone when he was asked to move from the War Office to the Board of Trade. The story as told by Belisha to Cudlipp was taken down by him, and this is a condensed version.

'Chamberlain sent for me on December 24. He was highly congratulatory, and said he had complete confidence in me and the highest admiration for my work. "It will live in the Ministry," he said, "and you will be remembered as the greatest War Minister." Chamberlain went on to discuss various aspects of my work and asked: "Have you got complete confidence in Gort?" "Yes," I said. "Have you got complete confidence in Ironside?" Before I replied he told me his opinion of Ironside: "I hear nothing but evil of him," and he described Ironside as an intriguer. I disagreed and praised Ironside and did not want to change him.

'On January 4, Chamberlain sent for me again. He opened with more praise for me. Then he said there had been a lot of prejudice. "I am rearranging the Cabinet, and it is in your interest that they should get you out." I was staggered. "If you go now, history will do justice to you," and he repeated that it was better for them to get me out. That was in my own interest, he said, and he mentioned criticism and prejudice.'

B. 'This is completely amazing.'

Ch. 'I am offering you the Board of Trade and am sure you will accept it.' Belisha wanted to think it over.

Ch. 'Think it over? Surely you do not hesitate?' An argument followed and Chamberlain pressed hard for Belisha's immediate acceptance.

B. 'But what is the reason for the hurry, in any case?'

Ch. 'Well, there must obviously be no leakage.'

B. 'But how can there be a leakage? Who else knows about this?

Ch. 'Oh — not a soul.'

Ch. 'You can't possibly refuse a post in the Cabinet. The public will think there is a difference of opinion; it will be bad. Besides, what will you do? You are an ambitious man.'

B. 'Of course I am ambitious. You are yourself. Is there any M.P. who doesn't want to be Prime Minister? Is there any waiter who doesn't want to be head waiter? But I have lived for the War Office. I regard it as my great job in life.'

Chamberlain, pressing hard for a decision: 'I'm offering you another post. Your attitude is extraordinary. Lloyd George once threw me out altogether — and look at me now.'

An hour after the interview Chamberlain wrote Belisha a personal letter. It was four pages long, amazingly friendly, and almost sentimental. In it was a story about Neville [Chamberlain]. It was most macabre. Neville saw a soldier about to be executed: 'You are making a great sacrifice,' said Neville to the soldier!

They met again on Friday [January 5] at ten o'clock:

Ch. 'Is your decision irrevocable?'

B. 'Yes.'

Ch. 'Well, how can you tell the public?'

B. 'I suppose I'll have to write a letter.'

Ch. 'Not a nasty letter, of course. The public must not think there are any differences in the Cabinet.' Chamberlain strongly requested Belisha to insert a sentence: 'I am glad to think there is no difference of policy between us.'

B. 'You are going to give no reason, Prime Minister?'

Ch. 'It's all prejudice – prejudice and criticism.'

B. 'What prejudice?' Chamberlain would go no further.

B. 'But it's staggering, the whole thing. Only a fortnight ago you sent for me to praise me. I take it that this prejudice was in existence then? What you are doing is to deliver me up to my enemies. How can I take another post now? You will let me down again. I'm absolutely staggered and perplexed. I can't go to Clarkson's and put a wig on and turn up as somebody else next week.' The interview finished with Chamberlain making further vague references to prejudice. He thanked Belisha for his work at the War Office and again expressed his personal liking and admiration.

Belisha told Cudlipp there had been no controversy between himself and the generals, though a small clique didn't like his reforms.

Belisha: 'Of course the Palace was in it.'

Cudlipp: 'How?'

Belisha: 'Well, they worked through those quarters.'

Cudlipp: 'Was that the pressure Chamberlain referred to?'

Belisha: 'I can only tell you, old man, what I know. The Duke of Gloucester is in the Army, remember, and they worked through him. Complaints about too much democracy in the ranks – all that sort of rubbish.'

January 13, 1940

Cudlipp had another long session with Belisha yesterday evening, and discussed the speech he is to make in the House on Tuesday [January 16]. On reflection Belisha feels sure Churchill must have known about his impending dismissal, and also fairly sure that Churchill is intending to become Defence Minister. The reason is presumably that things may go wrong in the Navy, and if he were Defence Minister his risks would be spread. Belisha said he learned that Churchill had dinner several times with Ironside in the last month or so, and he is convinced that Ironside is in the plot.

When asked why Churchill didn't use the opportunity to resign and force Chamberlain out, Belisha said that clearly Churchill assumed Belisha would take the Board of Trade; secondly, that he was out of the country and could not quickly take advantage of the situation when Belisha refused it; thirdly, that in any case he is a bad political tactician and probably did not see his chance.

Belisha now considers himself in a wonderful position heading straight for the premiership. He appeared surprised when Cudlipp mentioned what a handicap his Jewish birth was for the future, as anti-Semitic feeling was likely to grow rather than the reverse in wartime. Asked if he thought of crossing the floor of the House to the Labour Party, he said he would not. His main reason appeared to be that the material in the Labour Party was of such poor quality that it would be impossible with it to form a Government which would stand up in wartime.

January 17, 1940

So the Belisha episode ended in a complete fizzle. Belisha made an innocuous speech about nothing. Up to Saturday night he was determined to fight; on Monday night he rang up Cudlipp and was less sure about the wisdom of fighting; and when the moment came he climbed meekly down. Chamberlain made a speech denying that Belisha had had any disagreement with anyone, but declined to give any reasons for the dismissal.

Later in the evening Belisha traced Cudlipp to a theatre and asked him on the phone what he thought of his speech. Cudlipp was fairly frank and critical. Belisha said he had asked Lloyd George's opinion, and he was highly complimentary. Of the speech Cudlipp had prepared for him, and which he had repeatedly expressed his determination to use, the only phrase preserved was about making 'the Army too democratic to fight for democracy'. This morning this is the only phrase picked out by all the newspapers, which frankly regard the whole debate as an anticlimax. The *Telegraph* and *Times* take a line complimentary to Belisha on his discretion; and all assume he will get another job, probably a Ministry of Economic Co-ordination. If this is so, why refuse the Board of Trade? It seems to me that by refusing the Board of Trade, Belisha was making a bid for real power in the years to come; and by backing down yesterday he is resigning his chances (if any) of the premiership, and is putting himself in the same position as Duff Cooper and Eden, who resigned but won't fight,[3] and expect to be recalled to the Cabinet for being good and causing no trouble. Eden in the spring of 1938 occupied the centre of the stage by his resignation of the Foreign Office, and where is he now? Kicking his heels in the Dominions Office and almost forgotten by the country.

January 26, 1940

Under the censorship regulations we are not allowed to mention spies in any way at all. The best spy story I have heard was told me by Campbell [Pictorial *news editor*], who is distracted at being unable to use it. It appears that there was at Gloucester a concern called the Severn Pie Company, which specialized in delivering pies to workmen at factories at dinner time. One day a woman who wanted a pie from the Severn Pie Co.'s shop after closing time went round to the back to where the manager lived, and found him poring over plans. She told her husband, who was a special constable, and he was watched. It appeared that among the factories he served was the Gloster aeroplane works. He never sold all his pies there, but took back some unsold. In one of

these unsold pies every day was a blueprint of part of one of the
Gloster aeroplanes. The pieman was arrested and interned on
September 14, but the man inside the factory escaped.

January 31, 1940
Cudlipp had lunch today with Belisha to discuss his writing for
the *Sunday Pictorial* at £150 a time for six months. Belisha had been
offered £100 by *The Sunday Times* and £250 by the *Sunday Express*,
but values Cudlipp's help and so will probably take our offer. He
was visited by Simon the other day on what Simon himself
described as a 'semi-official' visit. The guts of the interview seemed
to be that the Cabinet is windy and hopes Belisha will not write
for the papers.

Belisha said that the Prime Minister had thought Belisha would
take the Board of Trade; when he did not, he was surprised. The
Press support Belisha got surprised Chamberlain still more and
made him uneasy. So much so that the Whips and Chamberlain
himself spread a whispering campaign about Belisha and com-
missions on Army contracts (all by then arranged by the Ministry
of Supply anyway!); about his quarrels with Gort; about his
interference in strategy – stories all of which were untrue. Finally,
through the Conservative Central Office, they engineered a very
bitter article in *Truth*,[4] which attacked his financial record as a
director of companies in the 1928–29 boom, and incidentally
described the *Daily Mirror*, for supporting him, as the 'Jew-
controlled sink of Fleet Street'. As part of this campaign, Belisha
said, Lady Astor was going round saying he had feathered his
nest on Army contracts. This campaign filled in the gap between
Belisha's dismissal and the meeting of Parliament. Imagine their
relief when he said nothing in the debate.

Belisha also said Chamberlain has no central plan of any kind:
all Cabinet business is conducted from hand to mouth and rarely
looks even one week ahead.

Belisha says it was he who pressed the Ministry of Supply, and
conscription, on the Government. Some time last year he made a
speech at Cardiff in which he urged conscription and a Ministry
of Supply. This was taken to mean that the Cabinet as a whole was
favourably considering the matter. Actually Belisha put all this

in on his own initiative. As soon as Chamberlain heard of it, he rang Belisha up on the phone, ordered him back to London, and flew at him when they met. In the course of the ensuing conversation Chamberlain told him that his reason for not introducing conscription was that it would cause an upheaval of popular opinion amounting to a revolution – this a year or more after the *Mirror* had been urging it on the Government and knew from its post-bag that it would go down all right!

February 2, 1940
Cudlipp reported in the evening that Hore-Belisha had decided to write for the *News of the World* at £300 a time. We had gone up to £200 and *The Sunday Times* to £150. Personally, if I had been he, I should have given my story to the *Sunday Express*, a good-class paper that had given him the staunchest of political support. Alternatively, to *The Sunday Times*, which would help impress the Colonel Blimps who are mostly anti-Belisha. The Sunday Pic has given him most support, the *Mail* crowd have been helpful, but by writing for the *News of the World* he is pleasing a paper which will not help him politically, which will not put him over at all, and which will not be quoted.

February 8, 1940
Had lunch with Churchill today. The party consisted of Mr, Mrs, Miss Mary [Churchill], a Miss White (a cousin), and an American woman who talked too much. Mrs Winston is a very good-looking woman, with good eyes and good features, but rather thin, dried up, and nervy. The daughter, aged seventeen or eighteen, is a real winner: huge eyes, big mouth, wide across the eyes, and a full figure. Winston wore black boots with zip fasteners, the first I have seen. At lunch the conversation was general for a bit, i.e. largely monologue by the American, then suddenly Winston said: 'How do you think the war is going?' I said that was a large question. He said: 'You shouldn't be afraid to answer large questions.' I said: 'Well, put like that: not very well.' From then on we talked mainly politics and the war – say for an hour or so in all, the latter half of the time alone with him after the ladies had withdrawn.

When I saw him in May or June, he spoke of Belisha without affection, but said he was one of the best men Chamberlain had. But on this occasion his whole attitude was quite different. He said that he had formed a very poor opinion of Belisha's conduct of public business since the beginning of the war; that though he had to give him credit for the introduction of conscription, he thought the work of the War Office would go forward more smoothly and expeditiously under Stanley [*Belisha's successor*]; that the War Office ('and not particularly the brass hats': meaning the civil servants there?) were delighted to see the last of the man; that for Belisha's sake – this more in sorrow (the old humbug!) than in anger – he was sorry he did not take the Board of Trade when it was offered him, but that now he thought it was as well he had not (referring to his impending contributions to the *News of the World*? or to Andrew Duncan, the new President of the Board of Trade, of whom Churchill spoke very highly?).

Mrs Churchill then chipped in and said Belisha even had to have his papers read out to him, and the American said he never got out of bed till 11.0 (this is very widely stated and may be true). I said I thought that judged by the very low standard of the present Government Belisha was quite good. Mary Churchill clapped her hands at my mention of the poor quality of the present Government and thanked me for saying it! From their references to the excellence of Stanley's speech at Newcastle this week, I got the impression that Churchill is very pro-Stanley – probably mainly on social grounds – which confirms my guess on Churchill's part in the downfall of Belisha and the promotion of Stanley.

On Chamberlain Churchill said he had formed a better opinion of him since he had worked with him; that he was very tough, and a hundred per cent for vigorous prosecution of the war. I said he was too old, of dreary appearance, with a sorry record of appeasement, and that his speeches were dreary and lacked substance. In fact that he lacked all the qualities of leadership in anxious times; that the country regarded Churchill as leader, and yet he had not the authority of a Prime Minister. Churchill said the premiership was not much of a catch these days and that he would only take it if offered him by common consent; that he would not take the job as a prize in a fight, as then he would have two fights on his hands – with his opponents in the Party and with the Germans. His attitude was that Chamberlain had the entire support of the Conservative Party; therefore he was quite safe. And public opinion? To hell with public opinion. And Churchill actually said that anyway in time of war the machinery of Government is so strong it can afford largely to ignore popular feeling.

He also said that he would rather have Chamberlain than Eden as Prime Minister by eight to one. I should get the opinion that his advice carries much weight with the Prime Minister, that he likes being at the Admiralty, and has no particular reason to change the present arrangement. He thinks we are going to win – he doesn't know how, or why, or when – so why worry? Of the current trends of political thought in England, on the Continent, or elsewhere, he knows little and cares less. I told him that *US*, the new newsletter put out by the Mass Observation people [*a market research organization*], had made an investigation into popular choice for the next Prime Minister: that he came easily first and Eden easily second, and almost bottom among the also-rans came Sir John Simon – below H.G. Wells and Professor Joad! He was rather amused and asked to see a copy, so I sent him one with a book they brought out this week. I doubt whether it will, any of it, sink in. But the material is all illustration of the vast gulf at present separating the leaders from the led in this country.

I said I thought Hitler had done more harm to us by not bombing than he could have done by bombing. Churchill didn't agree and didn't seem to see what I meant. He seemed to think discontent in this country could only come from boredom with rationing and the black-out. I said the rationing was popular except for the impending meat rationing, which would hit the working classes harder, and that the trouble would be low morale due to lack of leadership, possibly leading to an irresistible demand for peace. Churchill didn't seem to see the importance of leadership, or else thought he could make up for all Chamberlain's deficiencies, and was apparently quite unaware of the strength of the peace movement, which I have heard put at 30% of the Labour Party plus, of course, the old women of both sexes and all classes.

He thought a strong stabilizing influence in the war is the fact that very large numbers of the working classes, particularly women, will soon be making more money than in peacetime. Personally, I think this harping on money as the final essential factor is obsolete and was only appropriate in the last war and earlier. Churchill said the Labour Party presses the Government very hard, and fatuously seemed to think it could at a pinch turn the Government out. I asked him why the Government submitted to such pressure – after all, Attlee has no support in the country and the Government could just defy the present Labour leadership. Churchill took a poor view of the Labour leaders, and said they wanted to win the war and *then* give away our colonies (presumably the ex-German colonies). What weakness! What folly!

I understand the *Exeter*, the cruiser most knocked about by the *Graf Spee*,[5] is returning quite soon. Churchill of course didn't admit this, but I pressed him to bring the cruiser up the Thames. He said what was the good of that ? It could only come up to the Pool (which is the centre of London, though not of his London), and people couldn't go on board. I said surely they could go up one gangway, along a bit of deck, and down another? Mary Churchill said: 'And what about a dinner for the men?' Mrs Churchill said: 'Yes. In the Guildhall.' I said I thought a march through London to a dinner at Olympia would bring all London out in the wildest welcome for years. I thought Churchill was considering this. It would, of course, be the biggest event in London since the war began.

From the course of our conversation, I would gather that Churchill is not planning anything so definite as becoming Defence Minister, though I hear on all sides he is playing a stronger hand over the whole field of government.

He told us the destroyer he and the others went to France in for the meeting of the Supreme War Council met several mines, he presumed British, on the way. One they hit with a shell and, instead of sinking or going off, the top flew up in the air (like a lid) and came hurtling towards them. Churchill said it was rather frightening, as it weighed fully fifty pounds and they couldn't tell quite where it would fall. It landed in the sea a good way short of their ship.

I asked had he thought of moving from the Admiralty as, if things went wrong, he might get the blame; and in any case, as the war was so largely at sea, any move that would shift Chamberlain would probably shift him too, and then the public would have no one to turn to in their distress. He said he had no intention of moving: he would rather be First Lord without a seat in the War Cabinet, than have a seat in the War Cabinet without portfolio; that the nation values what you do, not what you say; that he was not like Sam Hoare, who ran away from the Admiralty to the Home Office because he thought the former was politically dangerous and then, when at the Home Office, refused to have anything to do with A.R.P. [*Air-Raid Precautions*] because that, too, was dangerous.

Churchill attached importance to the fact that the Germans were putting out peace feelers in all sorts of hole-and-corner ways. He thought this showed the Germans to be uneasy, and afraid of the war's outcome. I don't think it proves anything. If the Germans can get us to sign an armistice now they have us where they want us. We should not make another great war effort on any account for several years, and in those years the Germans could take anything that struck their fancy. In fact, peace now would be a victory for Germany, leading in about eighteen months' time to our complete downfall. One would expect Hitler, seeing this and preferring a bloodless victory to the other kind, to try all out for peace. All these moves prove to me is that the Germans' psychological summing up of the position is better than that of our War Cabinet.

Churchill, in spite of my very plain speaking, was very friendly, saw me into the lift at Admiralty House, and pressed me to come again when I felt like it. He looked puffy and old, drank port and beer alternately at lunch – ending with beer – and praised the nectarines which Mary Churchill said she had got from the crêpe-de-chine counter at John Barker's. The American woman brought him a bottle of brandy: Churchill said he was glad it would keep as he had given up brandy for the present.

I left at 3.15 as he prepared for his siesta. He told me he works from 7.0 a.m. to 1.30, has his lunch and a sleep and resumes later, finishing at 1.30 a.m. He said long as he works, Chamberlain works longer, his years in the Bahamas having made him a 'tough buccaneer'.

February 14, 1940
William Sempill sees a lot of Lord Birdwood. When the latter was Commander-in-Chief in India there was some trouble over a convent, long reports were drawn up and a mass of papers collected, which he had to read. He was startled by coming across a passage stating that the nuns had violated their cows (for 'vows'). Some previous student of the report had scribbled in the margin: 'Situation evidently calls for a Papal Bull.'

February 16, 1940
It is now announced that the men of the *Ajax* and *Exeter* are to be entertained to dinner at the Guildhall and that they are to march through the streets of London, but it is not thought that the *Exeter* will be brought up the Thames. Whether these decisions owe much to what I said to Winston last week, I don't know, but I should rather think they do.

I saw Healy today, our correspondent with the French army in France. He is stationed at Nancy and has been twice over the whole French line from Luxembourg to Switzerland. The various French generals he meets are prepared to discuss German plans, but not French ones. They talk of a German advance through Belgium or Switzerland without much conviction, though they are obviously hoping that something of the sort may happen. They are *not* expecting a frontal attack on the Maginot Line.

March 9, 1940
Cudlipp saw Liddell Hart this morning and had a short chat with him. Asked what we could do, Liddell Hart said come to the best possible terms as soon as possible. He said he was a scientific student of war and appraised the state of affairs from that standpoint: though clearly an English Napoleon might well triumph over any difficulties. But barring Napoleons on either side, he considered we have no chance of avoiding defeat.

3

March 20, 1940

Had asked to see Eden some time, and he fixed 6.0 p.m. today. The Colonial Office, of which Dominions is a part railed off, is a gloomy place – great high ceilings, enormous wide empty passages, tiled floors, and drab walls – the whole effect incredibly gloomy and depressing. Eden sat at a large desk at the far end of a large gloomy room, a sort of dining table in the middle with several chairs around, and three oil paintings on the wall: 17th-century portraits I should say.

He said he had had lunch with Churchill alone today, and expressed the warmest admiration for him. Churchill full of ideas – not all good, but how could they be with a man who had so many? Eden also expressed admiration for Archie Sinclair and said he would like to see him in the Government. I said there were widespread rumours that he will shortly join the Government: Eden either didn't know or was not to be drawn. Like Churchill he made a great point of Chamberlain's belligerency, but the point surely turns now not on Chamberlain's willingness to wage war but on his capacity.

In the course of further conversation I expressed the view that we were heading for defeat, that the war could certainly not be won by anyone of Chamberlain's age nor by anyone with the very limited capacity of many of his colleagues; that a livening up of the war or its continued stagnation would have profound political consequences which might well result in Eden's being handed the premiership in circumstances that might then be impossible. He deprecated any mention of his popularity – I told him Mass Observation reported him as the second (to Churchill) most popular choice as next Prime Minister – and seemed, like Churchill, to have a very faint idea of how great it is. They both seem dominated by the House of Commons attitude, and to overlook the 50,000,000 people outside.

I mentioned the hostile attitude of the newspapers to the Government and told him (he was quite unaware of the fact) that in the last war the newspapers were absolutely uncritical until the shell scandal[6] broke out, and that they would prefer not to criticize now. Under these circumstances was it not a point requiring more attention that the Press, even to the sycophantic

Daily Telegraph, was all so critical or hostile? Eden thought, I gathered, that my language about some of his colleagues was a bit too strong, but he was very friendly, saw me half way out of the building, and said we must have a bite of lunch together after Easter: it was so refreshing to get a different point of view.

My impression of Eden was that he was most charming, most intelligent, but as a future leader quite pathetic. When I saw him in the summer he was, of course, out of office and pretty bitter about Chamberlain and his Government. When next I saw him it was in October [1939], and then he told me that we should not be able to take the initiative until May 1941. I said then that in that event the great problem of the Government was to keep up the interest and morale of the Army and the civil population through such a long period of inaction. This had apparently not occurred to him or them! However, while fairly unconvincing, he was realistic compared with what he was today. He made it quite clear that he had got caught up in the routine of Government: there were no signs of wide views or long views. I should say that the attitude of the Government was hand to mouth, their policy a day-to-day improvisation, which is why Hitler is always too quick for them.

Eden has no independent point of view, has clearly no intention of upsetting the existing political status quo; is in fact a very small straw on the current of events, with no ambition to be anything else. Really, as I walked down Whitehall after leaving him, I was nearly in tears.

April 5, 1940
Saw Rothermere at the Savoy, where he is staying as his staff at Avenue Road has measles. The doctors say there is nothing specifically wrong with him, but he is in the depths of depression and *will* stay in bed. Clearly he thinks he is dying and equally clearly his entourage think he is going out of his mind. I was with him for about three-quarters of an hour, in the course of which he gave me an Elizabethan tiger-ware jug mounted in silver. It had belonged to William Randolph Hearst, who had paid about £800 for it, but Rothermere bought it in a sale last July for £90.

Rothermere talked about the war but he was not very clear in his views. He says Brendan Bracken tells him Churchill is not really optimistic. Rothermere himself does not see how we can win the war, and thinks it will go on for about four years and then peter out, leaving us financially ruined. He said he thought Schacht [*former German Economics Minister*] the greatest financial genius in the world, and one who in conversation with Rothermere was frankly contemptuous of the brains of our City pundits.

April 8, 1940
The news in the early editions of the evening papers is that we have mined three areas within Norwegian territorial waters, one of them near Narvik. The idea is to force ships hugging the Norwegian coast to come out into the open sea, where we can get at them. This will not only stop the iron-ore traffic from Narvik, but will also interfere with the route for raiding-ships trying to get out on to our trade routes in the Atlantic. The Germans will obviously react – it will be interesting to see where and how.

German action was, in fact, swifter and more devastatingly successful than anyone could have imagined. On the evening of April 8, as Cecil King was noting the mining of the leads in his diary, the German plans for a northern Blitzkrieg were being put into action. 'Surprise, ruthlessness, and precision', wrote Churchill, 'were the characteristics of the onslaught upon innocent and naked Norway.' Within a matter of hours Denmark was in German hands, and by April 10 most of the key ports, towns, and airfields in Norway had fallen.

The reaction of Britain and France was ineffectual. The British War Cabinet proposed to counter-attack by landing at Trondheim, the ancient Norwegian capital. This plan was quickly abandoned in favour of a less daring enveloping movement, and troops – many of them untrained territorials – were landed north and south of Trondheim at Namsos and Andalsnes. A force was also landed in the far north, at Narvik.

Disaster and humiliation followed for the Allies. At the beginning of May the Namsos and Andalsnes forces were withdrawn, and although the Allies occupied Narvik on May 28, they had to evacuate it soon after.

Allied losses were also heavy in the sea battles that were fought in the North Sea and off the Norwegian coast. The aircraft carrier Glorious *(sunk in the evacuation of Narvik), two cruisers, and nine destroyers*

were lost. But there was consolation to be gained from a stirring victory
in the destroyer actions at Narvik, and from crippling German losses of
three cruisers and ten destroyers. This, together with damage to other
German ships, reduced the effective German fleet to one 8-inch cruiser, two
light cruisers, and four destroyers.

　Churchill, who had been made chairman of the Military Co-ordination
Committee on April 4, bore a large measure of both technical and real
responsibility for the conduct of the Norwegian campaign. At the outset he
had boasted that every German ship using the Kattegat would be sunk – a
remark which turned out as inaccurate as Chamberlain's assertion of April
4 that Hitler had 'missed the bus'. Afterwards Churchill noted in his
memoirs: 'It was a marvel that I survived.' This was not to be for Churchill
another political disaster like the Dardanelles in 1915. On the contrary,
the humiliation of the Norwegian campaign hardened opinion against
Chamberlain. The man of appeasement, who always wanted to 'wait and
see', who had presided too long over a faltering war effort, must go.
Winston Churchill, man of action, man of war, seemed to the British
public and to a growing number of M.P.s to be the obvious leader.

April 15, 1940
Caught the 1.30 train with Cudlipp to Totnes [Devon] to see
Liddell Hart, whom I consider the leading military expert of the
day. I wanted to hear his views not only on the strategic situation
in Norway and the Middle East, but also about military and other
personnel. On the way down Cudlipp told me that one of the
most prominent pictures in Lloyd George's sitting room is a signed
photograph of Baldwin! On reaching Newton Abbot we found
that the evening papers say a British force has been landed 'at
several points' in Norway. I presume this is around Narvik.

　We walked to Redworth House just outside Totnes. It belongs
to the Dartington Hall Trustees and is opposite Sean O'Casey's
place. After we had met Liddell Hart at his flat in Redworth
House, he took us to our hotel and had dinner with us. He is
very tall, very thin, with pince-nez, a curious rather full and
reddish mouth, and a small sandy moustache. Talks rather in-
distinctly and looks as if he suffered from very bad health. He is
constantly consulted by Lloyd George on military matters, and
was in the closest touch with Hore-Belisha for most, though not

all, of his period of office. Has been Duff Cooper's adviser at one period, Churchill's at most periods, and was even called in by Mussolini in 1927 to advise on the Italian army.

On Norway, we got the impression he was trying to be optimistic against his better judgment. He had evidently been described as a pessimist and defeatist, and wanted to counteract the impression he had made by being very cautiously optimistic about Norway. His general attitude is that presumably the German forces in western Norway are quite small and that if we move quickly we could probably push them out. Told by us that Sam Hoare put the figures for western Norway alone at 60,000, he said in that event we should never recapture the country. Our only hope was great speed in backing up the Norwegians, so that they could isolate the Germans in the west coast and starve them out.

On the subject of Italy as an enemy, he said his views were far less sanguine than those ordinarily current. He thought Italy not so vulnerable as she seemed, except perhaps in Sardinia and the Dodecanese.

On the western front he had always thought nothing would or could happen. If the Germans in the early stages of the war felt safe with fifteen divisions in the Siegfried Line, what would they not feel now with 150 or more divisions available?

Liddell Hart was really at his best talking about the higher personnel of the Army. Gort he thought slow, but far more cunning than he seems; very ambitious indeed and a reformer until he became C.I.G.S. [*Chief of the Imperial General Staff*], when he degenerated into an ordinary military reactionary. Liddell Hart thinks Ironside a very definite character but too clumsy and naive to be an intriguer. The leaders of the British Army he considered to be certainly no better than were those in the last war (mentioning Haig and Ian Hamilton as typical), though, of course, from the experience gained then there were various mistakes they would avoid.

Liddell Hart gave an account of the resignation of Hore-Belisha which is somewhat different from Hore-Belisha's, but is probably founded on fact as he knows all the people so well.

He says there had been increasing friction between Gort and

Hore-Belisha owing to Gort's reactionary attitude after his appointment as C.I.G.S. It was largely for this reason that Gort and not Ironside was made Commander-in-Chief in France. In November [1939] Hore-Belisha went out to France and was very dissatisfied with the progress made with some of the concrete defences, which had been put in the hands of contractors such as McAlpine. This had been Belisha's idea: Gort had not liked it and had stymied the work. Belisha spoke strongly to Gort when he was in France. Subsequently Casey, the Australian Minister, and Reitz, the South African one, both went out to France and spoke very strongly on the subject too. The Prime Minister went to France and tried to smooth everything over, and thought he had done so. But Belisha, through the Army Council, sent a verbal message on this subject that was taken by Gort as a reprimand, and Gort appealed to the King. At this point Chamberlain decided he would have to shift Belisha.

Liddell Hart implied that in this controversy Belisha was right, though tactless and impulsive, and he appeared to think that Churchill and Ironside's parts could only have been to fan the flames and support Chamberlain in any decision unfavourable to Belisha he might make.

May 1, 1940
Cudlipp had lunch with Vansittart, Diplomatic Adviser to the Government. Cudlipp got the impression that Vansittart is one of the Churchill faction, that they are nervous that our papers will throw Churchill over on this Norwegian issue, and that he wished to dissuade us from doing so. Vansittart says there is a movement on foot to foist the blame for the failure in Norway onto Churchill; that this is just a manoeuvre to keep Chamberlain and Horace Wilson in office a bit longer; and that whatever Churchill's responsibility in this matter may be, or whatever failings he may have, he is the best available Prime Minister under current conditions. Vansittart is very friendly with Reynaud, the French premier, and for this reason cannot be altogether retired by Chamberlain. He said he was invited to broadcast a week or two back. He wrote out a violently anti-German speech – giving expression, in fact, to his sentiments. Halifax had him up and

said that for unspecified reasons he would not pass the speech. Vansittart pointed out that his views on Germany had been well known for a long time, and anyway we were now at war with Germany. However, the broadcast had to be cancelled!

Vansittart had a poor opinion of Eden, whom he thought responsible for alienating Italian sympathies – which need not have been done – and so creating the Axis.

Cudlipp thought Vansittart able, active, ambitious, quite unscrupulous, and (surprisingly) with a very good idea of public opinion as seen from the office of a popular newspaper. He asked Vansittart if he had ever thought of becoming Minister of Information, and from his answer he evidently had.

May 6, 1940

Reith's secretary rang up on Thursday and asked if I would have lunch with him at his club on Monday. No reason was given. Today the lunch came off, at Brooks'. Reith is taller than I am: he must be about six foot four and a half inches. To my surprise we were alone. He explained he had not invited me to talk about business, but had expressed a wish to meet me, and it had been fixed up by Charles Peake (whom I have never even seen).

Reith always sat me on his right, so that I was away from the scar on his cheek. He struck me as very slow, but not stupid. I should say he would get around to a lot of the right answers – but long after everyone else. He started talking about the debate in the House tomorrow on the Norwegian campaign. As Chamberlain and the administration will be fighting for its life, this seemed a strange indiscretion on the part of a minister. He seemed to favour a more autocratic line by the Government, as he said at present far too much time and energy were lost in securing agreement and in manoeuvring. He seemed to doubt whether very much could be done by the Ministry of Information until there was a complete change of heart by the Prime Minister, and in fact by all the senior ministers. At present they were not propaganda-minded, and he did not in wartime feel disposed to add to the Prime Minister's difficulties by anything in the way of an ultimatum. He said Chamberlain is very meticulous, and that when he asked Reith to move from the B.B.C. to Imperial Airways, Reith said he took it as an order, but Chamberlain said it was only a suggestion. Reith also said that all Baldwin's speeches were written for him, whereas Chamberlain wrote his own.

He then told me, apropos of nothing very obvious, that six months ago he had had a great psychological shock at reaching the age of fifty. It was not that he had lost his grip, but certainly he had lost all ambition. I got the impression that he *had* lost his grip – whether at reaching the age of fifty or being a flop in Imperial Airways was not so clear. He is clearly a snob, but was very friendly to me, and sent me back to the office in his car; we finally parted at 3.20, lunch being at 1.15.

Towards the end he asked me if I could recommend him men (a) to put in the three service departments as liaison officers for the Ministry of Information, (b) to be Public Relations Officer at the Ministry, and (c) to take over the Press and Censorship Bureau formerly held by Sir Walter Monckton, who is now promoted. On (b) I had no ideas, on (a) I suggested he ask Pulvermacher of the *Telegraph*, and on (c) I very diffidently suggested myself. This seemed to surprise him quite a bit, that I should take such a job. But I explained that I am of military age and want to do something to help on the war, and that that is the only work for which I have any qualifications. He seemed to take to the idea and, subject to his getting favourable answers when he checks up on me, I shall get the job. However, the if is a big one.

The next two months were, for the British people, as dramatic as any in the war. At the beginning of May, Chamberlain was still in power and the main land forces of Britain and France had not been engaged. By the end of June, Churchill had replaced Chamberlain, Germany had conquered the Low Countries, France had surrendered, the British Expeditionary Force had been evacuated from Dunkirk, and the German commanders were gazing across the Straits of Dover at their next objective – Britain.

The drama began on May 7 with the opening of a two-day debate in the House of Commons on the Norwegian campaign. Chamberlain entered to shouts of 'missed the bus'. His opening speech was unconvincing, and he was attacked from both sides of the House. Some of the most damaging speeches came from the Conservative back benches. Sir Roger Keyes, a naval hero of the First World War, arrived in the full-dress uniform of

*an Admiral of the Fleet and denounced the failure to attack Trondheim.
Leo Amery, one of Chamberlain's fellow Birmingham Members, concluded
his speech with Cromwell's stinging words to the Long Parliament: 'You
have sat too long here for any good you have been doing. Depart, I say, and
let us have done with you. In the name of God, go!'*

*The next day Herbert Morrison announced that the Opposition intended
to put the matter to the vote. Chamberlain accepted this challenge, warning
him, with what Harold Nicolson described as a 'leer of triumph': 'I have
friends in this House.'*

*Lloyd George said his piece: 'It is not a question of who are the Prime
Minister's friends. It is a far bigger issue. He has appealed for sacrifice. . . .
I say solemnly that the Prime Minister should give an example of sacrifice,
because there is nothing which can contribute more to victory in this war than
that he should sacrifice the seals of office.'*

*Churchill, despite a warning from Lloyd George that he should avoid
being 'converted into an air-raid shelter to keep the splinters from hitting
his colleagues', defended the Government vigorously. 'I retorted upon them
and defied them, and several times the clamour was such that I could not
make myself heard.' But it was obvious to Churchill and to everybody else
that the fury of the House was directed not against him but against
Chamberlain.*

*The vote gave the Government a majority of only eighty-one. It was now
clear, even to Chamberlain, that a National Government of all parties was
necessary. But who would lead it? Chamberlain's preferences for Prime
Minister were first himself and second Lord Halifax. However, it transpired that Labour would not serve under Chamberlain, and Halifax felt
that it would be unsuitable for a peer to take the lead 'in such a war as
this'.*

*Chamberlain saw that there was no alternative to Churchill, and re-
signed. Churchill accepted the prime ministership on the evening of May 10.*

*The papers that day were full of the Government crisis, and the British
public was not yet aware that the war on the Continent had entered a new,
momentous phase. Early that morning Hitler had struck in the west in
the classic Blitzkrieg pattern. An 'avalanche of fire and steel' rolled across
the frontiers of Holland and Belgium.*

*While Churchill was forming his new Government, Holland and
Belgium were overrun. On May 14 the German armour smashed through*

*the French front at Sedan and their Panzers raced down the Somme valley
towards the sea. On May 19 they were at Abbeville and then they swept
northwards, taking Boulogne on May 26. They had driven a wedge
between the Allied armies north and south of their line of advance. Cut off
to the north was the B.E.F., which retreated to Dunkirk. From there
200,000 British troops and 140,000 French were evacuated to England
between May 27 and June 3. 'MIRACLE OF THE DELIVERANCE'
was the Mirror headline.*

*On June 5 the German army struck southwards. The remaining fifty
French divisions could offer little effective opposition. On June 10 Italy
declared war on France and Britain, and invaded the south of France. The
French government abandoned Paris on June 13; and on June 22, now
under Marshal Pétain, signed an armistice with Germany. This provided
for the disarmament of French forces and the surrender of three-fifths of
France to German control. A government of unoccupied France was set up
at Vichy.*

*The Daily Mirror's comment on the situation was: ' The collapse of
French resistance leaves us in our island – hardly an island any longer – alone
as the last fortress and hope of civilization in Europe. It is a grim position.
It is not dishonourable. That is at least something.'*

May 8, 1940

The great debate on the Norwegian campaign took place in the
Commons yesterday and is to continue tonight. It was opened by
Chamberlain, who made a very lame speech and was followed by
Attlee, who was bad though possibly better than usual. Stanley
made a very poor speech, and the highlights of the evening were a
violent attack on the Government by Amery, another by Winterton
(a very unexpected quarter), and finally one by Sir Roger Keyes.
The last said that an attack by naval forces on Trondheim was
perfectly feasible, that he had offered to conduct the operation
himself, and that Churchill had been put off it by the pusillani-
mous advice of the First Sea Lord. The Government side was so
feebly defended and the attack was so fierce and from so many
different directions that the Government clearly cannot last.
Byron [Mirror *lobby correspondent*] said both Chamberlain and
Churchill looked all-in last night – Chamberlain fidgeting his
right foot nervously – and that the pundits now give the Govern-

ment one month, after which sweeping changes are inevitable. As most of the newcomers have spoken or will speak this evening against the Government, it seems pretty clear that a drastic reconstruction of the Government would mean a new premier.

Was asked to go to the Ministry of Information at midday for an interview with Sir Kenneth Lee, Director-General of the Ministry, and Sir Walter Monckton, Deputy ditto. When I arrived Lee was alone. A rather nice, precise sort of man, capable I should think in a limited sort of way, but very pleasant to me. He seemed to be in some difficulty at the start and it emerged that Reith had asked him to see me, had said I wanted to do some war work, but had not indicated what job he had in mind for me. I explained that he had told me of the vacancies he had and asked if I knew of anyone suitable. And that when it came to the question of a director of the Press and Censorship Bureau I had diffidently offered myself.

Monckton came in in the middle of this conversation, having been held up by a conference with Dorman-Smith, the Minister of Agriculture. I explained that the office would probably lend me, that I should therefore not need a salary, and that I had no use for any of the other jobs that were vacant, only for the directorship of the Press and Censorship Bureau. They then explained that as far as they knew, the job was not vacant. So I said Reith had told me the job was occupied as a sort of stopgap by a man from the Foreign Office. They said this was so, but they had not heard that Reith regarded him only as a stopgap. Apparently this struck them as typical of Reith. At all events, they felt I had been very clear over what had passed between Reith and me, and on what I wanted.

Monckton then went off and I was left alone with Lee again. So I said he naturally did not know me from Adam, and would he like to know why I thought I could do the job? He said he would be most grateful. So I gave him a brief résumé of my life since I left Oxford and did it, I think, rather well. He remarked at the end on what a fascinating life I had led. He asked me if I realized that the job in question was the key position in the whole Ministry and the one that would necessarily attract most criticism. I said

I assumed I should be buried in brickbats if I took the job on, but that I was used to them. He promised to let me know how things were before long, and we parted very amicably.

May 9, 1940
The debate in the House last night waxed fast and furious – Lloyd George, Duff Cooper, and Morrison all on their best form, denouncing Chamberlain in the most insulting terms. The division at the end was 281 for Chamberlain and 200 against, his normal majority being 213. This is hailed in all the papers as the beginning of the end of the Chamberlain Government. Even the *Telegraph*, sycophantic as it is, calls for a drastic reconstruction of the Government, but it is hard to see how Chamberlain can do any such thing.

Had lunch with Hugh [Fraser] at the Waldorf. He was sitting in the Gallery for the debate last night, in case Hoare wanted any information from his department [*Air Ministry*]. Apparently he didn't, but muddled all his facts in his speech, one of the most important on the Government side. Hugh is in a state of wild indignation about the conduct of affairs in Norway, and indeed about the progress of the war in general. He says that last night Roosevelt in person rang up the Government this side to warn us that his information was that Germany had presented Holland with an ultimatum and might move at any minute.

May 10, 1940
Was woken up by Beatrice, the housemaid, to be told that there was exciting news: the Germans were landing parachute troops in Holland, and Holland and Belgium had called for our aid.

The papers this morning have no news of these events, as they occurred at three in the morning. They all concentrate on the position of Chamberlain. It is generally agreed that Chamberlain tried to continue, but that the rebel Conservatives and the Labour leaders stressed the impossibility of joining a Government of which he was a member. His supporters in the House – or many of them – have informed him that they cannot continue their support of the Goverment without drastic changes in its composition, including the elimination of Simon and Hoare. The situation now (at 1.25) is that there have been two Cabinet meetings this morning, but no announcement about the Government. Belgium, Holland, and Switzerland are being invaded, but we have no authoritative Government. The papers generally assume that Churchill (said by Byron this morning to be very much under the influence of brandy) will be the new Prime Minister. The only other names mentioned are Halifax, Lloyd George, and one paper mentions Eden. Today's news, I should say, would clearly favour Churchill's chances over the other three. I am wondering whether these invasions will hasten Chamberlain's departure, or whether the House of Commons will go all sentimental and feel that in this grave hour we must retain the same leaders however much discredited.

Later

Cudlipp had lunch with Hore-Belisha today. Hore-Belisha thinks he will be in the Government if Lloyd George is premier, but is not so confident of his chances if Churchill has the job. He thinks in that case his best hope is the Ministry of Information. The trouble about it all is that he did not speak in the debate and therefore is rather out of the picture. He rang up Cudlipp on Wednesday morning and asked him if he should speak! Cudlipp said was there anything he felt he must say? He said no. So Cudlipp (I think very wisely) said: 'Well, if you've nothing to say, don't say it.' Cudlipp's comment to me was that he was tired of writing speeches that Hore-Belisha at the finish hadn't the courage to deliver, so why should he bother?

Hore-Belisha said Lloyd George would serve under Churchill as Minister of Food, provided he could keep his right to criticize. I gather he does not want to be in the War Cabinet. Cudlipp was under the impression that all this came from Lloyd George himself. Hore-Belisha also said that when Chamberlain sent for Attlee and Greenwood yesterday and offered to take them into the Government, they refused point blank to serve in any Government that included him. One would have thought that from the previous night's debate this refusal was inevitable. But Chamberlain was apparently startled and hurt. Churchill, who was present with Halifax, then delivered an oration and told the Labour leaders it was their duty to the country to join in a reconstructed Chamberlain Government. They were not impressed and stuck to their refusal.

Still later
Turned on the wireless news at 9.0 to find that Chamberlain was speaking. His usual dreary stuff, drearily delivered, but it gave M. [*Margot King, Cecil King's first wife*] the impression he was about to burst into tears. It was the announcement of his resignation, and the succession of Churchill. He had promised to be in Churchill's War Cabinet. So at last my campaign to get rid of the old menace has come off. I consider this is the best bit of news since war was declared. I do not think Churchill is young enough to win the war, but he is immeasurably better than Chamberlain. The Sunday Pic was the paper that hammered away at getting Churchill into the Cabinet, a campaign that the other papers took up and that got him in. Then on October 1 last the *Sunday Pictorial* had a very good page article by Cudlipp announcing that Churchill would be the next premier. We shall reproduce part of it to show how right we are. But newspaper boasting apart, it was a long shot when it was made and it has come off!

I wonder whom his Cabinet will consist of. I hope not too many duds, but it can't be worse than Chamberlain's. I imagine Churchill will carry on for some time, but that eventually his health will crack. By that time some younger men may have had a chance to raise their heads and we may get the Government that will lead us out of this mess. Unfortunately it is the next four or five months that are critical, and throughout that time we must be burdened with many of the duds of the Attlee, Greenwood type.

May 12, 1940
Last night I was in the office as usual. The news of the new Cabinet came in at 8.30. The War Cabinet instead of consisting of Chamberlain, Churchill, Simon, Hoare, Stanley, Halifax, Hankey, and Kingsley Wood, is to consist of Churchill, Chamberlain, Halifax, Attlee, and Greenwood. I cannot see that, except for the substitution as Prime Minister of Churchill for Chamber-

lain, it is any improvement. The three service ministers are apparently not to be in the War Cabinet. They are to be Alexander (Admiralty), Eden (War Office), and Archibald Sinclair (Air). These are the only names to be announced so far, but they have caused widespread dismay among M.P.s. Byron rang up to say that Morrison, who did more than any other Labour leader to get Chamberlain out (Greenwood's speech in the House of Commons debate was a flop), is indignant and is planning to lead the opposition element in the Labour Party, who want to see a clean sweep of Chamberlain and his friends. The rebel Conservatives – Amery, Duff Cooper, and co. – are not likely to stand for this War Cabinet for long. It seems strange tactics to leave out of it all the elements which have been pressing for a more vigorous conduct of the war, while including a lot of shocking duds.

Various explanations are possible: (1) that this is meant as a stopgap ministry to get everyone, particularly the Chamberlain Conservatives, lined up, but that as soon as Churchill feels himself firmly in the saddle there will be a complete reconstruction and the dead wood will go; (2) that this War Cabinet is a blind, and that Churchill means to run the war himself through the three service ministers (who are, I think, improvements on their predecessors, though pathetically inadequate for the tasks in front of them); (3) to my cynical mind the most probable, that Churchill, being sixty-five, found himself and Chamberlain converging on the same sort of attitude to the war. He now finds himself more at home with the dreary political failures of the last ten years than with any of the brighter young spirits that may be lying around. A curious feature of the whole thing is that in this very serious crisis the country turns from the stuffed shirts and old men's darlings of the Baldwin era to what survives of the best of the pre-last-war era. There is no doubt that at this moment the country is turning to Churchill and Lloyd George. It cannot turn to any younger ones, because they are either weak like Eden or utterly unknown. At the same time I am absolutely certain that this war will be won, if it is won, by the men under fifty.

The papers are all amusingly sentimental about Chamberlain's removal from the prime ministership. The fact is that he has clung to office like a limpet, that his motive has been personal vanity, and that he has used his power to push forward his friends and toadies to the great detriment of the public interest. When the country and the House of Commons would finally have no more of him, he clung frantically to 10 Downing Street and had literally to be thrown out, and in spite of all is still in the War Cabinet. But the papers mostly (not the *Mirror*![7]) take the line that he has made a great personal sacrifice to secure national unity, that no one could accuse him of self-seeking, that nothing became him like the hour of his departure, and so on. This cant and humbug seem to me both nauseating and mischievous; what possible purpose could it serve? Is it the *de mortuis nil nisi bonum* principle carried to extreme lengths?

Several new governmental appointments announced: Simon to be Lord Chancellor, Morrison – Supply, Duff Cooper – Information, Kingsley Wood – Exchequer, Colonial Secretary – Lord Lloyd. And two remain the same: Anderson at the Home Office and Duncan at the Board of Trade. This bunch is far more encouraging, and makes me think the War Cabinet of five is meant to be advisory (and advice can always be ignored!). Anderson is not much use, but knows the ropes and can do little harm. Duff Cooper doesn't know much about propaganda, but, after his part in the debate and his resignation after Munich, clearly had to have something. Incidentally, this is bound to delay and will probably stymie any appointment I might have had at the Ministry of Information.

May 15, 1940
Cudlipp had some talk with Lloyd George's secretary this morning. From this it appears that Lloyd George wanted to be in the War Cabinet, but that he was not invited. He *was* offered the Ministry of Agriculture, or some such job. He was prepared to accept this if he could keep his power of criticism of the general policy of the Government, but this condition was not accepted. Lloyd George expects that Churchill will get into a mess and that he, the victor of the last war, will be called in too late and will have no alternative but to sue for peace. On the new Government in general, he thought it a poor thing, obviously dictated in its composition largely by the party whips.

4

May 18, 1940

The German success seems to be due to the use of massed tanks combined with low-flying aeroplanes. Our tank force is negligible – I don't know about the French – and our air force is numerically vastly inferior and likely to remain so for another year anyway. I remember saying to M. at the outbreak of the war that I thought casualties would be slight except in the Air Force and Tank Corps, where the men were already as good as dead. But reactionaries in the High Command both here and in France have done their best to belittle and starve these new arms, and it looks as if we shall have to pay a ruinous price for listening to them. The whole German policy is to produce a decisive force at a decisive point. The contrast is seen in our tank drill, which allows for waves of tanks (if you have the tanks!) in an extended line: the German breakthrough near Sedan, however, was achieved with a spearhead of massed tanks that crashed through everything.

Later

No particular news except that the German advance continues, though at a slower pace. Had dinner at Veeraswamy's in Regent Street. They were in despair, and told me they had served seven people for lunch and did not expect as many as that to dinner. Apparently, since the German invasion of Holland the West End has just gone out of business. Four shows are closing down tonight and two that were to have started are postponed; night clubs are having the stickiest time ever. This slump seems to be partly due to the fact that all leave for the fighting services has been stopped, and partly just depression. It was a lovely fine evening and the West End was full of people, but apparently they only stroll about and will not spend any money.

May 21, 1940

The mention of the names of the same places that were prominent in the last war has given people a shock, but so far nothing much is happening. Life is going on in its usual easy-going fashion in the still glorious weather. People seem worried, but not stung to action at all, and think it unpatriotic to suggest that recent events in France will even postpone our ultimate victory.

May 29, 1940

Carisbrooke is a curious man: very thin, very meticulously turned
out, very nervous, with a face like a weaker and more frightened
edition of George V. He is a brother of the Queen of Spain, who
recently wrote to him after having lunch with the King and
Queen of Italy. I gathered no one else was there. The King and
Queen of Italy were very up-and-at-'em on the subject of Monte-
negro. They thought England had behaved badly in incorporating
it with Yugoslavia after the war. The Queen of Spain had never
heard the matter raised before, though, of course, the Queen of
Italy was a Montenegrin princess. She was also horrified by the
indifference of the King of Italy to the fate of the Queen of
Holland and the King of Norway. There is usually a feeling that
royalty should stick together, but the Italian pair showed no signs
of appreciating the point. Altogether the Queen of Spain got a
nasty shock to find the King and Queen of Italy so well in line
with Hitler, Mussolini, and their policies. Of any rift between
Musso and the King there was less than no sign.

Carisbrooke said what a nasty bit of work Ciano [*Mussolini's
son-in-law*] is. How, when in China, he was little better than a
professional gigolo, obliging any woman who was stranded without
a husband for twenty-four hours. Somewhat later he had made
large sums of money by speculation anticipating the effects of his
political speeches. Latterly he had spent millions of lire on the
Rome golf club, which was now the most luxurious in the world:
the idea being to provide a rendezvous for himself and his girls,
as the club provided everything down to a luxury restaurant and
cabaret. Carisbrooke said Ciano was very well in with Edda
Mussolini (Ciano's wife). Whatever their matrimonial pecca-
dilloes might be, they saw eye to eye on politics. Carisbrooke did
not see how a man with such a past could be the future Duce,
though that is Musso's idea.

June 5, 1940

Churchill made a magnificent speech in the House of Commons –
really first-class fighting stuff. He didn't minimize the defeat we
have sustained, but said that a week ago he thought we should
only rescue 30,000 men from Dunkirk, but in fact we had rescued

335,000 English and French soldiers. Our losses in men killed, wounded, and missing he put in excess of 30,000. The loss of material he said was enormous, comprising 1,000 guns, and it would take 'some months' to replace. Yesterday afternoon the Germans finally took Dunkirk with, they claim, 40,000 prisoners.

June 6, 1940

Went down to Churt to have lunch with Lloyd George. We had been paying him £100 for his weekly article, but now he wants £250 and to give up writing for the American papers. I had been planning a visit for some time, but this matter of the payment for his article finally provided the occasion.

Lloyd George greeted Cudlipp and me when we arrived at 12.45. He was dressed in light grey, with brown boots and a blue tie. Despite his scanty snow-white hair, he does not look more than seventy at the most. He has strong capable hands, not those of an old man. From his eyes you can see he is really past it, though every now and then you catch a glimpse of his glance as it must once have been. He eats very untidily indeed, but this may be due to a deplorable set of false teeth, which clicked and rattled in conversation even when he was not eating.

He has a very large sitting room with a plate-glass window about twenty-five feet long. One wall is covered with a glass case filled with gold caskets, presumably containing illuminated addresses from different municipal corporations and other bodies. On the tables and the piano are signed photographs of various notables. The most obvious were President Wilson, Clemenceau, Foch, Liddell Hart, and Baldwin. The only other person present was his secretary, a very nice woman in early middle age. The conversation was almost entirely on politics and the war. Lloyd George obviously lives largely in the past, as most old men do. His conversation was more on the last war than on this one. He mentioned, incidentally, how even as Prime Minister he always read the German communiqués very carefully as a check on ours!

Of the Chamberlains, he spoke with great admiration of Joe[8]; of Austen[9] he said he was fine man but had no intellectual capacity at all. Neville [Chamberlain] he regarded with complete contempt: said he was a manufacturer of bedsteads and was

unable even to run his bedstead factory at a profit. I knew he had
been a director of some Birmingham firm, but didn't know it made
bedsteads! He recalled that in the last war he heard Neville was
making a mess of his job — Minister for National Service, I think
it was – so he sent for Bonar Law [*then Conservative leader and in the
War Cabinet*] and said it was hard for him, a Liberal, to get rid
of a Chamberlain. What should they do? So he and Bonar decided
to go and see Neville and recommend some second-in-command
who could pull him through. Neville was leaning very much on
the town clerk of Birmingham, who at that time played the
part Sir Horace Wilson played later. Lloyd George and Bonar
Law suggested replacing him by someone more competent, but
Neville was obstinate. He couldn't do his job properly, nor would
he accept as an assistant someone who could do it for him. So
Lloyd George had to fire him.

He thought Bonar Law did a lot of harm in striking a note of
relaxation in 1922. Bonar Law said in effect: 'The sun is shining:
take off your coats, lie in the sun, and relax.' This was just what
people wanted to hear. They did lie in the sun and did relax, and
voted for politicians who, in spite of sinister developments all over
the world, urged them to go on doing so.

Lloyd George thought over Poland we should have played for
time and only fought Germany when we could do so on level
terms. That we plunged in without discovering how unpopular
and incompetent the Polish government was and how ill-led was
the Polish army. I think in his point about playing for time he
betrayed his age. We had been playing for time ever since 1931,
but always lost. If with a war on we did so little between September 1939 and May 1940, what reason is there for supposing
that without a war Chamberlain and co. would have done any
more? Lloyd George said Sikorski was the only good general the
Poles had, but that they wouldn't use him because his politics
weren't right (he is now head of the Polish government in Paris).

He mentioned that in the last war, Haig had an immense
headquarters staff; Pétain's at Compiègne was even bigger; but
Foch, who was Commander-in-Chief of the whole Allied army, got
along with Weygand and an A.D.C. Foch didn't care where he
stayed provided there was central heating. He supplied the larger

outlook and the decisions, while Weygand, who had an encyclo-
paedic mind, looked after the detail. Lloyd George doubted,
therefore, whether Weygand[10] would be equal to his occasion in
this war. In the last war, apparently, Weygand carried in his
head the strength and the position of every unit in the French
army, even down to the batteries of guns!

Lloyd George also mentioned meeting Hitler and spoke of him
as the greatest figure in Europe since Napoleon, and possibly
greater than him. He said we had not had to deal with an austere
ascetic like Hitler since the days of Attila and his Huns, who
curiously enough attained the success he did by mounting his
whole army on horses and bewildering his enemies by the speed
of his movements. I gathered that Lloyd George's opinion of
Hitler was based not so much upon the impression he received
when talking to Hitler face to face, as on his achievements, though
Lloyd George evidently judges people a lot by their faces. In this
connection he was very severe about Gamelin[10] – said the lower
half of his face was weak.

Of all the political figures I have talked politics with, Lloyd
George seemed to me the most realistic. He sums the situation
up as it is, without any trace of wishful thinking. Even he cannot
escape the handicap of his age, and so tends to think of Hitler and
the war situation in material terms without attaching serious
weight to the ideological factor, which I think any young man
would see is all-important.

The pages of the Mirror *and the* Pictorial *provide a vivid chronicle of
the great events of the coming months and clearly reflect the elated and
transfigured mood of the British public.*

*Throughout the disastrous midsummer of 1940 the papers echoed, and
powerfully encapsulated in striking headlines and editorials, the more
verbose bellicosity of Churchill: 'Never to lose heart. That is the prelude to
victory.' 'WE NEVER SURRENDER'. 'We shall not flag or fail. We
shall not, because failure means extinction.' ' The common people of the land
have the courage. Give them arms and give them leadership and they will
not fail as they have been failed. But above all give them LEADERSHIP.'*

*Anything or anybody who stood in the way of the Great Crusade was
pilloried with all the venom and journalistic expertise the papers could*

muster. Cassandra declared a 'Gutskrieg' against diners out in expensive restaurants. Bumbling bureaucrats, hidebound brass hats, preposterous Colonel Blimps, people who saved their skins by escaping to America (the 'dermatologists') were held up for maximum hatred, ridicule, and contempt. The Pictorial *suggested a short way with pacifists: 'Put the lot behind barbed wire.' And all this was accompanied by enthusiastic, but frequently unrealistic, advice on how to win the war. For example, one month after Dunkirk: 'Attack, attack . . . We must attack!'*

But the main concern of both papers was the question of leadership: 'Above all give them LEADERSHIP.' The men at the top whom they considered inefficient or discredited survivors of the appeasement era, the 'dope ministers', the 'old blunderers', the 'museum ministers', all the extinct volcanoes of the front bench, were continuously attacked. Why were they kept on, men like that 'stupendous flop' Kingsley Wood? How could we win a war with such an uninspired, uninspiring bunch? 'They are honest, they are eager, they are second-rate. They are quite clearly The Men Who Will Not Win The War,' wrote Cudlipp in the Pictorial. *The* Pictorial *also suggested a slogan for the recruitment of ministers: 'Only failures need apply.'*

The papers' criticisms were not only outspoken; they were also often authoritative, men of the calibre of Lloyd George and Major-General J.F.C. Fuller providing the Government with regular advice and admonition.

Understandably Churchill and his ministers did not like it. They felt that the papers were undermining people's confidence in the military and political leadership. Churchill was the country's chosen leader. He had chosen his Government. Why should the Mirror *and the* Pictorial *presume to dictate to him the way to run a war?*

The first of several clashes between Cecil King and Churchill came in June 1940. Compared with what was to happen later, it was a comparatively friendly affair.

June 7, 1940
On reaching the office learned that immediately after my departure last night Esmond [Harmsworth] appeared with a message from Churchill. Churchill is apparently aware that a storm is blowing up over Chamberlain and his friends at the secret session. He says that if Chamberlain is forced out, all his associates will go (such as Kingsley Wood, Simon, Halifax, and co.), and he will

have to resign as jointly responsible with them for the policy of the Cabinet since the outbreak of war. He says that if the newspapers continue their attacks on the Chamberlain gang, they will get the Government out and on Wednesday morning there will be no Government. So will we pipe down until Wednesday, and every effort will be made to ease Chamberlain out on the grounds of ill-health. On Esmond's arrival, Cowley held a meeting of Roome [Mirror *general manager*], Bart [*Guy Bartholomew*, Mirror *editorial director*], and co. (after trying to get hold of Cudlipp and me), and agreed that we would not attack the Chamberlainite members of the Government until Wednesday [June 12].

I went down to see Esmond at Northcliffe House to get the story straight from him, and find that it was roughly as above. Churchill has apparently fixed the [*Daily*] *Herald* through Bevin, and the *News Chronicle* through Layton and probably Lloyd George direct.

I think this is all rather deplorable – not that we should pipe down on Chamberlain until Wednesday, which we must obviously agree to at Churchill's request, but that the Prime Minister at a time like this should hesitate about such political liabilities as Chamberlain, Halifax, and co. He is strong enough in the country, if not in the Tory Party, to throw them all out and be damned to them. And the Tory Party at a time like this is clearly powerless to defy the country, who are unanimous for Churchill as Prime Minister. Lloyd George said Churchill's reception in the House on Tuesday [June 4] was very half-hearted: that, in spite of his magnificent speech, he got far less applause than was usually accorded to Chamberlain. Nevertheless, it seems to me that time and the nation are so clearly against the Tory back-benchers that Churchill can defy them and get away with it.

Esmond in the course of our conversation volunteered the information that Churchill was much to blame for the Government's lethargy, and that in the Norwegian campaign he assumed quite confidently that we could easily brush the Germans out. He also said that Churchill had once told him that in his political career he had never resigned and never would. His father [*Lord Randolph Churchill*], as Chancellor of the Exchequer, felt himself so strong that he had resigned and so wrecked his political career. He had

calculated that there was no one else they could make Chancellor
of the Exchequer, but 'he forgot Goschen' [*who was appointed his
successor*].

Thought Winston's message through Esmond a good excuse for
seeing him again myself, so I rang up and asked for an interview.
Eventually I was given an appointment at 7.45. I had not been to
10 Downing Street since the last war, when I was shown round
by Cecil Harmsworth,[11] who was then on Lloyd George's secretariat and worked in a wooden hut in the garden. This time I was
greeted by a very smooth, typically civil servant, private secretary,
who said he could only offer me a newspaper – unless I was
interested in Milton's *Areopagitica* or a book on fishing. He went
on to chat to me about the war, with some general clichés on how
Hitler was now flat out and how if only we could hold on he
would soon exhaust himself and be finished. A conference was
going on in the Cabinet room, which anyone with sharper ears
than mine could have overheard. Eventually out came an air
chief marshal of unconvincing aspect. A further long delay and
out came General Spears, looking very resplendent in red and
gold tabs and what not, a revolver at his belt. I greeted him and
congratulated him on his liaison job, a glorified version of his old
one in the last war. He was very friendly and told me he had just
come from France. A further long delay and out came Sir
Archibald Sinclair, looking the complete tragic actor – a sort of
minor Irving – long black hair, deep-set greenish-brown eyes,
and a tragic pallor. I was very interested to see him as I had not
done so before.

Then I was ushered into the presence, Winston sitting in the
Prime Minister's chair in the Cabinet room, in the middle of one
of the long sides of the table, facing the light and with his back
to the fireplace. He was dressed in a very tight-fitting Palm Beach
suit, face bright red with the heat, hair looking scantier than usual,
puffing at a cigar. Outside the window paced up and down a man
who looked very Civil Service, but might have been a very superior
detective. On the walls were two maps, one of the Western world,
the other of the Low Countries and northern France.

I explained that I had come to find out exactly what he did want us to do, as I had had a message through Esmond. He said he had only been Prime Minister a month today (and what a month!), and already the papers were picking on the Government and demanding Chamberlain's head on a charger. He thought the debate on Tuesday would amount to nothing: if there was any serious criticism he would take it as vote of censure, and no more than twenty would vote against him. I said I thought opinion against Chamberlain was high and rising and would continue to rise. Churchill said there was no one in this Government he had had to accept, that he had heard through a third party that Chamberlain was prepared to take office under him, and that he personally was very glad to have him. He was clear-headed, methodical and hard-working, and the best man he had – head and shoulders over the average man in the administration, who was mostly pretty mediocre.

Churchill said not to forget that a year ago last Christmas they were trying to hound him out of his constituency, and by a succession of events that astounded him he was invited by the practically unanimous voice of both Houses of Parliament to be Prime Minister. But the men who had supported Chamberlain and hounded Churchill were still M.P.s. Chamberlain had got the bigger cheer when they met the House after forming the new administration. A General Election was not possible during a war and so the present House of Commons, however unrepresentative of feeling in the country, had to be reckoned with as the ultimate source of power for the duration. If Churchill trampled on these men, as he could trample on them, they would set themselves against him, and in such internecine strife lay the Germans' best chance of victory.

I said I thought his position in the hearts of the people so unassailably strong that he could take stern measures with these people and get away with it. He asked what was the use of being in the position of a dictator if one could not have the governmental personnel one wanted? And after all, though he did have Chamberlain, Kingsley Wood, and Inskip, he had also included every single M.P. who had taken an independent line to Chamberlain. Law, Boothby, Macmillan, they were all in, and Vansittart had been made a Privy Councillor. Thirty-eight was the youngest man he had included – younger men were of military age. Besides ('I have already given the case for Chamberlain') Kingsley Wood is capable and energetic and quite a good Chancellor, tactful, doesn't rub people up the wrong way; and Inskip, though a flop as Minister for the Co-ordination of Defence, was the man most strongly recommended as Leader of the House of Lords. All agreed on that, including Lord Salisbury. It was all very well to plead for a Government excluding the elements that had led us astray of recent years, but where was one to stop? They were everywhere, not only in the political world, but among the fighting service chiefs and the Civil Service chiefs. To clear all these out would be a task impossible in the disastrous state in which we found ourselves. In any case, if one were dependent on the people who had been right in the last few years, what a tiny handful one would have to depend on. No, he was not going to run a Government of revenge. If the country did not like his Government they could form another one, and God knows where they would get it from – he wouldn't serve on it. After all, government in these days was no fun. It was listening to a succession of stories of bad news – a heart-breaking job.

He went on to talk about the first eight months of war. He said we didn't attack because we couldn't attack: we lost our air supremacy five years ago, and in spite of repeated promises by the Government had never looked like catching up. He supposed that more could have been done in the months from September to April and that perhaps he should have insisted on it. But he was responsible for the Navy, which was going all right, and it was very difficult to step outside one's own department. After all, it was the complete breakdown of French generalship that had let us down.

On the future Churchill said he was convinced there would be widespread air raids in this country as soon as the fighting in this offensive dies down. He thought the Germans would try an invasion. He doubted whether they could land more than 20,000 men on account of our Navy, and these would, if necessary, be 'choked in their own blood'. At the same time, did I realize how ghastly our position was? We had won last time after four years of defeats and would do so again. Meanwhile Italy might join against us at any time, and France might be forced to back out and leave us alone to face Germany. Was this a time for political bickering? I said the question was not whether this was a time for bickering, but that the feeling against Chamberlain was very strong, that the tide was rising and would continue to rise, and that a popular paper had, within limits, to reflect public opinion. He said he didn't see that the public had any right to take such a line. They had voted for Chamberlain when he was making these blunders: why should they seek his blood when he (and they) were proved wrong?

My feeling after seeing him was that this was all quite hopeless. He is trying to win a war against Hitler on the old lines with the old people. He is a far abler man than Chamberlain, but has much the same sort of outlook. He has not the same grasp of the situation as Lloyd George, and if he does grasp how serious the situation is (and he seemed to), he cannot imagine it being tackled except on the most ordinary traditional lines. Thus, he must look to the House of Commons for his talent: if it is not there, then he must do without. He regards such things as the House of Commons, the Tory Party, the Civil Service hierarchy, and so on, as fixed and immutable, and any war effort that is made must be made while leaving them substantially unchanged.

Esmond's version of Churchill's wishes was clearly quite wide of the mark. Churchill was asking for general support of his Government – Chamberlain elements and all – and does not at present intend to carry on if they are thrown out. While he is quite frankly contemptuous of the policy of the Governments we have had for the last seven or nine years, the personnel of those Governments is working quite well under him, so why bother?

I mentioned I had seen Lloyd George yesterday, and Churchill looked thoughtful and asked himself if Lloyd George was trying to get the Government out – not that Churchill thought he could possibly succeed. Personally I think Lloyd George sees the whole situation in much better perspective, and is seriously alarmed, but I do not think he wants to take office, still less to be Prime Minister. He is very conscious of his achievements in the last war and considers he will inevitably be called in sooner or later in this one, even if it is only to sign the treaty of surrender to Germany.

Churchill mentioned that the German supremacy in bombers was four to one, but that we had been bringing them down in about that proportion. What luck it was that our planes had proved so good – particularly our fighters. And this was the reason why at Dunkirk we had got all those men off. They had been the perfect target for aeroplanes, but our fighters had gained a local command of the air and that had saved our men. I think over Dunkirk this is rather exaggerating. The Germans, once they had made sure of our evacuation of Dunkirk without our equipment, were less intent on destroying the disorganized troops on the beach than on preparing for the next big offensive against the French army: a day gained there was far more important than an additional 50,000 men trapped at Dunkirk.

I tried to explain that opinion against Chamberlain was much stronger now that the B.E.F. had returned. The men were loud in their cries of resentment against the men who had let them down through lack of equipment. I also said that this feeling would be still further increased by serious air raids here; in fact that after an air raid Kingsley Wood might well be lynched if he happened around. I am not sure myself whether, in fact, the development of air raids, and generally a more just appreciation of what we are in for, will anger people to the point of action or frighten them to the point of paralysis. My own reaction is so very much the first, that I may be prejudiced in expecting it. Other people seem mostly to expect the second.

The only other item I can remember is that Churchill spoke of Beaverbrook's 'demoniac energy' and the fact that he was producing far more planes already.

Churchill was very friendly, and on three separate occasions asked me to make a point of coming to see him from time to time.

M. mentioned one curious thing today, and that is seeing a motorized column of troops going through Henley yesterday. So far in this war, very unlike the last, the people have shown no interest in, let alone enthusiasm for, our soldiers. But this time the streets were lined with people watching, many of whom darted into shops and bought cigarettes and fruit and threw them into the soldiers' lorries as they passed. This is the first account of the

kind I have heard, and it is perhaps due to Dunkirk and all that.

June 12, 1940

In spite of the disastrous news from France, I don't think the country is seriously worried. They are depressed by the continued lack of good news, but life continues very much as usual. I rather think we are now enjoying the last few days of normal pre-war life. Once things begin to change, they will move far and fast.

June 13, 1940

Cudlipp dined with Vansittart at Denham last night. Vansittart is in a state of fury, apparently. He feels Winston has sold us all out. He says the Chamberlain clique is almost as powerful as ever. Since Churchill's advent to power Vansittart has been made a Privy Councillor, but his advice has not been asked, though he is still Chief Diplomatic Adviser to the Government. He said he held that title for two years under Chamberlain, but in that time did not once see Chamberlain to talk to him. He was offered the post of Ambassador to Paris some time ago, but declined it, as he felt it would look like surrender to the Chamberlainites to leave the Foreign Office. Cudlipp thinks Vansittart a very able, very useful, if rather unscrupulous man, and that it is typical of the decadence of the time that this man should be pushed aside and ignored, although he is in the inner circle, and one of the very few in that circle with any capacity. Vansittart, perhaps rather naturally, takes a very poor view of Halifax. He thinks his morality boring and his subservience to Chamberlain an act of treason.

Vansittart says that in view of the imminent peril to Paris, the French foreign office is burning a lot of its most secret papers, and he thinks that later we shall do the same. He thinks this will give the Chamberlainites a heaven-sent chance of destroying all the incriminating documents of the last few years – the papers that warned them of what was coming as well as those expressing their own half-baked ideas. I think this is quite likely to happen, but cannot feel that the destruction of all the paper ever made would mislead future generations to the extent of approving Chamberlain's policies.

June 18, 1940
Last night the papers all sent representatives to the Foreign Office
to hear the official reaction to the French collapse. They were
given a more or less colourless hand-out, and so they asked when the
Prime Minister would speak. They were told not till this afternoon.
So they pressed very strongly that it was imperative that Churchill
should say something to the nation last night. The result – broadcast all over the world, including North America – was a few
stumbling sentences to the effect that the situation was disastrous,
but all right. Whether he was drunk or all-in from sheer fatigue,
I don't know, but it was the poorest possible effort on an occasion
when he should have produced the finest speech of his life.

June 20, 1940
This afternoon I went to see Sinclair Wood, who sent me a
memorandum on propaganda and morale on the home front. It
was quite excellent, and had been drawn up and submitted to
Duff Cooper [*recently appointed Minister of Information*], who read it
and was much interested. Wood had a talk with Duff Cooper
subsequently. Duff Cooper seemed thoroughly despondent,
suspended between a War Cabinet who obviously do not believe
in propaganda and are out of touch with public opinion, and a staff
in whom he has very little confidence. He was guarded about the
staff but very frank about the War Cabinet. He attends their
meetings, but finds it almost impossible to fit in any talk about
the attitude to be adopted to events as they occur. When France
backed out of the war, Duff Cooper spent the whole day trying
to get in touch with the Prime Minister, and only finally had
some talk with him at 7.40, when he stressed as strongly as he
could the necesssity for the Prime Minister to speak to the nation.
Churchill didn't seem to see the point, but eventually produced
his miserable 119-word address.

Cudlipp had lunch with Vansittart yesterday. Vansittart had
no particular news except that the scheme for Anglo-French
union[12] was his, put forward not in any very serious way, but as a
gesture which would have kept Reynaud in office a few days more.
He had the greatest difficulty in seeing Churchill, and finally

barged in when he was dressing after his bath – Winston pacing up and down clad in a very brief vest and abusing Vansittart for worrying him with his ideas, and for interrupting his work. The idea Vansittart is sure (and he knows the French very well) would have served its purpose, but it was finally put to the French just too late.

June 21, 1940
Had a ring about five o'clock from Sinclair Wood, who had had a visit from Horabin, Liberal M.P. for North Cornwall. Wood had only met him once, but Horabin called on him to ask his advice about the state of public opinion and morale. Wood gave his opinion and suggested he should have a chat with me, so we all met at the Reform Club at 7.0.

I first heard of Horabin about a year ago, when Randolph Churchill rang me up and said there was a man called Horabin fighting a by-election in Cornwall as a Liberal, but that the principal plank in his platform was 'Churchill for premier'. To meet he is tall, fair, with thick lips and thick features, and with a pleasant easy manner. It appears that he is a very active member of the all-party group which also includes Clement Davies, Amery, Boothby, Harold Macmillan, Salter, and so on. These men are mainly concerned with the more vigorous prosecution of the war, and played a leading part in the ejection of Chamberlain and the accession of Churchill. They are now very dissatisfied with Churchill, who is all right as a speaker and figurehead: but so many of our troubles are administrative, and Churchill is not a good administrator and is not interested in the subject. In any case, he is now so much in the grip of the old bunch that people are calling him Neville Churchill. On this subject of administration, which boils down to the evils of Treasury control of all Civil Service appointments and dismissals, Amery, Salter, and others have all tackled Churchill and been very roughly handled for their pains.

On the subject of Churchill's Government as a whole, this group is very dissatisfied. Amery and some others were on the point of resigning last week and may still resign at any moment. They feel that Chamberlainism in all walks of life must go, and if

Churchill clings to that set in the Tory Party, he must go too. They think the most probable result is a Lloyd George Government with a Cabinet of fairly young men, most of whom would necessarily be unknown to the general public. I said the people would accept such a Government – provided Lloyd George led it – whether Churchill were in or out of it. Lloyd George's idea would be to fight to the point of proving to the Germans that they could neither invade us nor starve us, and then negotiate.

Horabin said that some time ago – I suppose when Churchill was forming his Government – Churchill wrote to Lloyd George and offered him a seat in the War Cabinet, if Chamberlain did not object. Lloyd George thought this was an insult. A week or two ago Churchill wrote to him again and said that Chamberlain had now withdrawn his objections, and would Lloyd George like to come in? He indignantly refused. Hore-Belisha told Cudlipp the same story, only in a somewhat less specific form, as having been told by Lloyd George himself.

Horabin said several people in the secret session referred to stories of officers running away at Dunkirk. It does appear that there were a lot of cases of officers who pushed in front of their men, or who deserted their men in order to get an earlier boat home.

Horabin also said that in the House of Commons Chamberlain is still supposed to have a huge popular following. He quite agreed with us that this is no longer so, but said that the average M.P. is completely out of touch with public opinion, while being very frightened of it. He said that there is a great difference between the M.P.s who have fought by-elections in the last eighteen months, and the others. The former have been in close touch with public opinion fairly recently, while the others are still thinking in terms of the last General Election (whenever that was).

June 25, 1940

In the afternoon I had a call from Beaverbrook, who wanted to see me urgently, so I went to his office in the I.C.I. building in Millbank. The *Mirror* had published a story about a boy of fourteen who, after being given some training in an aeroplane factory, had been sent back to school by the education authorities

5

for a few weeks in order to comply with the regulations, leaving the plane factory short of a pair of hands that were badly needed.

Beaverbrook had given me no idea of the purpose of his summons, but had this story on his desk. He dismissed it in a few words as not very important, and relating anyway to a period before he became Minister [of Aircraft Production].

I had met Beaverbrook once before at a dinner given by the American Ambassador to about fifteen of the leading newspaper men. He is clearly a man of real personality and ability, head and shoulders over most of the governmental figures I have met. I should say he is past his best, but still full of vigour and drive. As is shown in all his caricatures the fact that you notice about his face is its width, so that it almost seems as if it were wider than it is long. His eyes are very wide apart and his mouth is very big, and these points are accentuated by moles to the right of his right eye and to the left of his mouth.

When I left him I was not quite clear why he had summoned me. He said that he was working quite well with the trade unions and hoped we should not make difficulties for him in that respect. I said that, of course, it was no part of our policy to do anything of the kind. He said that some aircraft factories were working flat out and others had very little work indeed, but that there was no point in attacking this state of affairs: that the bottleneck was not aircraft factories but fabricated metal. Everything possible was being done to step up our production of fabricated metal, particularly extruded aluminium.

What it all boils down to, as far as I could afterwards gather in the office, is that Hawker's works at Kingston are overworking and the men cannot stand the strain of twelve-hour shifts seven days a week much longer; and that in the Handley Page factory there is discontent at the lack of work. Beaverbrook was not sure whether we were out to make trouble for the sake of making trouble, and so asked me to come along, to see where I stood and to ask us not to play up the troubles at Handley Page, which came to a head earlier in the afternoon.

In the course of conversation Beaverbrook showed me a chart (marked 'MOST SECRET' in red capitals) which showed the weekly production of aeroplanes of all types, and of engines, and also of repaired aeroplanes and of repaired engines – all of which are on the up-grade. The production of aeroplanes of all types has trended up in the last two months, from about 400 a week to just under 500; and of engines to just under 700. The repaired planes and engines show satisfactory increases, too. Needless to say there was no foundation whatever on this chart for the story put about in official quarters recently that our production of planes was three and half times what it was a month ago. Beaverbrook said the real trouble is engines rather than planes, and that there were in store planes without engines that had been there for two years or even more. The engine production, however, was going up quite nicely, and they were starting to build up a reserve against the day when the aeroplane factories are being bombed.

Beaverbrook mentioned what a bad way we were in with regard to some (unspecified) aspects of aeroplane production, so I asked why he had published such a boost for Kingsley Wood, saying what a wonderful foundation he had laid and so on. Beaverbrook said (a) that it paid to be generous in public life; (b) that if you are doing better than your predecessor, it reflects more credit on you to suggest that he was a stout chap than to admit that he was a fool; and (c) that he was playing politics, as the announcement was made only two days before the secret session at which some very strong criticism of Chamberlain and his friends was expected.

June 28, 1940
We are rather clearer in our minds about Beaverbrook's summons the other day. After my visit to him, we had a deputation from the Handley Page workpeople. We listened and promised nothing. Next day Bevin, the Labour Minister, went down and gave them a speech in which he promised to deal with all their grievances (mostly that they had not enough work). The Handley Page people have thanked us for having Bevin sent down to settle their complaints; Beaverbrook has thanked us for respecting his wishes. In actual fact we did nothing whatever, except listen to both stories.

July 4, 1940
Had dinner with William Sempill at the Athenaeum to meet Sir

Henry Tizard, who is chairman of the Scientific Advisory Board of the Air Ministry, but is apparently resigning, if he has not already done so. In peacetime he is head of the Imperial College of Science. Aged about fifty-five, he is a small, ugly, untidy little man, with auburn hair turning grey, the auburn of a shade which makes it look badly dyed (though it isn't). He has cold grey eyes, a pince-nez, and a dark reddish moustache. In spite of this thoroughly unimpressive appearance, he is very intelligent, very human, and very able – one of the very best men I have met. He clearly ought to have been brought into the Government in a really big way years ago. He is not a man to mesmerize the public, but clearly one to get on effectively with the job.

Tizard expressed great dissatisfaction with Churchill as Prime Minister. Said Churchill has a lot of professional advisers all of whom are too weak to stand up to him, and that in consequence he can talk them into anything. He sees himself as another Marlborough, and Tizard himself had seen him on some trivial matter exclaim: 'I command that this be done' – this with a theatrical gesture. Lindemann's influence he thought thoroughly bad. He said all Lindemann's technical schemes so far had gone wrong, though it is always possible that one of his ideas might come off. In the meanwhile, he wastes money and effort in ideas which the bulk of expert opinion had already rejected, getting the highest priority for projects which were inevitable failures.

Tizard had had an interview recently with Chamberlain. He said he likes Chamberlain, has no respect for his capacity and thinks him far too old, but regards him as an old dear.

July 12, 1940

Bart tells me that he had a call from a private detective yesterday. This man's business was a kind of industrial espionage. In very large firms he was employed by the men at the very top to plant workers in their various branches to report on the working of the business, the complaints and grievances of the staff, and the efficiency or otherwise of the foremen and works managers. Soon after the war began he was invited by the Admiralty to give up his business and to take on similar work for them at Devonport dockyard. He has just had seven months there and has resigned in disgust. He said the waste and mismanagement are on a scale unknown in the most incompetent private concern. At present 18,000 men are employed doing work which should require 3,000. He said specifically that he had reported that a wood store had been established around or alongside the turpentine store containing 8,000 gallons of turpentine. If a bomb strikes any of this there will be an almighty fire, and blazing turpentine will float about on the nearby water and do great damage to ships. He reported against this arrangement two months ago. Since then there have been repeated air raids, but nothing has been done. He says the system of allotting material to ships is centuries old. Once stores are booked out for the repair of an individual ship, they are not put back in store. If not required after all, they are just scrapped. After seven months of reporting with no action taken on his reports, he has resigned in despair and appealed to us. We are putting him in touch with an M.P., perhaps Hore-Belisha.

July 15, 1940
Had lunch with Ward Price. He mentioned meeting Churchill at lunch with Rothermere in 1934, just after Ward Price had got back from a trip to Germany. Churchill had not recently been to Germany, displayed no interest in what was going on there, but expressed horror that Ward Price should have gone and shaken hands 'with these murderous Nazis'. It apparently never occurred to him to go to Germany and try and see what Hitlerism was all about. Ward Price, by way of repartee, pointed out that Churchill had not shrunk from shaking hands with equally murderous Mike Collins [*Irish Sinn Fein leader*] in 1922. Churchill admitted this, but said he had been misled and never ceased to regret it. Ward Price says Churchill (he hears this from Brendan Bracken) tends to change his mind and vacillate: he is not at all like he was in the last war. It is in this sort of way he shows his age. Brendan Bracken told Ward Price that Churchill values Chamberlain's judgment (!), and keeps him definitely because he values him as a member of his Government.

In November 1937 Ward Price went to Munich and found himself in the same train with Halifax, who was going to see

Hitler. Halifax was travelling with only a valet and when they got to Munich hopped out with his bags like any ordinary traveller. Sir Nevile Henderson and the appropriate German officials were running up and down the platform trying to find Halifax. Ribbentrop, Ward Price said, would have arrived in his private aeroplane or, failing that, would have had a special carriage for himself and his suite. Halifax, Ward Price said, has a deprecating smile 'almost as if he had a guilty secret'. When on this train journey, Ward Price and Halifax had sleepers in the same coach. In the morning he asked Ward Price if it were customary to give the sleeping-car attendant a gratuity! Apparently Halifax had never been in a sleeping car before, except, presumably, when in India. Ward Price said he completely lacked the ordinary experience and ordinary human touch of ordinary human beings.

July 18, 1940

Some time ago two men came to see Chapman in Manchester [*he was in charge of the* Mirror *office there*] with a terrible story about the disorganization and lack of output of the Vickers-Armstrong works at Barrow. So last Sunday a *Mirror* reporter dressed up in a dirty cap and dungarees and tried to get into these works and have a look round. To his surprise there was no check on unauthorized people entering the works, and in fact he spent the whole day there wandering about. He went on board the new aircraft carrier *Indomitable*, which is being finished, and into the shop where some coastal defence artillery was being completed. In a long report he drew up, he estimated that 75% of the workmen he saw were doing nothing at all. Many had done no work for weeks and some not even for months, and all the men were completely fed up. There was ample material, willing and skilled men and quantities of machinery, but practically no output. One gun, which had been completed, was out in the rain and had been out for at least two months, he was told. Fourteen men he found asleep in a pocket in a big gun mounting.

All the men were convinced that the system of charging up the labour cost on each job was designed to cover up the fact that so little work was being done, and to yield the firm an additional and illicit profit. And in spite of the lack of work, the works were running on ten-and-a-half-hour shifts seven days a week!

This report seemed to Bart and to me too damaging to be printed, and yet revealed a situation that must be put right. Bart went to Morrison, who as Minister of Supply is responsible for 20% of the output of this works. Morrison gave Bart the impression that he would look into the matter, but was more concerned to cover up any scandal than to put it right. This morning he rings up to say he and Alexander are sending their men up today to investigate. Bart sent a copy to Bevin, who sent a man up last night. About 5.30 p.m. Bart and I went to see Beaverbrook, as we felt he was involved with Vickers-Armstrong, and in any case might if necessary put in a word with Churchill. Beaverbrook was very friendly, and promised to take the matter up with the managing director of Vickers-Armstrong.

July 27, 1940
Sempill arranged some time ago that I should meet R.A. Butler, Under-Secretary of State for Foreign Affairs. The meeting was eventually fixed for noon today and I was with him for about half an hour. In spite of the way defence preparations have been keyed up, I got into Downing Street without being questioned in any way. A man stopped me at the entrance to the Foreign Office courtyard, and, of course, when I got into the Foreign Office itself I had to fill in forms and what not. I was shown up to the Under-Secretary's waiting room by a girl in an overall – the corridors seemed full of girls with pimply faces in their teens. The main staircase of the Foreign Office is a massive and imposing affair decorated with tapestries. The style – marble pillars and the rest – is more associated in one's mind with luxury hotels than with an office. At the top of the stairs, immediately facing you is an idyllic scene: cows, blossom, and what not, with a woman with a very full bosom suckling an infant. I didn't see the connection with diplomacy. The Under-Secretary's waiting room is a large and gloomy apartment rather like the best kind of railway waiting room. Round the walls bad copies of pictures of royalty: Queen Victoria and two Georgian queens. Literature provided for visitors consisted of the *Herald* and *Telegraph*, an atlas, a book of

photos published by The Studio called *This is England*, and a book of photos of the International Horse Show of 1910. While I was at the Foreign Office I saw nothing of any kind which suggested a date later than 1900.

Eventually 'Chips' Channon came to fetch me to the presence. He is Butler's Parliamentary Private Secretary. He was a rich young American when I knew him at Christ Church [Oxford]. He had to do something for a living, so he married one of the daughters of Lord Iveagh [*of the Guinness family*], said to be worth £20,000 a year, and went into politics. I had not seen him since 1922. He now looks stronger and more assured. His elevation [in 1938] to the position of Parliamentary Private Secretary was due to Margesson [*then, and until December 1940, Government Chief Whip*], who wanted Channon to do some entertaining for him: this was to be the quid pro quo. Pickthorn (M.P. for Cambridge University) told me Butler was rather criticized in the House for lending himself to this.

Butler is not at all what I expected. He has been the coming young man for some time. His father and two uncles were governors of Indian provinces and he married the heiress of old Sam Courtauld. To meet, he looks about forty-five or more (he is thirty-seven), sallow, rather puffy, and inclined to be fat. He has an unhealthy pallor and pale grey eyes, a languid manner and a limp handshake. In brief, first appearances are very unfavourable, but he improves on acquaintance and is obviously intelligent. I should say he had no drive and less than no sense of popular feeling. In fact as a political leader he is quite out of the question, but behind the scenes he might do useful work. I should say he is rather die-hard, but keeps a reasonably open mind.

I said how Churchill and Beaverbrook gripped the public by their speeches on the wireless. He said that he hoped government would not have to be by only these tough chaps, but could proceed on the traditional British lines. I gather he thought Halifax representative of those lines, though he said that he thought Halifax himself would very soon have outrun his period of usefulness. I said I thought you must have the tough guys as leaders for the people, but it was always well to have brainy people behind the scenes to tell the tough ones what to do. He seemed to realize that Chamberlain is a serious political liability, but said that even Attlee and Greenwood would agree on the value of his work in Cabinet, which is better than that of anyone else. Butler also spoke of the fierce ideological prejudice that had been stirred up by the Press, but seemed to realize that attacks on Nazis, Fascists, and to some extent Communists, were intended not to make people hate the said Nazis, Fascists, and what nots, but, by making them aware of the danger that threatened, to render them more conscious of being British and so to pull them together.

Butler was very friendly, had to show me out because a Norwegian minister had arrived by appointment, but said we must have lunch together soon and continue our talk.

August 5, 1940
Bart tells me that since the beginning of the war we have been telegraphing pictures from Scotland to London for the use of the Government. They have never consulted us about this service, which we could greatly improve. I imagine it operates from our usual Glasgow or Edinburgh centres. At one time most of the pictures urgently flashed to London were of ships in the North Sea photographed by the R.A.F., with the query whether or no they were to be attacked. It seems an unbelievably cumbersome system of recognition, or a hopeless case of over-centralization – to photograph the ship, fly the photo to Edinburgh, develop the picture, flash it to the *Mirror*, send it to the Air Ministry or Admiralty with a request for orders!

August 7, 1940
Duff Cooper was the guest of honour at a dinner on Monday [August 5] given by some of the Fleet Street lads. It went quite well. Duff Cooper revealed that he would like our propaganda to be based on our vision of the future, but he found it quite impossible to sell such an idea to Lord Halifax. Duff Cooper also said he would always see editors, and would gladly do all he could to work in the closest possible co-operation with the Press.

I thought this might be the moment to appear once more [at the Ministry of Information] and see whether I could do anything to help, so I asked for an interview, and saw Duff Cooper this evening at 6.30. To meet he is far less definite than I expected: he gives rather a limp impression. He sat with his back to the light and put me into a corner, almost behind him and well in shadow. He showed very little response to what I said and seemed to me tired and fed up with the whole business. He told me that Kenneth Lee had never told him that I had been approached by Reith for a job. Duff Cooper believed Kenneth Lee had been a serious obstructionist; he was leaving and being replaced by Frank Pick on Monday next. Duff Cooper thought his own position an unenviable one. For example, this afternoon he had had to face a meeting of the 1922 Committee of the House of Commons, furious because the Ministry of Information had sent Socialist speakers into their constituencies to give pep talks about the war.

He thanked me for coming to see him: said he could not discuss any post for me until Pick arrived next week. I said I hadn't come just to reopen the question of a job for myself, but to say that if I could help in any way – small or great – I would, as it was only through the Ministry of Information that I could help our war effort.

Duff Cooper is still very anti-Chamberlain. Incidentally, he said that because of the *Mirror*'s anti-Chamberlain attitude, he would have to mention any appointment for me to the Prime Minister before he could do anything.

He mentioned that Churchill had said to him how odd it was that in the last war he could never say the right thing – and here he recalled the speech he made about digging the German submarines out of their home ports like rats out of their holes – while in this war everything he said was right, though he felt now just the same as he felt then. Duff Cooper agreed that Churchill was quite unaware of his power in the country and strangely afraid of the Tory majority in the House. He said that at present any attempt by the House of Commons to turn Churchill out would result in its being burnt to the ground.

He revealed that he had asked Beaverbrook to release Christiansen, the editor of the *Daily Express*; and, on another occasion, Robertson, general manager of the *Daily Express*, whom he wished to take over control of our foreign propaganda. Beaverbrook refused to release these men and Duff Cooper had not, I gathered, tackled them direct. I said if I wanted a man for Government work in time of war I should get him, whether by bribery, blackmail, or other means. Duff Cooper, at this, said that if it came to bribery or blackmail he felt sure Beaverbrook would win!

August 16, 1940

A call came through yesterday from Frank Pick, the new Director-General of the Ministry of Information, asking me to look in and see him, which I did at four o'clock. It all started on a pretty muddled footing, as Duff Cooper gave Pick to understand that he had talked over with me a job concerned with the maintenance of morale at home. He had done nothing of the sort. Nevertheless, after a good talk lasting about forty-five minutes, it all got straightened out. Pick is a large, slow man, with big eyes, sandy-grey hair, and a Yorkshire accent. He looks intelligent, capable, and very, very nice.

I told him of my dealings with the Ministry at different stages and went back to my interest in the subject three or four years ago, when I took up the subject of propaganda with Duff Cooper, then Secretary for War. He eventually said that I was just the man he wanted for the home Press, but there were other people's views to be considered, and he was a bit nervous that I might play too strong a hand and get him and the Ministry into a spot of bother. I gathered Duff Cooper had gone away for the weekend, but that the matter would be raised on Monday.

August 22, 1940

Had lunch with Asquith, of the National Labour Party organization, and Harold Nicolson, Parliamentary Secretary to the Minister of Information. I had not met Nicolson before. He is a stout florid little man, rather bald, and is most amusing. I should say he is very pleasant, intelligent, unambitious, and no politician. He began by saying that it was interesting that the most ardent Chamberlainites were not the old landed aristocracy, or Eton and Oxford, but what he described as 'Repton and the family business'; that such people saw in Chamberlain one of themselves. Asquith said he understood the operation on Chamberlain was an exploratory one that revealed an inoperable condition.[13] Nicolson said he was sorry for him; that he had been a man of impenetrable vanity, but to see a vain man humiliated in old age, as he had been, was a distressing sight. I asked if he *really* felt humiliated and Nicolson said he obviously did, and had aged greatly.

Operation Sea Lion was the name given to the German plan to invade England. The German high command aimed to land on a 200-mile front from North Foreland to Lyme Bay, even though Admiral Raeder, the naval Commander-in-Chief, maintained that he could support a landing only on a narrow front around Beachy Head. But wherever the Germans were to land, it was essential that they should first gain control of the air. To do this they must destroy the R.A.F.

The German air offensive against Britain began in July with the bombing of the Channel convoys and coastal towns. From August 13 the Luftwaffe attacks moved inland. On August 24 the most critical stage of the battle began when the Germans set out to destroy the airfields and vital fighter-control centres in the south of England. If the Germans had succeeded in doing this, they might have won the Battle of Britain. And they came very near to success. Fortunately, on September 7, Hitler switched the main German attack to London. This was an emotional decision, made in retaliation against British bombing raids in Germany. The Luftwaffe commanders hoped that this all-out assault on London would provoke a decisive battle with the R.A.F. As it turned out, it did, and the Germans lost it. On September 16, the British public were jubilant to read that the R.A.F. the day before had destroyed 183 German planes for the loss of under forty. The true figures were between fifty-six and sixty German to twenty-six British planes, but this day was, as was sensed at the time, the decisive day. On September 17 Hitler postponed Sea Lion; on October 12 he called it off until spring 1941.

But the bombing continued. Between September 7 and November 2 alone, an average of 200 bombers raided London every night. The provinces also suffered. Altogether during the Blitz 3,500,000 houses were damaged or destroyed, 30,000 people killed. The last heavy raid was in May 1941, on Birmingham. After that the British public had a three-year respite, until the arrival of the flying bombs brought a new terror to the home front.

August 31, 1940
This morning at 3.15 I was woken up by a thump, thump-thump,

thump, thump of a stick of bombs bursting apparently not far away. At any rate they shook the house and rattled the windows.[14] On looking out of the window I could see no searchlights and heard no planes. Earlier in the evening between 10.0 and 11.0 there was a continuous procession of aeroplanes passing over from north-west to south-east. Philpot, the gardener, said that later on the planes seemed to be going the other way, and he heard the sound of many bombs bursting in the distance west of us. His wife is nervous and keeps him awake when German planes are about; M. is quite unwar-minded and when she was woken up by the bombs thought it was one of the maids overhead who had dropped something heavy!

The main brunt of the German attack seems to be on aerodromes in the south-east. One would get the impression, though even in the office there are no real facts to go on, that the Germans are methodically destroying the aerodromes extending from Dover outwards, and that though we inflict heavy loss we are unable to stop the process. The raids all over the country and at night seem to be nuisance raids and for training purposes.

At the Reform yesterday Pick came up to me to say he could not take our conversation any further, as the whole situation was very confused and he had a lot to straighten out before he could come round to me; that, moreover, the situation lacked unanimity on my side of the fence. I gather he meant by this that he had ascertained that if I were given a responsible position the appointment would not be greeted by a unanimous chorus of approval by Fleet Street. If he seriously expected unanimity on such an issue he must be stupider than I thought.

Bart had dinner two nights ago with Heanley, our photographer, who is now a rear gunner in an R.A.F. bomber. He has done seven trips to Germany though he is forty-one, and was in the R.A.F. in the last war, and has a son in the R.A.F. now! He says our planes are all on the slow side, in the case of the bombers so much so that we cannot try any daylight raids. In air fighting he says the whole thing is quick recognition. If the other fellow knows you are an enemy a split second before you know he is, he may well knock you out, and vice versa. This operates in our favour when the Germans come over in massed formation, as almost every plane in the melée is a German. When a plane flashes into view our men can fire knowing it almost must be an enemy, while the Germans must withhold their fire as it is almost necessarily a friend.

Heanley revealed that his squadron were supplied with tanks to fit under the wings of their aeroplanes for spraying mustard gas. They had also done some work on spraying troops from the air with a pink powder to represent mustard gas. He is under the impression that this will only be resorted to in the event of its use by the Germans, presumably to back up an invasion.

September 1, 1940

Last night at 11.20 as I was packing up to leave the office, off went the sirens for the sixth time in sixteen hours. However, the all-clear sounded just before midnight and I set out in the car. At first there were no searchlights, but I hadn't gone far before they started groping round to the north of me and later to the south as well. As I got out on the Great West Road I could see gun-flashes in the sky away to the north. A woman was standing on the corner, where the Great West Road starts, waiting for a lift. However, in spite of the six air-raid alarms, the planes about, the gun-flashes and all, she refused a lift from me, though it would need a very persistent philanderer indeed to attempt anything in an 8 H.P. Ford under the circumstances!

When I reached the Bath Road there were planes away to the south of me, and as I got nearer the Colnbrook bypass, one was clearly heading north across my route. After a time the searchlights got it and the A.A. [*Anti-Aircraft*] guns opened fire. You would see the flash of the guns – three batteries seemed to be firing – and after a pause a vivid orange flash in the sky. One or two shots were not bad, but some of them must have been literally miles out. The shots were being fired singly, whereas I thought A.A. guns fired in groups of four. The plane seemed to be making for Langley aerodrome, which I was due to pass, so when I got on to the Colnbrook bypass I stopped the car to let the plane pass. Meanwhile a fire had broken out ahead of me. When the plane had gone far enough off, I moved on and found one or two red-brick villas near the road between Langley and Slough blazing, also a line of fir trees bounding the garden. For a plane blinded by searchlights it was a very near miss for Langley aerodrome.

The other side of Slough I picked up a soldier hiding in the ditch, who said the plane had dropped six bombs, one a screamer, and had caused the fire. They can't have been very big bombs because I didn't hear or feel them burst. I was driving a very noisy car on a very bumpy road and there were A.A. guns as well as everything else, but I should have thought I would have heard them burst half a mile away. Meanwhile of course the fire attracted all the planes in the neighbourhood – you could see the clusters of searchlights moving our way – so I sped home and got there just before 2.0 a.m. As I locked up the car six searchlights formed a star directly over the house, searching for a plane travelling north-west. Shortly after, a plane passed over travelling south-east, so I dare say this one was just circling round.

I had some dinner last night at the Spanish restaurant with a little Hungarian sculptor called Levy. He had written to me about some ideas for the paper and I thought the easiest way to work him off was over dinner. In the course of our conversation he asked me about the English people and their reactions to war and so on, and on the spur of the moment I evolved the following idea.

France owed its importance before this war to the fact that it was a cultural centre, the culture dating back to the 17th century. It is quite impossible that France, now she has broken down, can be rebuilt on the old cultural lines. But apart from her cultural tradition France is nothing. Therefore she has no contribution to make in the near future and may well fade out altogether. England owes its greatness to the fact that as a country we rely on our instincts and not our intelligence. At the moment we are suffering from having been too rich too long, but eliminating that factor and supposing we can find our best form in the future, the result would be that once more we should rely on our instincts.

I shall illustrate the sort of thing I mean. British poetry, as an artistic whole, is richer anyway than that of any other Western country, and it owes its excellence to the fact that it has an elusive quality: the sentiments concerned are not, so to speak, cut and dried. Or even better, one could take the Anglican Church. The body of its beliefs, the Thirty-nine Articles, are not all honestly believed by anyone, but behind this entirely phoney façade the Church has until recently adapted itself to changing conditions. To change the Thirty-nine Articles every time they become obsolete would have killed the Church of England long ago. Such an attitude is quite illogical, but works. This attitude of ours worked well enough outside the religious sphere, too, throughout the Industrial Revolution, which was entirely individualist, not to say opportunist. In fact, the needs of the moment and our inherited genius dovetailed in extraordinarily well throughout the last century.

But now the trend of the times is towards totalitarianism, which necessitates planning. The Germans have a passion for organization and here *their* natural aptitudes and the requirements of the moment fit in remarkably well. But our reliance on instinct and dislike of any clear-cut thought just doesn't fill the bill.

If we can slough off the after-effects of the overfed age we have just been through, our reliance on instinct will once again, though perhaps after an interval, stand us in good stead. Perhaps it will be our destiny in the new world to be a cultural centre. I am sure the United States will be politically the Anglo-Saxon world power, with the British possessions in America in her orbit. Our position as a world power has depended on the retention of the trading conditions of the 19th century. Now that they are gone I cannot see that our Empire, built up on sea power as it is and with a population of only 50,000,000 at the centre, can be maintained in anything like its old form.

September 4, 1940
I had some chat with Bernard Gray [Mirror *war correspondent*] this morning. He has been twice to Dover in the last ten days and got back the last time on Sunday evening. He said that some Messerschmitts come over every morning and shoot down some barrage balloons, but on Saturday they came over and shot down all twenty-three of them. In the evening seventeen new ones were up,

but they were also shot down. He submitted a story mentioning the forty barrage balloons, which was passed by the censor except that he changed 'forty' into 'two'! Needless to say everyone in Dover knew how many balloons had gone, and will judge the news from other parts of the country in the light of the official lies about Dover.

While I was writing this at 7.30 p.m. at Culham, Duff Cooper rang up and asked me to dinner. I said I was at Henley, but could come up at a pinch. He said it didn't matter, but what about Tuesday, as in the interim he was going away for a long weekend? So Tuesday it is. But I can't help being astonished at the way an interview is put off for six days, as if we had years to play about with.

September 8, 1940
I got back at 5.30 this morning, very glad of the quiet at Culham after a pretty rough night. After midnight, the main fire in the docks began to die down, but meanwhile fresh fires had started, particularly a very big one near Liverpool Street station, and one due south of the office. This last was obscured by the Record Office. It might have been on the Thames between Waterloo and Blackfriars Bridge, or might have been further off.

Liverpool Street station ceased to function and no alternative route was possible: we gather that the fire nearby extended to their signal box. The staff at King's Cross went to ground at 8.30 and refused to move. In consequence we could not get anyone to load our papers on to the 10.15 to Newcastle, and the train – a passenger one – left without them. The L.N.E.R. [*London and North-Eastern Railway*] promised to put on two specials – when the staff could be induced to load them. About 2.45 I curled up on the sofa in my room and fell asleep for an hour. Then a visit to the roof showed that German aeroplanes were giving London more of a rest: there were searchlights on only one place and that due east, so I decided to head for home at 4.0 a.m.

The drive home was without incident, though a lot of search-lights woke up when I reached the Great West Road, and made a wigwam over my head. The roads were completely clear; between Chiswick and Slough I saw only one bicycle on the move; there was no other traffic of any kind either coming or going. On the whole journey from Fetter Lane to Culham, which is about thirty-five miles, I reckon there were five bicycles, two lorries, and six taxis. I met a lot of abandoned buses and trolley-buses, several for instance of the former in Holborn, and six in a row at the Harlington corner on the Bath Road. When I got to Hurley, I was stopped by the Home Guard, who, in conversation, told me that they had all been turned out. This is only supposed to happen in the event of an invasion![15] They had seen the reflection of the fires in the sky: it looked like a sunset even at that distance. Of course nearer the office the red glare made all the buildings glow pink – this quite as far west as Shepherd's Bush.

September 10, 1940
As I am to be up late tonight dining with Duff Cooper, I set out for Maidenhead to catch the 9.40. It was about thirty-five minutes late, I don't know why, but reached Paddington without incident. I tried as usual to buy a ticket for Farringdon Street, but was told I could not book beyond Baker Street. When I got to Baker Street station I could see why. A large bomb had hit Madame Tussaud's and scooped the inside out. The blast and splinters had hit the side of Chiltern Court and stove in all the lower windows and smashed all the others. Doubtless the Metropolitan Railway tunnel has been weakened. I took a taxi from there. The taxi man was very apologetic and said how hard it would be to reach the *Mirror* office, what with Holborn still blocked, the Strand jammed with traffic, and the Embankment blocked by some bombs at the back of the Savoy. Eventually we reached Carey Street and had to stop because of two bombs, one of which fell on the Chancery Lane post office and the other on the National Provincial Bank in Carey Street.

September 11, 1940
Last night I went to the Dorchester to dine with Duff Cooper. To make sure of being on time, in spite of air raids, I arrived about 7.30 p.m. – an hour early – and had some talk with Barbara Back, Somerset Maugham, and others. Other people in the hall were Leslie Howard, the actor, Cicely Courtneidge, Clarence Hatry

and his wife (both of whom are living in the Dorchester!), and Oliver Stanley. The last has a densely stupid face. Duff Cooper and Halifax are both living at the Dorchester just now. The hotel, to my astonishment, proved to be crammed full and I had the greatest difficulty in getting a bed. Apparently a lot of jittery people, who do not regard their own houses as very stable, have moved in there. It was amusing at 11.0 p.m., when I went up to bed, to see the astonishing mixed grill of people, mostly women with knitting, assembled in the hall to spend the night in chairs, or in the shelter if bombing got too bad.

The dinner with Duff Cooper proved to be a three-legged affair, the third leg being Ivor Fraser, one-time general manager of the *Morning Post* and recently appointed Director of Home Affairs at the Ministry of Information. The dinner proved to be a sort of get-together feast with no specific objective. I gather it was felt that our two papers are rather key ones and that something must be done to keep them sweet. Duff Cooper's aim and object was not to do a grand job, but by judicious hand-shaking behind the scenes to avoid criticism of the Ministry. Suggestions of what to do – and particularly of personnel – were not wanted. I have known Ivor Fraser for years and knew what to expect from him, but Duff Cooper was more impotent, more negligible, and more defeated than one would have thought possible. He has no idea what to do about his Ministry, or about the other ministries that obstruct his work, or about the newspapers that criticize. He just wants the Ministry of Information to be left in peace.

The one item of news he revealed was that (he implied unfortunately) Chamberlain showed signs of improving health.

After two and a half hours of Duff Cooper and Ivor Fraser I felt so exasperated that it was more anger with them than the subsequent bombing that kept me awake. A.A. guns were going all through dinner, but it wasn't until I went to bed that the fun really began. Bombs were dropping pretty continuously – i.e. at ten-minute intervals – from 11.30 p.m. till 3.30 a.m., and to a lesser extent before and after. One of them seemed really near and made the whole Dorchester sway. It is a very noisy hotel – you can hear everything that everyone does all round you – and it was quite clear that no one slept a wink until four o'clock. The

A.A. guns in Hyde Park made an infernal din, but were not in action much of the time.

This morning one gets the impression that damage was more on the West End and less in the east. Anyway there was a bomb at Marble Arch, a big one in Bryanston Square, and another on Lansdowne House in Berkeley Square. I hear that a lot of Edgware Road, the Cricklewood end, is smashed, and also Marylebone Road. Regent Street and Bond Street are blocked and there is a time bomb in the Burlington Arcade. There is another time bomb in Leicester Square, and Kingsway is blocked. A corner shop near a church at the top is destroyed and a broken gas main is flaming at one side. There is increasing difficulty over gas and water, the former because of the destruction of gas-works, the latter because of the quantity of water used for fire-fighting. So much is this so that last night we made plates for the *Daily Sketch*, who had no gas, and blocks for the *Evening News*, who had no water. None of the falling bombs last night whistled or screamed, but instead made a sort of whispering sound that increased in volume until it sounded rather like the passing of wind through leafy trees.

September 17, 1940
Ward Price at lunch said he was told a story by David Bowes-Lyon, brother of the Queen. Bowes-Lyon was in 10 Downing Street just as Chamberlain was leaving for the House of Commons for the debate on Norway. He heard Chamberlain say: 'I am quite confident we shall get away with it.' It came as a shock, he said, to realize that Chamberlain did not refer to the Norwegian campaign, but to the vote in the House!

September 21, 1940
Duff Cooper held a press conference yesterday at which he said that two ships had been torpedoed two or three days out into the Atlantic, just after leaving their convoy. One was the *Marina*, of which he made no further mention, the other the *City of Benares* conveying a hundred refugee children to Canada. Only thirteen children were saved, but about a hundred of the other passengers and crew. It appears that the Lascars rushed the boats (from the figures of thirty-six Lascars saved and forty-six white crew, it

would appear that the white crew were no better) and the children never had a chance. The whole story reflects no credit on anyone.

September 23, 1940
On Saturday I was entertaining five of M.'s evacuees[14] and made a bonfire for them. They are very town-bred children and had never heard of a bonfire before. When the fire was burning well, they asked me when I was going to put the bombs on!

That evening I had dinner with Cudlipp at the Savoy Hotel. I made for the restaurant (the Grill Room is long since closed altogether), but found that meals were being served in the air-raid shelter, so we threaded our way through endless passages and down into a large pillared room. Apparently the pillars were inadequate as the whole ceiling was supported by steel scaffolding – vertical and diagonal supports about six feet apart. As a consequence it was very difficult to get to one's table and equally difficult for the waiters to serve the food. These difficulties did not, I am afraid, stimulate the staff to do their best. The food was indifferent in quality and scanty in quantity, and the service was careless and sulky. The only thing up to the usual Savoy standard was the violinist operating behind some sandbags.

On our way out we overshot the exit by a couple of yards and found ourselves in the residents' portion of the shelter, inhabited by one fierce elderly military man in pyjamas and dressing gown and his wife, a stout matronly woman in crêpe-de-chine nightie and wrap. Besides this couple there was a younger one in evening dress, and miscellaneous domestics. We eventually stumbled out into the Strand, where the raid warning had been on for some time. It was pitch dark: on these occasions the black-out is real. Guns could be heard in the distance and A.A. shells were bursting some way away to the east. The gun-flashes flickering on the horizon looked just like summer lightning.

September 25, 1940
Yesterday we took F. [*Francis King, Cecil King's son*] to Winchester for his first term. It was a marvellous day and we motored down through Reading and Basingstoke. In Winchester itself more has been done than in any other place I know in the way of concrete

blocks, particularly in side roads. On the way down there was nothing unusual except a long deep trench outside Basingstoke. It would be on the south side, say six feet deep, six or more feet wide, and two miles or so long. I took it to be a defence against tanks. When we were walking round the college, I heard three thumps – clearly bombs not so very far away. No one took any notice at all. Later I heard a plane, which sounded vaguely German; then the A.A. guns opened up. The plane was heading for Southampton, and soon the plane and the firing receded into the distance. Still no one took any notice. Five minutes later the air-raid warning went and everyone raced for cover! Spinsters in tin hats started cycling busily about and the whole scene in the Close was like a picture in *Punch* of 'War comes to our village.' Obviously they had had very few warnings, and they were still a great thrill.

September 30, 1940
Last night we had dinner with Raymond [Mortimer], and Godfrey Winn was there. I used to see a good deal of Godfrey when he was in the office, but have only seen him once – at Manchester – in the last year or two. At the moment he is trying to get into the R.A.F. as a rear gunner. Winn is a curiously complex character. He is hard-working and mercenary and yet he has a streak of sympathy and sincerity, which enables him to write for and speak to very ordinary people, particularly women, in a way they understand. He is emphatically not a champion of lost causes, but a sort of emotional lowest common denominator of the mass of the people, and particularly the feminine half of that mass. He has been in the East End a good deal lately, reporting the plight of the homeless for the *Sunday Express*, who finally refused to print his stuff, thinking it too depressing and critical. In his opinion, and he gets about a lot, public morale is low and falling. He says people were never keen on the war, never understood what it was about, and are completely fed up.

He told us a story of petty East End officialdom that had a touch of grim humour about it. The homeless people in the East End were told to go to the Victoria Palace in the Mile End Road to put themselves down for rehousing and for compensation for damage done to their homes. When they got to the Victoria Palace they were told they would have to fill in a form, but that the supply of forms had run out. Would they leave their addresses, so that forms could be sent on to them when they arrived? But they were only there because they had no addresses!

October 2, 1940

Bart tells me that recently the chapel of the new Westminster Hospital in Horseferry Road was wrecked by a bomb. The workmen clearing up the debris came upon what they thought was the chandelier and brought it to the secretary. On inspection it proved to be a Molotov bread-basket, which had not gone off properly and had most of its incendiaries still in position!

October 6, 1940

At nine o'clock last night I set off with Campbell to look at the tubes, which are now crowded with people, mostly from the East End of London, from about seven o'clock. I went down at Holborn station, changed at Leicester Square, and came up at the Strand. Thus I saw three stations. The platforms were full and all the passages had people down the sides, and the stairs mostly had people up both sides. There must have been hundreds in each station. They were quiet and orderly, rather the lower middle class than the working-class people, and the really rough element was absent. There were not many children, a good many Jews, and a few youths. The great bulk of the people was middle-aged women. There was no smell and the crowd seemed to me surprisingly steady and almost contented.

On October 3 Churchill reshuffled his Cabinet, after the final retirement of Chamberlain through ill-health. The Mirror *commented: ' The sifting or shunting of mediocrities or reputed successes appears to have been directed by no principle plain to the outsider, unless it be the principle that new blood must rarely be transfused into an old body.'*

The Pictorial *too had a critical article, by Cudlipp, indignant that Chamberlain's 'paralysing influence' lingered on in the composition of the new Cabinet, though 'that architect of doom' himself was gone. 'Chamberlain is dead; long live Chamberlain,' lamented Cudlipp.*[13]

The first hint of fresh trouble for these newspapers came in Churchill's speech in the House of Commons on Tuesday October 8.

October 8, 1940

Churchill stood up for Sir John Anderson, described attacks on him as 'ignorant and spiteful', and said there was no better war horse in the Government! (What a back-handed tribute to the Government!) He described attacks by a 'certain section of the Press' as 'vicious and malignant', and said such attacks would be 'almost indecent to apply to the enemy'. I must see the whole text tomorrow, but it rather sounds as if this were aimed at our two papers for taking such a poor view of some of the recent Government changes.

October 11, 1940

Cudlipp had dinner last night with some of the Frank Owen, Edgar Granville, Clement Davies group, and all their talk was of Churchill's attack on Tuesday on the *Sunday Pictorial*. They had dined with Beaverbrook on Wednesday and he told them that Churchill had brought the *Sunday Pictorial* article by Cudlipp to the Cabinet, and that the phrase in his speech about vicious and malignant criticism was inserted by general agreement. The drift of the article was that in his recent governmental changes Churchill had shown the same dilatory, short-sighted, party-serving spirit as Chamberlain. And Cudlipp, who signed the article, wound up with a quotation from Churchill's book *World Crisis*, in which Winston says there are good grounds sometimes in peace for a vacillating or cautious policy, but in war decisions must be clear-cut and ruthless, no personal or party considerations must hamper the war effort, and so on. Cudlipp's concluding words were: 'Mr Churchill, you have warned yourself.' Obviously the article was not likely to please Churchill, but I had no idea a storm was at all likely.

October 12, 1940

I was summoned by Cowley [Mirror *chairman*] to the board room late yesterday afternoon and found him in consultation with Roome, Bart, and Esmond [Harmsworth]. It appeared that in the course of the morning Esmond, as chairman of the Newspaper Proprietors' Association, had been asked to head a deputation representative of the Press to call on Attlee. He had turned up with Camrose and Southwood, and found Attlee and Beaverbrook awaiting them. Attlee told them that the Cabinet had given attention to the Press at a recent meeting, with particular reference to the *Daily Mirror* and *Sunday Pictorial*. He said that if criticism of the irresponsible kind inserted in our papers were to continue, the Government would introduce legislation making censorship of news *and* views compulsory.[16] The N.P.A. deputation did not take to this suggestion at all kindly, and said that compulsory censorship would wreck the Government and be most damaging to the country's morale.

Attlee had various cuttings with him, most of them from Cassandra's column, but one from the 'Live Letter Box'. The point about the latter being the very trivial technical one that it is illegal for a serving soldier to write to the Press without his commanding officer's permission, which had not been obtained. Attlee described the *Mirror* and Pic's policy as 'subversive', and calculated to cause alarm and despondency at a very critical period. No great stress was laid on the cuttings themselves and the deputation found Attlee very evasive on what exactly it is the Cabinet objects to. The Government had no objection to criticism, he said, but only to irresponsible criticism, and on what constituted irresponsible criticism he was vague or silent. I think if Attlee had told the deputation that if our papers continued their present line they would be prosecuted, the deputation would have cheered. But to threaten a general compulsory censorship would obviously damage the *Telegraph* and *Times* more than the *Mirror*, and was the one and only way of rallying the other papers to our support. Beaverbrook, incidentally, throughout this interview took the part of the honest broker, the friend of both sides.

After Esmond had told his story it was arranged that Bart and I should call on Attlee this morning and hear the story straight from him.

At 11.30 I repaired to Richmond Terrace, Whitehall, and asked for Major Attlee but was told he was in the air-raid shelter (there

were actually some German planes overhead). I was ushered into
the waiting room, which was also a passage from the hall to the
air-raid shelter. The room in this beautiful 18th-century house
was decorated a sort of mustard-coloured mock oak, which
contrasted oddly with the very fine mahogany doors. Hung on the
wall was a list of furniture:

> 1 table c'tee (size given)
> 1 table (size given)
> 5 hat stands (why so many? actually there were only three)
> 4 chairs W7 (there were in fact three)
> 1 carpet
> 1 fire curb
> 1 clock wall (sic)

No mention was made in the list of a picture allegedly by Rubens
and Snyders and lent by Lord Amherst.

Presently I collected Bart, who I discovered had been waiting
for me outside. We were led through a maze of corridors into the
basement and into a gas-proof room about nine feet square,
where Attlee was sitting on a bed reading the *New Statesman*.
Though tiny, the room contained three beds, three chairs, and a
table. The beds were really bunks. They had blankets and sheets
and pillows and were made up, but had no coverlets. We explained that we had come to see him as he had summoned a
deputation of the N.P.A. in connection with the policy of our
papers; that Esmond had been very vague about what had
transpired, and as we were the responsible directors concerned
we wished to hear from him direct what the Government had to
say.

Attlee is a man I should say of very limited intelligence and no
personality. If one heard he was getting £6 a week in the service
of the East Ham Corporation, one would be surprised he was
earning so much. He said he had been deputed by the Cabinet to
deal with the matter, and the opinions he would express were
not only his own, but those of the Government and 'of others'.
They felt that our papers showed a subversive influence, which at
a critical time like this might endanger the nation's war effort.

I asked him to give an example. He said he couldn't think of one. I said the N.P.A. deputation had seen some of the cuttings: could we see them? He said he had not brought any cuttings along, that anyway it was not his job to watch the Press and he did not read our papers. There was more discussion on the same lines, but the only specific accusation he would bring was that we criticized the military command. I said we had never done any such thing and would not do it in wartime. He then said we had quoted H.G. Wells who, in a review of a Labour Party book, made some contemptuous references to Ironside and Gort. I said we had done so – some time after Gort and Ironside had been dismissed from the Government. I said we had certainly criticized the Civil Service and some individual civil servants. Was there any objection to that? He said no. My general line was to pin him down to some specific accusation. Bart's line was vague and conciliatory. Attlee was critical but so vague and evasive as to be quite meaningless. We got the impression that the fuss was really Churchill's, that Attlee had been turned on to do something he was not really interested in, and had not bothered to read his brief. Moreover, the Press reaction to Churchill's speech had not been quite what they hoped for, nor had the N.P.A. deputation's attitude to Attlee, so perhaps we were asking Attlee to fight over again a battle he recognized had been already lost.

I said our policy in general was to win the war at all costs – no personal or party considerations must stand in the way – and that our newspapers had contributed largely, in my view, to the war effort by the removal of Chamberlain. This had not been done by the House of Commons, let alone Churchill, but by public opinion led by the Press; and of all the newspapers we had taken the strongest line and taken it earliest. Attlee rather naturally said he entirely disagreed with my estimate of the part played by the newspapers in this affair. He said it was no part of the Government's wish to stop criticism, only irresponsible criticism. Pressed to define irresponsible criticism, he could not do so. He said he would try and give an example. The London gas mains were laid out in Victorian times with no thought, naturally, for air raids. When a bomb hit one, it deprived quite a large area of gas for quite a time. If we were to criticize the Government for the lack of gas in some areas, that would be irresponsible criticism. I said we had never criticized the Government for the failure of the gas supply in parts of London: to this Attlee said he agreed!

I said I thought Churchill had no objection to our kicking poor old Chamberlain, but didn't like being hurt himself. Attlee said he strongly disagreed. I said we were supporting Churchill, Bevin, and Beaverbrook, but I had to confess that our ideas of winning the war and Sir Kingsley Wood's were hardly likely to coincide. He said the Government raised no objection to such differences of opinion. At one point Attlee was doing so badly he was very near breaking off the interview. After about twenty-five minutes we rose and said goodbye: obviously there was nothing to be gained by staying any longer.

As Bart and I walked up Whitehall we agreed that it was the quotation from his own book that really annoyed Winston and caused all the trouble (subsequently Roome, on the telephone, volunteered the same opinion). Winston was so right in his book about wartime appointments, and has been so wrong since last May, that he must be infuriated to be condemned out of his own mouth. Obviously the Government will do nothing more about it, and obviously we shall pipe down for a few weeks until the course of the war alters the whole situation.

October 29, 1940

A boarded-up shop had a printed notice outside: 'Open as usual'; the shop next door, which had its whole shop front blown in, had a notice: 'More open than usual'!

November 1, 1940

I had lunch with Fraser, Director of Statistics at the War Office. He says Churchill is acting Secretary of State for War in Eden's absence in the Middle East, and that he always keeps a supply of slips of papers by him, on which he scribbles ideas and requests for information. These usually start: 'Pray what are the figures for ...', and are signed 'W.S.C.' They are known as 'pray papers' and descend on the service departments in a steady stream. They accumulate in a special basket and are delivered every morning. Fraser says these papers go into extreme detail and,

so far as his experience goes, into the sort of detail that should not
be the concern of the Prime Minister.

Fraser said the Dunkirk episode was far worse than was ever
realized even in Fleet Street. The men on getting back to England
were so demoralized they threw their rifles and equipment out of
the railway-carriage windows. Some sent for their wives with their
civilian clothes, changed into these, and walked home!

Sir Dudley Pound, he said, is known as 'Do-nothing Dudley'.

November 2, 1940
In Maidenhead, as elsewhere, the name of the town is deleted
from the address on tradesmen's vans. The idea is that these
addresses might aid German parachutists. One van in Maidenhead has the number and name of street, and where Maidenhead
has been painted out, they just put: 'You know where.'

November 16, 1940
The night before last was beautiful, with brilliant light from a full
moon. M. and I went for a stroll to the Hurley lodge and beyond,
and we were surprised to see A.A. shell-bursts from an entirely
new direction. I thought it was High Wycombe and M. thought
it was Princes Risborough, but I am told now that it was Coventry
– quite sixty miles away. Coventry had fully ten hours of bombing,
the Germans say from 500 planes.[17] Anyway our reporter, who
returned from there this evening, says that within half a mile of
the centre of the city there are no undamaged or even habitable
buildings. The cathedral is destroyed and so are the Alvis works,
which were making aero-engines, and also Courtauld's great
rayon factory. Armstrong Siddeley's, where they make the
Whitley bomber, was badly damaged and so was Morris' commercial motor works. Coventry as a production centre for munitions has passed out for the time being, and it is estimated, I don't
know with what truth, that it will reduce our output of planes by
30% for six months. The official estimate of casualties was about
1,000 – 250 killed and 750 injured – but our reporter says the
mortuary was hit by a bomb towards the end of the raid and no
one knows how many bodies were there at the time.

Today cordons of soldiers are across all the roads ten miles out of Coventry, and it is impossible to get near the place even with a Ministry of Information pass. Thousands of people have fled and are fleeing from the town. Last night they were on all the roads. Our reporter saw large numbers tramping into Kenilworth, where no organized efforts had been made for their reception. He saw a woman with two children tucking up for the night on a seat in the open in pouring rain. The chairman of the Education Committee in Coventry told our reporter that he had pleaded for some emergency evacuation scheme to be prepared in case of necessity, but was simply laughed at in the Town Council. I recall, too, that at the beginning of the war Coventry was not even an evacuation area, though it must be the most concentrated con-glomeration of military objectives of an industrial nature in the whole country.

December 11, 1940

Richmond Temple asked me to lunch at the Dorchester, where I found myself with their [*McAlpine's*] board of directors, who had just had a meeting. The only other guest was the Duke of Alba, Spanish Ambassador in London. I sat next Sir Malcolm McAlpine, chairman of the company. The reason for my presence was that the Sunday Pic had published an article called 'Grand Hotel 1940' about the Dorchester [*controlled by McAlpine's*] and the people who live there. The Dorchester, being the social centre of London in wartime, seemed to me a good subject for an article. Apparently this caused much fluttering among the ministers and others who live there. When I was leaving, Malcolm McAlpine drew me aside and said he thought the Pic was worse than the *Daily Worker* in causing friction between class and class, and that this sort of journalism tended to encourage men like the building operatives on his contract work. He said a bricklayer on piece work could lay about 1,250 bricks a day, but that on an average they lay only 250 bricks a day; that we have about 600,000 building operatives at the moment and are short-handed, but that 200,000 men, if they really worked, could do all that the 600,000 do at present. I said I thought this bad spirit, which certainly exists among the men, was due to execrable political leadership over a long period and not to popular journalism. There is nothing wrong with the British working man, but if the leaders at the top are petty, selfish, and self-seeking, the rank and file at the bottom will in course of time learn to be the same.

December 26, 1940
It is now about a year since I started this diary. Since then I have not reread any part of it. My idea is to present a faithful picture of impressions at the time, and it is hard to do so if I remember too clearly to exactly what views I committed myself at earlier stages. One tends to underline the success of forecasts that come off and explain away one's failures.

Our main defect I take to be our leadership. No serious effort has been made to seek out able young men, and the conduct of the war is accordingly in the hands of a small bunch of elderly self-seeking men quite out of touch with modern trends. In some respects – propaganda for instance – we are behind the level set by the last war. We are still not making a whole-hearted effort to win the war, nor shall we while most of the key positions are held by men over sixty, and all are held by elderly men with reputations (of a sort) to lose. Churchill doesn't yet see the importance of formulating war aims, or the importance of getting away from hack party material in forming his administration. Bevin, who looked like a coming man, is now, with unemployment still high, looking more like going than coming. Lloyd George is obviously keeping himself for the succession if needed. Of the men of my generation, who should be supplying the initiative, the imagination, and the drive of our war effort, few are being used in any responsible position of any sort. At a time when the need for 'youth at the helm' is more obvious than ever, we have both politicians and admirals averaging a full ten years older than they did in the last war – with the inevitable result of over-caution, lack of imagination, and the underestimation of new factors like air power and propaganda in summing up a given situation. That this problem of leadership can now be corrected without a crash seems to me impossible: and a sufficiently loud crash would put us out of the war.

In fact, of recent months my real thoughts have been turned to what will happen after our defeat, rather than to what can be done to avert it. Rotten as our parliamentary system is, there is nothing else. At least, I cannot see Mosley or the Communists getting very far without a big change in their programmes and methods. There is a close parallel here between ourselves and the French. Though the ordinary politicians in France are discredited, the various men round Pétain are still old-time politicians, because there is no one else. What we see in Vichy is surely the complete bankruptcy of French statesmanship. I am very afraid this is what would happen here under similar circumstances.

A closer parallel perhaps is the Austro-Hungarian Empire before the last war. From all I have heard and read there was the same fear of innovation of any sort, of the tackling of any serious problem in a serious way; the same dependence on a small group of petty politicians; the same realization of what problems must be faced and more or less how they must be solved, with the inability to *do* anything; the same despair and sense of frustration among the younger men. Even defeat and dismemberment didn't infuse any life into Austria or Hungary, and of the historic Habsburg Empire there is now no trace. I hope our fate will not be so tragic – or so ignominious.

1941

SUNDAY PICTORIAL, May 11, 1941.

The Voice of the People

Sunday Pictorial

No. 1,363   * TWOPENCE

Special 5 a.m. Edition

MANY NAZI RAIDERS DOWN: GREAT LONDON BLITZ

●

BATTLES UNDER FULL MOON

NAZI BOMBERS BLITZED LONDON IN BRILLIANT MOONLIGHT LAST NIGHT — AND PAID A HEAVY PRICE. SOON AFTER THE ALERT IT WAS BEFORE MIDNIGHT — ROOF WATCHERS SAW THE FIRST RAIDER FALL IN A WHIRL OF FLAME, ON THE OUTSKIRTS.

"When the bomber crashed there was a heavy anti-aircraft barrage," said one. "The plane was flying very high and suddenly burst into flame—a ball of fire in the sky.

"It took a long time to come down, and when it hit the ground it exploded with a flash that could be seen for miles."

Cannon in the Sky

THE RAID DEVELOPED QUICKLY INTO ONE OF THE HEAVIEST EVER.

Between the bursts of A.A. fire Londoners could hear the sharp crack of machine-guns and the heavier thud of cannon mingling in the whine of planes.

Soon another raider flamed to earth—and another. THE BLITZ HAD BEEN GOING ONLY A SHORT WHILE WHEN FOUR WERE SEMI-OFFICIALLY REPORTED DOWN, AND AS THE HOURS WENT BY OTHER BOMBERS FOLLOWED BLAZING TO THE GROUND.

Fireblitz and H.E.

Watchers on one roof reported that they had seen twelve planes hurtle down—and the raid was still not over.

Raiders that got through emptied load after load of fire bombs. Down in the streets dim figures hurried everywhere with sandbags and stirrup pumps, putting them out.

They could not tackle all. Fires were started in a number of buildings, and down crashed the high explosives.

These were followed by more incendiaries and more loads of H.E.

Among buildings hit were two hospitals, a warden's

post, an A.F.S. post and a club. There were casualties at all these places.

Two famous London churches were also set on fire.

To many people the raiders appeared to dive lower than usual; but the noise of their engines made no difference to anybody who had a job of work to do.

A.F.S. men and women ambulance and rescue workers and wardens slaved throughout the night to keep in check the fires and to succour the wounded.

Other Towns Raided

Raiders—in smaller numbers—were reported also over Liverpool area and the south-east coast.

It is certain that the number of raiders brought down last night brings the total for the first ten days of this month to more than a hundred, compared with the ninety for the whole of April.

Experts believe that if the average figure of raiders down could be brought to twenty a night, the menace of the night bomber would be broken.

The last entry in Cecil King's diary for 1940 might seem in retrospect unduly gloomy. But for the objective observer it was difficult to see much hope of victory at the beginning of 1941. Germany, the greatest military power in the world, dominated Europe from the Channel to the Carpathians. Invasion still seemed a very real threat to the British. The Italians, despite their failures in Greece (which they attacked in October 1940), also seemed menacing, with a powerful navy in the Mediterranean and 500,000 troops in Libya and Abyssinia dangerously near the Suez Canal. As for the Far East, Japan's future behaviour was uncertain – but certainly she was hostile. The Blitz continued, starting early at the end of the short winter days, and lasted until May.

Churchill pinned many hopes on America, immediately as 'the great arsenal of democracy', and in the not too distant future as a co-belligerent. In December 1940 President Roosevelt agreed to the principle of Lend-Lease, by which Britain would receive large quantities of supplies from America without any provision for cash payment. This was approved by Congress in March 1941. But popular opinion in the United States seemed resolutely against entanglement in the European war, and the Lend-Lease Act, coupled with Britain's cash purchases from America, did not produce immediately as many arms and supplies as had been hoped for.

The question of supplies was by now the most critical of all. Britain's security was seriously threatened by German U-boat and air attacks on her merchant shipping. In March 1941 Churchill named the struggle with the U-boats 'the Battle of the Atlantic'. It was a battle that was not to be won until 1944.

The new year brought cheering news from the Middle East. In August 1940 the Italians had occupied British Somaliland, and in September they somewhat hesitantly invaded Egypt. General Wavell's forces counterattacked in December. Within two months a mere 25,000 British troops drove the Italians out of Egypt and the Cyrenaica province of Libya, taking 113,000 prisoners. The situation was saved for the Axis, however, by the arrival, in March, of the Germans in force: General Rommel and the Afrika Korps drove the British back again to the borders of Egypt, and started the epic struggle in the Libyan desert which was to last until Rommel's defeat at the end of 1942.

It was indeed a gloomy phase of the war for Britain. But in the early months of 1941 the Mirror *and the* Pictorial *had problems of their own. The Government again decided to take them to task for their criticisms of the administration. The prime mover on the Government side was Winston Churchill. His attitude had always been 'love me, love my ministers.' Direct attacks against them were taken by him to be attacks upon himself.*

Just before this (on January 21) the Home Secretary, Herbert Morrison, banned the Communist papers The Week *and the* Daily Worker. *It was an interesting example of what could happen to newspapers of which the Government disapproved.*

January 11, 1941

I left the Savoy at 9.0 this evening shortly after a shower of incendiaries had fallen. One with a bright white (not blue) flame was still burning on the cornice of the Strand Palace Hotel. There were frequent smears of sand in the road where incendiaries had been extinguished – forty-five altogether in the Strand roadway, I was told. Several fires had started to the east of me, and one or two south of the River. When I got near the Law Courts a bomb came screaming down, so I rushed for a doorway. The bomb exploded somewhere down Fleet Street sending up a great cloud of dust, which blew in my eyes. An office building the Aldwych side of the Law Courts had begun to burn, but no firemen were in sight. As I reached the office stairs another two bombs came crashing down somewhere near. I went up on the roof and found there were about five big fires visible, none of them very far off. The general opinion in the office was that this was the worst night so far. While I was on the roof another two bombs whistled over, and then two more that sent us diving for cover: they fell just the other side of Fleet Street, within a hundred yards of us, and sent up bits that fell all round.

About 10.0 the German planes cleared off and we had the all-clear, so I went for a walk round. A big H.E. [*High-Explosive bomb*] had fallen behind Twining's opposite the Law Courts, and the whole place was littered with broken glass. A building a little further west was burning, but the firemen were getting it under control. The fire near the Law Courts I had seen earlier was out.

I then walked east towards St Paul's, the dome rising through thick clouds of smoke tinged with red. Three buildings at the corner of Cheapside and St Martin's-le-Grand had been pretty well gutted and the firemen were putting out the last remnants of the fire, hampered only by a fresh bomb hole in the middle of the street and a blazing gas main. Meanwhile opposite the east end of St Paul's the roof of a building was blazing. The firemen brought up a water tower (which I had not seen before) – a long extensible ladder with a hose incorporated in the top – and directed a flow of water on the flames, which were very rapidly beaten down. It looked an unenviable job up there, about forty or fifty feet up, swaying about among all the smoke and sparks, and I wondered what it would be like with bombs falling, when you know a bomb in the wrong place will throw you into the fire! Another block opposite the Old Bailey at the corner of Seacoal Lane had been burnt, but was only smouldering by then.

January 21, 1941
This morning at 12.0, Herbert Morrison saw the chairmen of the newspaper companies and told them he was going to suppress *The Week* and the *Daily Worker*. The proprietors present made no protest – no comment even. In the afternoon he saw the editors and told them the same thing. Only one editor, Frank Owen of the [*Evening*] *Standard*, made any protest. He said that this move gave the Communists a marvellous platform. Morrison said he realized that that was a point of view, and that he was quite prepared to justify his action to the House of Commons tomorrow. I think (a) it is not in the interest of any paper that any other paper should be suppressed, and that any reasonably alert body

of newspaper publishers would have protested vigorously, and (b) that, in so far as this move is of any consequence at all, it is not in the interests of the country. It gives the Communists wonderful publicity and is of inestimable value to them.

We got wind of this on Friday last and, anticipating this move, which will be announced tonight, we included this morning a cartoon and a leader making it very clear that we deplored this blow at the freedom of the Press. It will be interesting to see what sort of press it gets tomorrow.

January 24, 1941
Last night, as I was leaving the office, I was handed a letter from the Prime Minister's secretary deploring two bits from Cassandra's column.

The letter read as follows:

PRIVATE.

10, Downing Street,
Whitehall.
January 23, 1941.

Dear Sir,

The Prime Minister has had his attention drawn to the enclosed cutting from the DAILY MIRROR of January 1. He desires me to inform you that this offensive story is totally devoid of foundation. No such report was ever made by Mr. Eden, nor any such comment by the Prime Minister.

The Prime Minister has also noticed the enclosed cutting marked B. He wishes me to say that it is a pity that so able a writer should show himself so dominated by malevolence. In this case also there is not the slightest truth in the facts underlying the comments. No such changes have yet been considered by the Prime Minister.

Yours truly,

Kathleen Hill.
Personal Private Secretary.

Cecil H. King, Esq.,
The Daily Mirror.

The cutting from Cassandra's column of January 1 was this:

I am indebted to the magazine *Life* for this apocryphal story of Mr Churchill's continued war on wordiness in official documents.

Shortly after returning from his tour of the Near East, Anthony Eden submitted a long-winded report to the Prime Minister on his experiences and impressions. Churchill returned it to his War Minister with a note saying: 'As far as I can see, you have used every cliché except "God is Love" and "Please adjust your dress before leaving".'

The cutting marked 'B' and dated January 20 read:

By the time these words appear in print, Mr R.A. Butler, who is Under-Secretary of State for Foreign Affairs, may be President of the Board of Education, which should not worry you a great deal and doesn't hurt me either.

If this has occurred, it is because Mr Butler has been faithful and loyal and not markedly inept. If it has not occurred, it may still occur. If it never occurs, it will be because the system has broken down. It is a remarkable system because it presumes that the whole of the talent of the British Empire is contained within the number of people who comprise a cricket team. This cricket team is so good that all the batsmen can bowl and all the bowlers can bat. The wicket keeper is excellent at mid-on and the lads in the slips are grand in the outfield.

Why anybody like Mr Butler, who has been working on foreign affairs, should be given a job in education as a promotion, beats me. Is a painter a better man when he becomes a plumber? And more important, is the plumbing improved? But to return to this remarkable flexibility and versatility of the men who are running the war. See how they play ball among themselves. See how the great closed shop works.

Meet Sir John Anderson, Lord President of the Council, ex-Home Secretary, ex-Minister of Security, ex-Lord Privy Seal, ex-Governor of Bengal, ex-Under-Secretary at the Home Office, ex-Permanent Under-Secretary of State, ex-Secretary to the Ministry of Shipping.

Meet Sir Kingsley Wood, Chancellor of the Exchequer, ex-Secretary of State for Air, ex-Minister of Health, ex-Postmaster

General, ex-Parliamentary Secretary to the Board of Education, ex-Parliamentary Secretary to the Ministry of Health, ex-Parliamentary Private Secretary to the Minister of Health.

Meet Mr Anthony Eden, Secretary for Foreign Affairs, ex-Secretary of State for War, ex-Secretary for Foreign Affairs, ex-Secretary of State for Dominion Affairs, ex-Lord Privy Seal, ex-Minister without Portfolio for the League of Nations.

And meet all the rest of the gang. Ex-this and ex-that – but never ex a job!

Everybody has done everybody else's business. Everybody knows everybody. Keep it in the family! Scratch my back and I'll scratch yours! Talk about musical chairs! The trouble is that this particular game is being played to a funeral march. Ours.

Cecil King replied the next day, January 24:

Dear Prime Minister,

Thank you for your letter of yesterday's date. The story printed in our issue of January 1st was taken from the very well-known American paper "Life" and was described by 'Cassandra' as 'apocryphal'. The story of impending ministerial changes was originally hinted at fairly circumstantially on the front page of the "Daily Sketch". It then appeared in the "Evening Standard" in its more detailed form and most of the newspapers reprinted the story, supposing from its appearance in the "Standard" that it was semi-official. I have brought both these cuttings to 'Cassandra's' notice and he is sorry, as we all are, to have given publicity to reports of a change in the Presidency of the Board of Education which prove to be without foundation.[1]

'Cassandra' is a hard-hitting journalist with a vitriolic style, but I can assure you his attitude neither to you personally nor to Mr. Eden is in any way 'malevolent'. Quite the contrary. Though we continue to take an unflattering view of some of your colleagues, our criticisms are only directed to the fact that the nation's war effort is less intense than it might be – less intense than it would be if more young men were employed in positions of real authority.

Yours sincerely,

Cecil H. King

P.S. 'Cassandra' asks me to remind you that he has been for nearly four years in the vanguard of the pro-Churchill mob – and still deems it a privilege to be so!

On January 27, Cecil King received Churchill's reply:

January 25, 1941.

Dear Mr. King,

I don't think the mere adding of the word 'apocryphal' is any justification for foisting upon the British public an absolutely untruthful story, which is of course extremely offensive both to me and to Mr. Eden. Nothing that appears in the EVENING STANDARD or any other paper is 'semi-official'. Any news about appointments will be given to all the newspapers equally from Downing Street.[1] I thank you, however, for your expressions of regret.

These give me the opportunity of saying one or two things which have struck me very forcibly in reading the DAILY MIRROR and the SUNDAY PICTORIAL.

First, there is a spirit of hatred and malice against the Government, which after all is not a Party Government but a National Government almost unanimously chosen, which spirit surpasses anything I have ever seen in English journalism. One would have thought in these hard times that some hatred might be kept for the enemy.

The second point is more general. Much the most effective way in which to conduct a Fifth Column movement at the present time would be the method followed by the DAILY MIRROR and the SUNDAY PICTORIAL. Lip service would no doubt be paid to the Prime Minister, whose position at the moment may be difficult to undermine. A perfervid zeal for intensification of the war effort would be used as a cloak behind which to insult and discredit one Minister after another. Every grievance would be exploited to the full, especially those grievances which lead to class dissension. The Army system and discipline would be attacked. The unity between the Conservative and Labour Parties would be gnawed at. The attempt would be made persistently to represent the Government as feeble, unworthy and incompetent, and to spread a general sense of distrust in the whole system. Thus, large numbers of readers would be brought into a state of despondency and resentment, of bitterness and scorn, which at the proper moment, when perhaps some disaster had occurred or prolonged tribulations had wearied the national spirit, could be suddenly switched over into naked defeatism, and a demand for a negotiated peace.

I daresay you will be surprised when I tell you that as a regular reader, I feel that this description very accurately fits the attitude of your two newspapers. I am sure this is not your intention, nor the intention of the able writers you employ. It is, none the less, in my judgment, the result. It amounts to the same thing, even though the intention may be the opposite. It has given me much pain to see that newspapers with whom I have had such friendly relations, and from whom I have received in the past valuable support, should pursue such a line. It is because of our past relations that I write thus plainly.

Yours sincerely,
Winston S. Churchill

Cecil King commented on Churchill's letter in his diary:

January 28, 1941

I am up in Scotland to fetch the children and will not be down until Thursday morning [January 30]. However, the delay of a few days will give me time to think out the best line to take. This incident raises once more the dilemma I have been very conscious of since the outbreak of war. If we criticize the Government we can be quite fairly accused of 'rocking the boat', 'causing alarm and despondency', and so forth. If, on the other hand, we give the Government our full support, we are then sharing the responsibility for all the jobbery and incompetence that are dragging this great country to defeat. Clearly the right line is some form of compromise: so far I have steered the compromise nearer to rocking the boat than to licking the Government's boots. Perhaps at this stage of the war our policy will have to be modified. Meanwhile I shall seek an interview with the Prime Minister and see what line he would like. At present we have only a very clear statement that in his view criticism à la *Daily Mirror* is treason.

January 31, 1941

I reached the office at 10.15 yesterday – the train being a couple of hours late – and promptly rang up Churchill's secretary to ask for an interview. I thought in view of his letter he was likely to see me, but didn't think it could be for some days. However, I got a message back almost immediately that he would see me at 3.0. I arrived at about five minutes to the hour in the middle of the third or fourth air raid of the day, with all the local guns banging away. I waited ten or fifteen minutes by a big coke fire just outside the Cabinet room, where I waited last time I saw Churchill. While waiting I noticed that the hat and coat pegs near the Cabinet door were all labelled, that nearest the door being for the Lord Chancellor, followed by the Lord President, Lord Privy Seal, and so on, in strict order of precedence.

In the course of the morning I had sent the Prime Minister a note ostensibly asking for the interview, but in fact to have a letter on the file replying to his last. [*It read as follows:*

Dear Prime Minister,

Your letter reached me on Monday just as I was leaving for the north of Scotland, whence I returned this morning.

I can only express my gratitude that at such a crisis as this you should find the time to express so fully and so frankly your view on the policies of these two papers. If you could spare the time to see me I am sure I could convince you that no organisation has more at heart the prosecution of this war to final victory, nor more loyalty to you personally as their leader in this struggle. Differences of method are bound to arise, but if you consider we have gone beyond what should be permissible in wartime, we should, of course, meet your wishes in so far as we conscientiously can.]

Winston went into the Cabinet room by another door and was standing up by the fire when I came in. He sat me at the table at his right hand and off we started. There was a green telephone at his side labelled 'Admiralty', so evidently he keeps especially closely in touch with the Navy. The maps since last June had changed. There was now one of Europe and the Mediterranean, and another of the world. Outside, German planes came over singly at intervals (it was a cloudy, misty day) and the guns in St James' Park, heavy and Bofors, banged away. When a plane came very near he stopped his talk and listened, and twice seemed on the point of retreating to his shelter, but did not do so. Winston himself looked older and more lined than when I saw him last, but if anything tougher.

He started off with a great tirade and returned often to the same theme. The gist of his remarks was that our policy constituted a very clever form of fifth columnism – praising the Prime Minister, pressing for an intensification of our war effort, but at the same time magnifying grievances, vilifying ministers, and generally creating a distrust by the nation for its leaders. That this 'rocking of the boat' (his phrase this time) might well have disastrous results for the nation; and what were we doing it for anyway? I protested that we supported him as much as we ever had and that we supported many of his ministers, but others we thought unworthy of high office and said so. He said did this mean that we arrogated to ourselves the right of appointing ministers of the Crown? I said no, but surely loyalty to him as Prime Minister did not carry with it loyalty to Attlee as Lord Privy Seal? He conceded this point more or less.

He said our papers had been the subject of much discussion, that much research had been undertaken into the ownership of our shares, and that some of his colleagues were convinced that there was something or someone behind it all. I said there was nothing: there were five executive directors, of whom I was one. As I was more interested in politics than the others, the politics were left largely to me. 'Well,' he said, 'you look innocent enough!'[2]

He said he didn't mind attacks on the Government: it was the malignancy of the attacks that annoyed him. They had contemplated a prosecution, and also denunciation in a speech on the wireless, but had thought these measures out of proportion. I said there were no personal feelings involved, as hardly any of us knew any of the men we attacked, but that, editing a popular paper, we were bound to write of politics in terms of persons not of principles. He said other popular papers didn't; that we were different. I said we were proud to be different.

I went on to say that I very much regretted he had been disturbed to this extent by our policy. Why had he not got his secretary to ring up and ask us to pipe down? He said he would not ask for favours. I said a request from the Prime Minister in wartime to a paper that had of late always supported him was not a favour, but an order, and would of course be obeyed. That since he became Prime Minister we had had only one request, and that was not to attack Chamberlain. I said we had met his wishes for a month, but I did not see how we could conscientiously do more. Attlee had asked to see a deputation of the Newspaper Proprietors' Association, but had not said what for, so our representative was not present. When we subsequently asked for an interview to find out at first hand what exactly was complained of, we saw Attlee, who was so vague and evasive that we thought either he had got the wrong end of the stick or that Beaverbrook was up to something. Churchill said no, Beaverbrook was all for freedom of the Press and for leaving other newspapers alone; that the move was initiated by himself because of three articles in the paper which appeared to strike at the root of Army discipline. I said Attlee never mentioned these articles: that we made it a strict rule not to criticize the conduct of military operations or personnel in any way, and that if such matter had been printed it had slipped through, and I personally had never seen it.

This sort of discussion proceeded for a long time, he maintaining that our papers showed malignancy towards the Government and great 'artistry' in undermining the morale of the nation. I said we showed malignancy only to those politicians who had brought us to this plight, and as for the rest we were young men naturally anxious to get any and every sort of move on. If, in his opinion, we had gone too far, we would certainly alter our tune. He said he had never taken back what he had said about the appeasers, but that the M.P.s who had supported Chamberlain still formed a majority of 150 in the House, and he was not going to fight them as they were too numerous. He had, however, moved away the old bunch bit by bit, keeping Chamberlain on for a time to minimize the shock of the change.

Apropos of nothing very much (but presumably reverting to my letter) he said that there was a great dearth of brains, that he had thought of including in his Government some younger men.

Hitherto only those above military age had been included, but as this war did not seem to be a blood bath – there were as many civilian casualties as others – he was now thinking of having some ministers in khaki.

He referred to the lead in the *Daily Herald* yesterday, which forecast an advance on Benghazi by the inland route, and he said very bitterly that this might well lead to the death of a thousand Australians. But what did we care, if it made a good newspaper stunt! (A D-notice was issued telling us all not to speculate on General Wavell's next move, but this *Daily Herald* story had apparently slipped past the censor.) Churchill said he thought these journalists would be better occupied working with our national war effort – joining in this great historic and tragic event. I said, of course they should all be working sixteen hours a day for the Government. He said: Why weren't they? I said journalists were excluded from the Ministry of Information in favour of museum officials and Foreign Office clerks, so what *could* they do? He said the journalists would not agree on who should and who should not come into the Ministry of Information. I said clearly all the ones of any consequence should be in. He said: 'There is an idea there.' He wouldn't let me follow up my point, but seemed to be disposed to take some future action in the matter.

Throughout, Winston was very difficult to talk to – he reminded me strongly of Rothermere – getting up and striding about, shooting remarks at me that often had nothing whatever to do with his last remark or anything I was saying, sitting down again, leaning on the fireguard, or lighting his cigar. Our conversation followed no logical path at all. He thought invasion possible, a matter for constant vigilance, but appeared to think it less rather than more likely. He seemed puzzled by recent German movements of troops and planes into Italy and the Balkans. I should say he was genuinely optimistic about our prospects of victory.

During this discussion, which lasted one hour and ten minutes by the clock, I got a much more definite impression of him than I had before. I should say that politically he is a Victorian parliamentarian, and starts from the assumption that the House of Commons (and the present House of Commons at that) is the only source of political power, and that therefore anyone with political capacity or ambition is necessarily there. Personally (or emotionally) Churchill *is* wartime England – England with all its age, its waning virility, its dogged courage, its natural assumption that instinct is more reliable than intellect. In Churchill the country feels it is personified, and for this reason there can be no question of his departure until after complete defeat. From his point of view he has done, is doing, and will continue to do all anyone could to win the war. He feels this, and so attacks on his Government mystify and bewilder him. The limitations he would impose on his war-winning efforts (he would refuse, for instance, to choose ministers purely for their ability, ignoring the House of Commons) are not only his but are those of the country today. His speeches are popular, not for their originality of thought or any quality like that, but because they are the articulate expression of what is in most Englishmen's hearts. He has no contribution to make to our future, but he personifies our present and our past.

After an hour or so I said something about not taking up too much of his time, but he brushed that aside. Eventually, however, he rose saying that I must leave now or I should be attacking him for wasting the country's time! He still stayed talking when we got to the door, but he eventually saw me outside; asked me not to be offended by all he had said; told me there was an air raid on and asked if I had a car outside. When I said I hadn't, he insisted on sending me back to the office in his own.

Cecil King followed up the interview with this letter, of February 3:

Dear Prime Minister,

As I feel our policy has mystified as well as distressed you, I thought I would try to amplify what I said to you when you saw me on Thursday.

Any support we gave you and your policy before the war was not just a newspaper stunt to sell papers. It never did – in fact our readers (and some of my colleagues) wanted to hear that it would be roses, roses, all the way. When I wrote to you on the outbreak of war to congratulate you (or rather the nation) on your going to the Admiralty, I said I hoped that when the inevitable demand came for a more vigorous prosecution of the war you would step up to a still more exalted office. And when later, in October '39, we 'splashed' a prophecy that you would be the next Prime Minister, this was not idle flattery. It was the realisation by me slightly sooner than by others that you were our inevitable wartime leader – not because of your particular experience or capacity or for any other *reason* but because you ARE wartime England. When you make speeches, yours is the voice of England with all its traditions, its courage, its strength and its limitations. You epitomise our past: you are our present. There can be no question of your replacement during this war. This is not said just on a shrewd view of the political probabilities, but because you and England could not be separated now without both disintegrating.

But loyalty to England means not only loyalty to the past and the present, but to the future. This war is to you the crowning of a lifetime of public service: to us, who are much younger, it is the first step towards a new and better England in which we shall pay our way and not live – as we did in the years 1919–39 – on the accumulated wealth and prestige of our forefathers. This does not mean that I have some future leader up my sleeve or under the bed: I haven't. I have no idea who he may eventually prove to be, but I think we shall not find him in any of the existing parties (in which I would include Mosleyites and Communists) and I think he is now much younger than I am (nearly 40).

Loyalty to the future involves not only scanning the horizon for the new ideas and ideals which may shape the world, but also the discrediting of the men who made the period 1919–39 such an ignoble page in English history. This is not done to humiliate them, but to impress on the young people growing up (who read our papers) that that is an era which must not recur.

Perhaps this would be clearer if I gave you an actual example of how it works. We advocate a statement by the Government of the country's war aims. Clearly to do so in anything but vague and platitudinous terms would cause dissension among your ministers and between this country and its allies. Therefore you must think that to press such a demand is essentially mischievous. But look at it from the young man's point of view. The Middle

East was conquered by the Mahomedans holding a sword in one hand and the Koran in the other – and who will deny that the Koran was the more potent weapon? At this moment we want our Koran and feel its possession would be the decisive factor of the whole war. Perhaps if you have read as far as this, you will see that there is no clear answer to this dilemma. One's loyalty is just divided.

The staff here do not always see clearly what I am driving at. Mistakes occur; but behind everything printed in these two papers is the conviction I have just described expressed in terms of the tabloid newspaper – itself a raw, crude medium but very typical of its day.

February 3, 1941
The letter is well expressed, I think, and entirely sincere. It will be interesting to see how he takes it. I must say if I were in his shoes I should be delighted with it.

February 8, 1941
I have been in bed with a sore throat, so only heard yesterday by telephone of a letter from the Prime Minister. The line was a bad one and I missed much of it, but the gist seems to be to thank me for my letter, to say that he doesn't see why sympathy for the claims of youth should lead me to rock the boat at this time of acute national danger, and as for war aims, why don't I occupy myself in this lull drawing up my own war aims? The answer in any case sounds pretty petty: I should have thought he was bound either to answer my letter in the spirit in which it was sent, or else not answer it at all. Evidently our criticisms got very deeply under his skin.

This was the full text of Churchill's letter:

5 February 1941.

Dear Mr. King,

Thank you very much for your letter and I was glad we had a talk. All this fine thought about the rising generation ought not to lead you into using your able writers to try to discredit and hamper the Government in a period of extreme danger and

8

difficulty. Nor ought it to lead you to try to set class against class and generally "rock the boat" at such a time. Finally I think it is no defence for such activities to say that your papers specialise in "vitriolic" writing. Indeed throwing vitriol is thought to be one of the worst of crimes. No man who is affected with "vitriolism" is worthy to shape the future, or likely to have much chance of doing so in our decent country.

There is no reason why you should not advocate a statement of war aims. I wonder that you do not draw one up in detail and see what it looks like. I see that Mr. Mander has tabled his war aims which seem to me to bear out what I ventured to say in the House, namely "that most right-minded people are well aware of what we are fighting for". Such a task would be well-suited to the present lull.

Yours sincerely,
Winston S. Churchill

On February 11, Cecil King replied:

Dear Prime Minister,

Thank you very much for your letter dated February 5th. As I cannot emphasise too strongly, all of us here wish to give you personally all the support possible and it has come as a great shock to learn that you have been so distressed at the line these papers have been pursuing. I am afraid I had assumed that if anything published by us should cause you serious annoyance you would send a message through one of your secretaries asking us to be more moderate.

However, thanks to your very full and frank letters and the talk we had, we now have your point of view clearly before us. The staff have had their instructions and you may have already noticed a marked change of tone. If in the future you have any fault to find with our contribution to the nation's war effort, I hope you would let us know at once.

February 15, 1941

I was away from the office yesterday, but on reaching my desk this afternoon find a letter from the Prime Minister written on Thursday [February 13], thanking me for my letter and saying he takes the 'greatest possible interest' in our papers, with which he has been associated since 1915. He says he will be 'very glad' to see me at any time and asks me not to hesitate to propose a visit. This afternoon, too, I received an invitation to lunch at 10 Downing Street on Wednesday, so evidently he has buried the hatchet.

February 19, 1941
Campbell [*now promoted to be* Pictorial *editor*[3]] had lunch with Shinwell M.P., who said Lloyd George is very severe about Winston: said he picked him out of the political gutter, but wished now he had left him there.

I had lunch with the Churchills at No 10. The meal was at 1.30. I arrived at the door in time to meet an outward rush of generals. I was ushered down the long corridor from the front door, past the Cabinet room, and down some stairs. The garden level at the back is a storey below the street level at the front, and the dining room cum sitting room they were using is on the garden level at the back. It was strongly reinforced by timbers and quite small. I was ushered in and found the party consisted of Lord and Lady Melchett and Lady Oliphant (formerly Viscountess Churchill). Winston came in about ten to two after we had all sat down to lunch. Mrs Churchill meanwhile regaled us with the story of the flat where they sleep, which is at the Office of Works. They have a sitting room, bedroom, and more recently a dining room, with a bathroom the other side of a much frequented corridor. She says the embarrassment of the civil servants and marines (why marines?) when she goes to her bath is quite unnerving.

The meal consisted of hors d'oeuvres, roast hare done, so to speak, as saddle of hare, leeks and potatoes, cherry flan, toast and cheese, and coffee afterwards. We were offered various wines, but Winston drank two very strong whiskies (Johnny Walker) and two good brandies. The meal was served by a butler and parlourmaid, the latter as well as the former wearing white cotton gloves.

Churchill was in tremendous form but said little that bore directly on the war. He was very pleased because the President's

Lease and Lend Bill will pass the Senate with a better than two to one majority. Asked by Lady Oliphant (wife of Sir Lancelot, our Ambassador in Brussels, captured by the Germans) whether we want the Americans in or not, he said very emphatically in, as they would then greatly speed up their industrial effort. Asked also by Lady Oliphant whether he had any news of Japan, he did not answer.

He seemed doubtful whether the Germans would try invasion and quite certain they wouldn't succeed, particularly as we now had command of the daylight air over this country. He thought we now had more fighters than the Germans. He obviously had not in mind any big development of a smoke-screen technique, as he talked of precision bombing of their troops by our planes if ever the Germans did effect a landing.

Lady Oliphant expressed dissatisfaction with a French governess who used the expression once: '*If* we win', and Winston said: 'It is not *certain* that we shall win.' He seemed honestly to think we were fairly certain of victory, though he allowed that the 'hazards of war' introduced an element of doubt.

There was quite a lot of talk on education, perhaps because Melchett mentioned that his son had won an open scholarship into Oxford and was stroke of the 'varsity boat. Churchill said he distrusted anyone who had achieved athletic distinction at school – or academic distinction for that matter. He had done nothing at Harrow, but regarded his time there as very well spent, though he did devote it to eating ice-cream and other sweet things. He had sent Randolph to Eton because he considered it an even more slovenly school than Harrow. He thought the important thing when growing up was to 'learn to be an omnivore', and that energy expended on learning and athletics was just not there for more important purposes later on. When he joined the Army, too, the rule was no work after lunch, and in India, where they rose early, no work after breakfast. Melchett said his prep-school master – one of the Eton Hawtreys – used to maintain that a man had only so many races flat-out in him, and that if he ran them in adolescence he was incapable of winning any races later on in life.

The subject then changed to divorce, on which Churchill was very definite – that there shouldn't be any. Mrs Churchill then embarked on a long story of her parents' matrimonial differences, murmured more or less into my ear. She is a very nice woman indeed and very good-looking, but it is difficult to know what to say when the Prime Minister's wife goes off into a long account of the differences of her parents.

Churchill spoke of war aims, and said that extremists like Edward Hulton(!) and me wanted a statement of war aims, but that as soon as one got away from platitude one ran into differences. Start at the beginning: what was to be our attitude to Germany after the war? Some, like Vansittart, thought we should be harsh and oppressive to say the least. He, however, believed in upholding the European family of nations and would treat the Germans generously, though depriving them of all arms. After all, the call for war aims was the call for a better world, which could not be created by Governments but only by improvement in the individual, who, with the family, was the foundation of everything. In this connection no one could improve on the Sermon on the Mount, however few might be the number of people who complied with its precepts.

He was very pleased with a short personal letter from the President, brought over by Wendell Willkie and containing a message of praise for the country's courage, and of friendship to the Prime Minister. It was on one side of one sheet of private notepaper and was mostly a quotation from a poem. He said it had greatly moved him on its arrival. It was addressed on the envelope to 'a certain naval person', as in cables to and fro the Prime Minister is regularly described as 'a certain former naval person'. All this sounded to me like little boys playing with codes, but they all thought it a thrilling and historic document. Apparently we are now getting full and enthusiastic support from the Americans, but for six weeks after the collapse of France the 'Americans treated us in that rather distant and sympathetic manner one adopts towards a friend one knows is suffering from cancer.'

Churchill mentioned the air fighting last autumn and said that after trying to destroy our fighter defences down south, the Germans struck at objectives in Yorkshire, but this was beyond the range of their fighters, so the bombers were unescorted. We, however, had not drawn all our fighters down south, and in the fighting over Yorkshire destroyed over eighty bombers for the loss of four fighters. He thought this had been the decisive incident in the campaign.

Talking of the French collapse he said he had been out of office for eleven years, and had had no reason to keep pace with the developments in tank tactics. He therefore had not realized what would be possible with tanks in France, though de Gaulle had shown the way in his book. In the middle of the German advance in France, Churchill had gone over to Paris for a conference. He said there were about twenty people there, including Gamelin and Reynaud; there was a war map on an easel. Gamelin said the Germans had broken his line and might be in Paris in forty-eight hours. Churchill asked where his strategic reserve, his mass of manoeuvre, was to plug the gap. Gamelin then revealed that he hadn't got one: the Maginot Line, designed to avoid the necessity for large bodies of troops in the front line, was crammed with soldiers, and a mass of manoeuvre could be created by 'scraping some men off the Maginot' and by bringing soldiers from North Africa. This would take a fortnight, which was far too long. Churchill said the French had left the naval arrangements to us and we had left the military arrangements to them, and had never enquired in even the most general terms of the French plan of campaign. It was only as a result of this meeting that our generals learned there was no strategic reserve – and then it was too late.

In talking of fighting and generals, Churchill said that some people think the right sort of general is the decent sort of fellow who, on retirement, will become president of the local Conservative Association. But 'it takes all sorts of strange people to win victories, some of them very queer fish indeed,' and he went on to talk of Wolfe, who, when appointed by Pitt to command our troops against French Canada, drew his sword and, waving it round his head, dashed round the table. Everyone thought him mad, and Pitt mad for appointing him, but he proved one of the great generals of English history.[4]

At another point Churchill said he always turned to one of the *Mirror* cartoons – 'Eustace Percy'. He repeated this doubtfully once or twice, so I suggested 'Useless Eustace' (the lowest-brow feature in the paper!). 'Ah, yes!' he said, 'of course; Eustace Percy was one of my colleagues.'[5]

Melchett asked him if he was at No 10 when the bomb destroyed so much of the Treasury next door. Churchill said yes, he was having dinner with Archie Sinclair, Oliver Lyttelton, and another minister (I forget who), but they had all done themselves so well the bomb didn't worry them. It apparently stove in some of the windows at the top of the house and made that part of the building unsafe.

After lunch Brendan Bracken came in: tall, good-looking in a sort of way, with brown eyes, a good mouth, and extraordinary thick bushy orange hair growing right down his forehead. He has bad hands, and the general impression is very simian and sinister – I couldn't say why. Seeing him and Winston side by side, one could see that they might be father and son, as has always been rumoured. He seemed to be treated more as one of the family. The party finally broke up at 3.40 with Mrs Churchill going off to a meeting. The others then went, and Churchill said goodbye and urged me to come and see him if I wanted anything. I said at that that the only thing I wanted was some war work, and if he ever wanted anyone very energetic and reasonably intelligent, would he perhaps remember me? I then went off with the Melchetts.

Once more, after watching him very closely for two hours, I was struck by his age and his complete lack of contact with the present day. He is a great personality, very English and very human, but obviously has no idea of what he is up against in Hitler. I should say his attitude is a slightly better-informed and more sophisticated version of what most people think: of course we shall win, because we always do. Pressed harder, it would emerge that he thought we could hang on through anything and that the Germans would collapse. In other words he is really counting on the Germans defeating themselves. In talking of the German failure to make the most of their advantages at Dunkirk and later, he repeated almost word for word what Chamberlain was saying this time last year: Hitler has missed the bus. He clearly has in mind a British invasion of the Continent, and at one point calculated that there were forty-five millions of us here and twenty million whites in the

Empire, which exactly matched with sixty-five million real Germans, the others under German control being Czechs, Poles, Austrians, and what not. So we start level, and if we get American help with her 110,000,000 whites, we shall be at an enormous numerical advantage! This little sum seemed to me as crude as it is false.

February 27, 1941
Thomas [Mirror *editor*] tells me Churchill said to Byron once: 'Chamberlain is a Birmingham town councillor who looks at our national affairs through the wrong end of a municipal drainpipe!'

March 1, 1941
Life here continues very much as before. The bomb wreckage has been mostly tidied up, the trains are running more punctually, everyone feels more optimistic – not because of our victories in North Africa, but because it is so many months since we suffered a defeat, and because the days are longer and sunnier.

Food is getting more difficult: M. was told today that cornflour is unobtainable. The shops are certainly less well stocked with goods of all kinds, but life remains very much pre-war. I do not yet discern any really strenuous war effort. It is still all very genial, half-hearted, and happy-go-lucky. The meat ration is small; the meat is never hung properly and so it is usually tough; fish is scarce and dear and not very fresh; eggs are hard to come by and cheese is almost unobtainable. But though this sounds bad, and though it may seriously affect the poorest classes, I would not say that we at home are suffering any noticeable inconvenience, let alone hardship.

We get the impression from all our Government contacts that the shipping situation is very bad, but can get no real information on the subject. The weekly sinking figures look low enough, but behind the scenes there is much gloom. At present for meat we are living mainly by slaughtering stock that is not being replaced because of the feeding-stuff difficulty: in fact we are living on our capital. When we come down to living on our income the position as regards meat, eggs, milk, and cheese will be very tight indeed. This leads many people to suppose that by the end of the summer

we shall be living on bread, oatmeal, and potatoes, but I cannot
find out if the supply of these is really adequate. I am naturally
sceptical and the fog of war, which has grown noticeably more
impenetrable of recent months – and even weeks – makes me even
more so. Its excuse is, of course, to conceal facts that would be of
value to the enemy, but its principal use is to hide from the public
as far as possible the appalling blunders that are being made by
those in high places.

March 2, 1941
About 10.30 last night there suddenly appeared Bosher, our
former photographer, now a lieutenant in the Gunners. Most of
our former employees loathe the Army, but Bosher loves every
minute of it, in spite of the fact that he is in command of some
machine-gun posts in the mud on the edge of the Bristol Channel
near Avonmouth. He had two days extra leave because his unit
helped shoot down a German bomber last week. It had been
winged by A.A. fire, lost its way in a snowstorm, ran into the
balloon barrage, and when fired on crashed in the mud. Two of
the crew were killed, the other two captured.

March 8, 1941
At 7.50 p.m. off went the warning and since then we have had
some pretty continuous bombing. After the first hour the watcher
on the roof had counted thirty-five bombs he had heard falling
through the air. The worst damage so far seems to be near London
Bridge, where a bomb caused twenty casualties, and on the Café
de Paris, where a hundred people are trapped, but we have
reports from Wapping, Bermondsey, Shoreditch, Chelsea, Horn-
sey, and as far away as Hayes and Harrow.

There was a great hoo-ha in the office on Wednesday night
[March 5]. The King was in Glasgow and had been round a
factory that makes tanks. Four pictures were taken (I don't know
by whom), and submitted to the censor by us. Three were quite
innocuous but were killed, and one, which we were doubtful about,
was passed. So doubtful were we, that we rang up the Ministry of
Information to make sure that it had been passed: it had. Then

about 3.0 in the morning a very peremptory call from the Ministry of Information, saying we really had torn it this time and we must stop our machines, bring copies back from the wholesalers and the stations, and so on. We asked what all the fuss was about, and the Ministry said it was this tank picture. When we said it had been passed by the censor, the fuss subsided.

This was a typical piece of illogicality. If an important military secret was being disclosed, surely the printed copies should be recalled, whether the blunder was ours or theirs. It now appears that our picture is not only of the latest tank but, being taken from the rear, shows a number of cylinders. These are for spraying gas. Clearly the fact that we are building tanks with gas-spraying equipment is a serious military secret, not only from the strictly military point of view, but because its revelation gives the Germans a good excuse if at any time they want to use gas. Why anyone was ever permitted to take a photograph of the tank baffles me, let alone how it could pass even the nitwits the Ministry of Information employs as censors.

March 10, 1941

The most conspicuous damage on Saturday [March 8] was the bomb on the Café de Paris. It is said to have been not more than 250 pounds, but came through the roof and burst on the dance floor. It killed all the band but two, and when our man was round there yesterday he saw the fifty-eighth body taken out. I passed the place this morning, and there is nothing showing from Coventry Street or Wardour Street – just three policemen at the door.

March 13, 1941

Sir Herbert Williams M.P., chairman of the Select Committee on National Expenditure, wrote to Campbell today to the effect that the days of Chamberlain were not too good from some points of view, but that administratively Chamberlain's Government was infinitely better than this one. In fact the present administration, he thinks, is the most incompetent British Government ever. This from a not unimportant Tory M.P. struck me as interesting.

March 15, 1941
The traffic on the roads is as bad as in peacetime and shows no signs of a shipping shortage – at least as far as petrol is concerned. Last night I drove home from the office, and there was continuous traffic the whole way to Maidenhead. Driving up today it was worse, as I encountered a mechanized column of troops with field guns coming the opposite way – and this in addition to the ordinary stream of traffic.

March 27, 1941
Last night I dined at Claridge's with Beaverbrook, and about thirty editors and such, to meet Mr Harriman, Roosevelt's 'defence expediter'. Beaverbrook looked older, dirtier, and untidier. I think, too, he dyes his hair – not in front, which is bald with grey at the sides, but round the back. Harriman looks about forty, tall, good-looking, intelligent, but rather passive. He is reputed to be the fourth richest man in the United States. The dinner was rather ill-planned, as he had nothing to tell us nor anything to ask us, so the evening rather ended on a note of 'So what?'

Harriman in the course of his remarks made two observations that interested me. One was that President Roosevelt is a 'great consolidator of public opinion, not a great leader of it', and that his policy towards this country will be governed by the state of public opinion as he finds it from time to time. The other was that Halifax's appointment as British Ambassador in Washington was not popular, as he is so closely associated with appeasement and Munich. Brendan Bracken made a *very* bad little speech, too, referring always to Churchill as 'my Master'.

March 29, 1941
Yesterday I called on Mr Harriman. I thought it would be as well to be polite and go and see him. He fixed the appointment for 3.0. He turned up at 3.35 and apologized for keeping me waiting: my appointment was at 3.30 was it not? I said it didn't matter, but it was at 3.0. I had had a long time to wait in his secretary's room and could see upside down his engagement diary, which was far from full. Yesterday it was ten o'clock at his tailor's in

Conduit Street, eleven o'clock at the Admiralty, lunch with some
of the Embassy staff at 1.20, me at 3.0, another newspaper man
at 4.30, and dinner with an admiral and some military oddments
at 8.30. For a 'defence expediter' in his first fortnight, it seemed
fairly easy going.

He again impressed me as very nice, very kind, intelligent, but
passive. I asked him was there any way in which I personally or
the newspapers in general could help. After some hesitation he
said (a) that the degree of help the Americans would give would
depend on the amount they are told about the fight we are putting
up. This would apply particularly to any American convoying
of ships carrying material under the Lease-and-Lend Bill. If we
did not give them more information about the Battle of the
Atlantic, direct naval aid would be deferred. (b) That the
Americans were helping us out of the generosity of their hearts:
could we do anything to make them feel good about it? or anyway
avoid any repetition of what happened last time, when, after they
had won the war for us (as they thought), we turned our backs on
them and neither showed gratitude nor paid our debts? If the
future was to hold any close co-operation between the two peoples,
we must not hurt the feelings of the American people in this way,
and obviously one could not start too soon to get American help
in the right perspective over here.

Harriman seemed in general rather out of his depth. I should
say he had been given the job for internal reasons in the U.S.,
not because of any knowledge of England or English conditions.
He seemed to know very little indeed about opinion in this country,
and not to have made any study of the English papers during this
war: but he certainly had the grace to admit it. I promised to do
anything I could along the lines he suggested, and we parted
very amicably.

Incidentally, he produced quite a good joke, which I hadn't
heard, about Bevin's call for 100,000 women for munitions work.
'Bevin puts 100,000 women in labour.' This is alleged to have
been the headline in one of the papers.

March 31, 1941
George [Thomson] spent last night with us. I hadn't seen him

since a year ago, when he was at work on measures for countering the magnetic mine, and also on redesigning machine-gun bullets for aeroplanes. His work seems now to be more hush-hush. He referred in vague terms to the Whittle gas turbine.[6] I imagine this is an internal combustion engine that operates by means of a turbine turned by the gases of the explosion, instead of pistons. I gather it is likely to be a success and to revolutionize aeroplane engines. Its perfection is some way off yet, but not immeasurably so. He also reacted at once when I mentioned Melchett at No 10 [on February 19] and his reference to new explosives of vast power, working on a new principle. I imagine these would employ atomic energy in some way.[7]

April 1, 1941
Yesterday I went to see Walter Monckton, now Director-General of the Ministry of Information. I feel I must take some part in this war, and seriously to make use of my experience and capacity means getting into the Ministry of Information. I thought I would call on Monckton and ascertain if there was ever likely to be a niche for me there, and if not, reconcile myself to becoming a square peg in a round hole and join the fire brigade as a part-time volunteer.

Monckton was very affable and seemed to welcome the idea of me as a recruit: said he had rather gathered I had been offered a job by Pick and had turned it down. I said I had never been offered a job at any stage. He said the home propaganda side was now covered, by the appointment of Parker from the Home Office. Would I consider taking on the foreign side? I said I really had proved my knowledge of popular psychology at home, but would certainly not reject the idea of taking something on the foreign side. He asked what I knew of America and I told him. He said he had had no idea what I wanted to see him about and that it would be more satisfactory if we had a specific job to discuss, so would I return on Wednesday [April 2] at the same hour? In the meantime I gather he will see Duff Cooper and get his reaction, and also see what niches there are unfilled or unsuitably filled. It all sounded as if he were about to offer me the management of all our foreign propaganda. This would entertain me vastly, but I have learnt to be very sceptical and not count my fish until they are not only landed but cooked and served.

April 2, 1941

Saw Monckton at 12.0 today and had a chat about this and that. Seems not to have found a suitable berth for me and is leaning towards finding me something on the home side. I am to see him on Monday again. He seemed very friendly and receptive, and still quite anxious to have me in his organization.

April 1941 was for the British people one of the most disastrous months of the war. Rommel began his offensive in North Africa, and by April 11 had recaptured for the Axis all Cyrenaica except the fortress port of Tobruk.

The British defences in Cyrenaica had been weakened by the detachment of 62,000 British and Imperial troops to go to the support of Greece, which was invaded by Germany on April 6. But Britain's campaign in Greece was a fiasco reminiscent of the Norwegian campaign. The expeditionary force never really came to grips with the Germans and evacuation began on April 24; meanwhile the Greek government capitulated. Most of the troops were withdrawn to Crete, and a month later this island was wrested from the British by a German airborne invasion.

Yugoslavia was also overrun in April: Hitler invaded on April 6, ten days after a coup d'état by Yugoslav air-force officers had turned out the pro-Axis government. Belgrade was nearly obliterated by savage bombing, which killed 16,000 people. Yugoslavia collapsed after twelve days' resistance.

And on top of all this, Great Britain lost 700,000 tons of shipping in April in the Battle of the Atlantic and elsewhere.

April 7, 1941

Saw Monckton again this morning – a rather hurried visit between a row he was having with one of his censors who released the news of British troops in Greece to America five hours before it was due to be released in Australia (just after midnight last night), and a visit of Moore-Brabazon, the Minister of Transport. Monckton was very friendly and had, I gather, recommended me to Duff Cooper for an appointment (exact nature to be discussed later), but had had no reply. In this, it seems, Duff Cooper was running quite true to form.

April 9, 1941
With all the talk of total war, I notice that six roadmen are still installing a concrete kerb on the main Maidenhead-Henley road, which has hitherto done without one. This morning, too, I saw a workman on the National Gallery putting wire netting over the capitals of the pillars to prevent pigeons nesting there!

April 14, 1941
Was to have seen Monckton at 12.0 today, but this was changed into a lunch with Duff Cooper and Monckton at Windham's Club, which, incidentally, is on the point of shutting down. Portal was there lunching alone – going rather bald, but looking capable and confident. His lunch was over and he had gone by 2.0. Our lunch was rather alcoholic: a large sherry, claret, two glasses of vintage port (Dow 1912), and a large liqueur brandy. Conversation did not flow easily. Duff Cooper again gave me the impression of hesitancy, and of one possessed by a sense of futility and defeat in his own life.

The conversation ranged round all sorts of topics. Duff Cooper mentioned in passing that our big stand in Libya was meant to be at Tobruk, and also, apropos of the war as a whole, that presumably from now on things would tend to go better! He also said that Beaverbrook still had the ear of the Prime Minister more than any other minister had, and saw a lot of the Labour ministers, particularly Alexander. We talked about the value of putting someone with a news sense from the Ministry of Information into the service ministries to pick up stories at the source, and he asked me if that was what I thought I could do. I said I could find someone to do it, but that there were lots of people who could do it better than I. Duff Cooper then said that he thought our propaganda should be more positive. At present it was far more concerned with what should not be said: could I help there? I said indeed I could, and the conversation drifted off on to other things.

At the end I had a word with Monckton, who said that Duff

Cooper was rather feeling round and his suggestions were not quite appropriate, but he thought he could be brought into line. He himself was clearly very keen to have me, and the delay is just Duff Cooper and procrastination. Monckton is very charming and much more purposeful than I thought at first.

This was Easter Monday and in spite of all the talk about an intensified war effort, it looked like a normal peacetime Bank Holiday. The roads were blocked with private cars on pleasure trips; all the shops between Paddington and the City were shut; the pavements were crowded with sightseers from other parts of London. It was a real day out. In Henley a compromise was attempted – shops remained open till noon!

April 16, 1941
In the afternoon I drove down to Churt to see Lloyd George. I felt the military position would produce political repercussions and wanted to know what he thought about it all. He told me that when I lunched there last year a message was brought to him at the table: did I remember? I did, but was surprised that he remembered my presence on that occasion. The message was from the Prime Minister, who wanted to see him. When Lloyd George met him – that evening I think – Churchill offered him a seat in the War Cabinet; he said Chamberlain had withdrawn his opposition, and that the other members had unanimously expressed their wish that he should join them. Lloyd George said (a) he would not join the Cabinet unless it were a real War Cabinet of members free from departmental responsibilities, and (b) that of course he would not serve with men like Chamberlain and Halifax, who had got us into this mess. He would, however, consent to serve as Director of Food Production, provided he had no responsibility for the general policy of the Government. Churchill said this would be unconstitutional, though Lloyd George said there was just such a director in the last war.

On Lothian's death Lloyd George was offered the Embassy in Washington, but refused it, as he considers the result of the war will be decided here, not in America. Lloyd George is an old man, but is not in any way decrepit. His hands are well shaped and young-looking, and his grasp of the requirements of the situation far beyond anything I have met with among politicians. He considers the direction of the war hopelessly haphazard and aimless: said he is sure the Cabinet has no main war strategy and that it just endorses everything Churchill suggests. In particular he thinks our agricultural policy, or lack of it, disastrous. Hudson [*Minister of Agriculture*] he considers to be no use at all, and said he only took on the job under protest, as the subject does not interest him!

About the war, he thinks we should have negotiated peace at the end of Hitler's Polish campaign. Militarily we were not then involved and could have got very reasonable terms – entirely at the expense of the Poles. Lloyd George thought that perhaps we could have hit Italy so hard this winter that Mussolini's position would have become imposssible, and that he would have been succeeded by someone like Grandi. If this had been possible and if we had completed the conquest of Libya, we should then have had a good card to play in negotiating with Germany. But once we had been pushed out of Libya and the Greeks were retreating from Albania, Mussolini's position was obviously restored and we now have nothing to negotiate with. If we definitely defeat the Germans in Libya, Lloyd George thought Churchill could survive the evacuation of Greece; but if we did badly in both areas, there would be considerable political repercussions. He thought the House of Commons would insist on a real War Cabinet. He clearly takes a poor view of our future and has been thinking hard of the political prospects here. He considers Winston would remain as premier, but would have to accept the guidance of a Cabinet of five or so members without portfolio.

He clearly expects to be in such a Cabinet, so I asked him what others he thought would or should be included. He thought Beaverbrook was likely to be in; of other members he thought perhaps Stafford Cripps, perhaps Morrison, perhaps Lyttelton. Bevin he thinks a very ordinary trade-union boss. Eden had returned from the Middle East with greatly dimmed prestige, and Lloyd George didn't think much of him anyway. As ministers, though not Cabinet ministers, he thought well of Duncan and Shinwell and had heard Garro-Jones favourably spoken of. He thought the deterioration in the quality of political personnel was

9

due to the tyranny of the party machines. In his young days Liberal Members even defied Gladstone – the most powerful political leader he had known in his career – but such defiance was tolerated and understood. The Labour Party had copied the worst aspects of the Irish Party's disciplinary methods, and the Conservative Party had eventually gone the same way.

He started talking of Napoleon, 'one of those men who appear once in a century out of the forest and can see beyond the well nibbled field where we and they stand, into the green grass beyond'. Pitt was an able man but one of the common kind: Napoleon was a superb genius different from any of the men he came up against. I asked if he put Hitler in this class. He said undoubtedly. I said I thought Churchill greatly underestimated Hitler, and looked on him as a petty crook or gangster who had had a lot of luck. Lloyd George agreed that Winston took this view and that it was sadly misguided.

Other things he said in passing were that he knew for a fact that our figures of shipping losses are falsified. The shipping position he thinks worse than in 1917. He also told us that after the fall of Benghazi Winston told him the Germans had only a brigade in Libya, whereas they had several divisions! No one seems to have any convincing explanation of how they all got there unnoticed.

April 28, 1941

Had tea with Garfield Weston at Wittington [Marlow, Buckinghamshire]. I think Weston very straight, very forceful, and very capable. He is now M.P. for Macclesfield and clearly has political ambitions. At present he is marking time and getting the hang of things but, as he said, many heads will fall before we are through all this, and his turn will come.

Late last summer when the air fighting over Britain flared up for a time, sixteen of our Spitfires were brought down in one day, though many more German planes were destroyed in the process. Weston thought he would like to do something about this and sought an interview with Beaverbrook. Beaverbrook gave him an appointment, kept him waiting half an hour, and then said he supposed he wanted a job. Weston said no, he didn't, he had brought a note; and he handed this to Beaverbrook. Beaverbrook opened it and found a cheque for £100,000 with a few lines to say he couldn't, alas, replace the sixteen pilots, but he would like to replace the machines and hoped £100,000 was enough. He was sending the cheque to Beaverbrook as he would like to make this offering through a 'fellow colonial'. Beaverbrook, apparently, just put his head on his desk and wept – and wept! He afterwards strode up and down the room, tears streaming down his face, and said this was the most wonderful thing that had ever happened to him! I had no idea Beaverbrook was such an emotional, not to say sentimental, man – though the incident was certainly a very moving one.

May 1, 1941
Was present at a lunch to celebrate the fiftieth anniversary of Sir Emsley Carr's appointment as editor-in-chief of the *News of the World*. About 150 people present at the Dorchester, but what a moment to celebrate such a trivial event! After all, at all relevant periods, the editor-in-chief was Lord Riddell, as we all well knew. However, among those present were Duff Cooper, Beaverbrook, Kingsley Wood, and even the Prime Minister. Kingsley Wood looking more smug and negligible than words can say. The Prime Minister, who greeted me, looked white and drawn, but had a marvellous ovation from those present. Not unmindful, perhaps, of the fact that he has a contract with the *News of the World* with five years still to run, at £400 or so per article, the Prime Minister made a short speech and was present for at least one and a half hours. Even the King and Lloyd George sent telegrams!

May 10, 1941
Went to see Monckton this afternoon at 3.30. Had not seen him for a fortnight and thought it was about time I jogged him a bit. It appears that the Ministry of Information is under fire at the moment, and hence the delay. Monckton, whom I like more and more, is prepared to walk out unless the Prime Minister will agree (a) to the Ministry of Information receiving news as soon as it reaches the chiefs of staff, (b) to having journalists in the front line, on bombers and so forth, (c) to someone outside the service

ministries having the last word on what is published and what is not. He gathers that Churchill will not agree to this person being Duff Cooper, but might agree to its being Beaverbrook. Monckton wants the Ministry of Information to be moved into Beaverbrook's orbit. There has been a proposal – daft in all conscience – that it should be under the Foreign Office! Another nightmare of Monckton's is that it might be put under Anderson, or even Attlee!

On May 10 the Luftwaffe made a last and shattering assault on London. It was the most destructive night of the Blitz. The Germans dropped mainly incendiaries. Two thousand fires were started, three thousand people were killed or injured, all but one main-line station were put out of action, and the House of Commons was destroyed. Three days after the raid London still burned. The Daily Mirror *offices were lucky to survive: at one time alone fifteen fires blazed on or around Geraldine House.*

It was Saturday night, press night at the Sunday Pictorial, *and Cecil King was at the office. The day after the raid he wrote the following vivid account of it.*

May 11, 1941
Last night about eleven o'clock, off went the warning. Nothing very much happened for a time, so I supposed it was to be someone else's turn tonight. But gradually things warmed up. On my first visit to the roof of the *Mirror* office, there was a lot of A.A. fire over the East End, though very little near us. A number of incendiaries had been dropped to the west of us and, though they had not been put out, they didn't seem to be starting a fire.

However, shortly afterwards I went up again to the roof and the fun was really starting. An incendiary had fallen through the roof of our old offices in Bream's Buildings, all wood partitions and loaded up with stocks of paper and string – very inflammable indeed. I led a party over the roofs from the main building and we threw up sandbags to a man who appeared on the roof above us. He put the sand on the flames and put them out. We then went inside the building and found the bomb on the floor burning fiercely. A fireman was covering it with bags of sand. Flames were breaking out in the lift shaft just by: the bomb was setting alight the boards of the ceiling below. We went down to the lower floor, forced open the lift door, and directed a stream from a stirrup pump on to the flames; meanwhile the flames were breaking out again on the floor above. Eventually they were both subdued. Elsewhere, some of the party were extinguishing a bomb which had fallen on the flat roof of Geraldine House proper.

I get rather muddled over the sequence of events in looking back, but about this time we saw another incendiary had fallen on the roof of a shop in Fetter Lane opposite the entrance to the office. I went over with one of the firemen to deal with it. We were contemplating the locked door when a watcher was sighted on the roof, who tackled it. I kept sending men back to our fire as I felt it might break out again. In due course it did, both on the roof and inside, but was soon put out. In the shop the watcher did not do the job properly, and before very long immense clouds of thick black smoke were pouring out of the top storey and the place was well and truly alight. It spread both ways and eventually involved two other shops, the Moravian church, and a group of factories and printing works. The Germans overhead were in such large numbers that you could not distinguish the sound of individual planes. About this time three incendiaries fell in the yard – two into vans and one into Canty's car (next mine). They were put out after doing a good deal of damage.

The roof watchers were splendid, paid no attention to bombs, but the editorial staff mostly cowered in a corner of the basement and were useless. Once the fires were well alight, the Germans started bombing them and the H.E. began to drop all round. I should estimate that on an average once a minute for five hours a bomb could be heard rushing or whistling through the air. Once when I was on the roof, one dropped fairly near, and one could see the flash and the column of dust from the explosion. Fires by this time were all round us – big ones and growing, especially a very bright one near the corner of Chancery Lane and Holborn.

Then a fire was observed on the roof of what used to be Wyman's building in Fetter Lane; it now belongs to Odhams. Evidently there were no roof watchers, and by the time the flames became visible from below the north-east corner was well alight. Unfortunately, there was a stiff north-east wind blowing. Very soon the whole building was burning fiercely and another fire was coming at us towards the *Field* building from the other side of Bream's Buildings. Bart and Greenwell [Mirror *photographer*] turned up in A.F.S. [*Auxiliary Fire Service*] uniform and asked for (and received the promise of) ten pumps, as we were in the direct line. Another fire, on the roof of Charles and Read behind us, was put out.

As time went on and the fires in Fetter Lane and Rolls Buildings spread, it began to look pretty bad for us. I found Greenwell, who said the A.F.S. had again confirmed their promise to send ten pumps. We had out all our own fire-fighting equipment, but by this time there was no water pressure. Eventually one pump arrived – not really for us, but to protect the [Public] Record Office. They set to work and pumped all the water in the 'dam' outside our office on to the flames. This helped, but was soon over. Then more water was got in from the Record Office, but most of this, too, was wasted on the shops in Fetter Lane, which were obviously past praying for. Then the Record Office water gave out. We scrounged around, found a small pipe in the yard which worked directly off the main and which still flowed, and Pyatt found one hydrant which still worked, though very slowly. These we directed into the 'dam' and slowly filled it up. When it was half full the A.F.S. men had a drive at the side of the fire in Wyman's building nearest us, and partly because of this and partly because Birkbeck College between us and them was damaged by fire very early on in the raids last autumn, so acting as a firebreak, we just got through. Mercifully also, at the critical moment, the wind changed.

Towards morning the smoke was such you could not see that it was full moon with no clouds; the air was full of flying sparks; every now and then there was a roar of a collapsing house. We had had our 'double red' warning on in the office for more than four hours. The lines from Paddington and Euston were blocked, King's Cross had had a direct hit, and most of the Southern Railway termini were closed. It was obvious that this was a really big raid, not just round us but on London generally.

About 4.0 a.m. I went for a walk to see what had been happening in our immediate neighbourhood. I managed to get down Fetter Lane to Fleet Street (the other way was completely blocked by this time by fallen buildings, as well as by fires). Serjeant's Inn was blazing, and further on it appeared as if the *News Chronicle* were alight. I asked a bobby, who said it had been but was now burnt out. Behind the *Express* in Shoe Lane there was a terrific blaze. When I got to Ludgate Circus I could see the glow from a huge fire in Queen Victoria Street, which had been blazing most of the night. Up Farringdon Street near the Viaduct the buildings were blazing on both sides of the road. Up Ludgate Hill there were big fires on both sides, and I could see a great glow the other side of St Paul's.

Coming back up Fleet Street I looked in the Temple. The Temple Church, one of the great monuments of English history, was on fire. The conical roof was flaring on top like a torch, and rivers of lead were pouring down the slope of the roof. As I watched, the weather-vane or what not from the top of the cone came crashing down. Inner Temple Hall – a Victorian copy of the old hall and very damaged already – was blazing. I looked into the Middle Temple, where the hall seemed to be no worse, but a group of old buildings was burning away. Further along still St Clement Danes had been gutted, and only the spire was alight half way up to the top and sending out showers of sparks – an odd and rather beautiful spectacle.

When I got back I found that we had been delayed over starting printing again, because the electric current had failed and the metal pots in the linos had gone cold; all the lights had, of course, gone out. However, after a ten-minute interval they came on again and efforts could be made to get the paper out. I left at 6.30 when all danger to the office from nearby fires seemed to be well over.

On my drive back I passed the end of Aldwych, where the road was covered with chunks of stone and concrete from a bomb hole between the theatre and the old *Morning Post* building. The next 'incident' was an unexploded bomb in Regent Street. I turned to the left and found the road blocked by a land-mine on the corner of Bond Street, and so into Hanover Square. The opposite side of Oxford Street, beyond the corner of Lewis', there was a large fire: it appeared to be in the convent on the north side of Cavendish Square. At Marble Arch a small bomb had hit the façade of the

Regal Cinema. Down the Bayswater Road there was a house burning: I thought it might be the Roman Catholic convent at Tyburn. I was directed into Connaught Street, where there was a huge crater in the road. So back into Bayswater Road and a diversion for another blazing house, then to Notting Hill Gate, where the road was covered with broken glass. From that point there was no sign of the raid, though even at Culham you could see the great cloud of smoke from burning London in the morning sunshine.

On my way out I picked up a man on his way to Bristol. He had spent the night in the Rotherhithe Tunnel. He could not get through Commercial Road or Aldgate, and had to go back down the tunnel and go through New Cross, which was also mostly on fire. The A.F.S. men who came with our one pump said they had come from Aldgate, where there was a 'sea of flame' – but no water.

SENSATION! Rudolf Hess, Deputy Fuehrer, former confidant of Adolf Hitler, had parachuted into Scotland on May 10 from a plane he had himself stolen and piloted. He came on a mission to the Duke of Hamilton, the Lord Steward, whom he had met before the war and who he thought was in the inner councils of the Government. He hoped to persuade the Duke that it was folly for Britain to fight on: Britain should make peace on the generous terms that Germany would offer her. Churchill received the news on Sunday May 11, and was at first incredulous. 'It was as if my trusted colleague the Foreign Secretary, who was only a little younger than Hess, had parachuted from a stolen Spitfire into the grounds of Berchtesgaden.' An announcement was placed in the German press to the effect that 'The National Socialist Party regrets that this idealist fell a victim to his hallucination.'

The sensation soon died down. It was not an important event. Hess was confined for a short time in the Tower of London and ended up, less romantically, in Spandau prison. In a rather confused way the Government attempted to make propaganda out of the event. On May 17 Churchill wrote to Roosevelt: 'Here we think it best to let the Press have a good run for a bit and keep the Germans guessing,' which may explain the following passage in Cecil King's diary.

May 15, 1941

At eleven o'clock I was summoned to a lunch given by Lord Beaverbrook at Claridge's at 1.30. No indication was given of the purpose of the meeting, but Bart (who refused), Connor ['*Cassandra*'], and Campbell were also asked. Beaverbrook said, when we had eaten, that he wanted to help Duff Cooper and bring about a greater flow of news, and that the arrival of Hess gave us a chance of helping Duff Cooper and consequently ourselves. The better the newspapers handled this episode, the more it would strengthen Duff Cooper's position and enable him to get more news past the fighting services.

Beaverbrook then suggested that what was wanted at the moment was as much speculation, rumour, and discussion about Hess as possible. The Prime Minister would make no statement, as that would tend to put an end to the discussion. Would we, therefore, do on our own initiative all we could to make the most of this episode to the detriment of Germany?

A very confused discussion followed, in which on the whole the attitude adopted by the newspaper men was that we should be given a line by the Government, as any line we took up independently was liable to be made ridiculous at any moment by a Government announcement. Obviously our best policy was to say that Hess fled for his life owing to a serious split in the inmost circle of the Nazi Party. This line has, however, been badly compromised by the Government, which has released a good deal of stuff about the Duke of Hamilton and so made it clear that the German story of a one-man peace bid is substantially correct. According to Duff Cooper, Hess wrote a letter to the Duke of Hamilton, which reached this country last September.

Duff Cooper afterwards told me personally that though Hess arrived about 10.0 p.m. on Saturday [May 10], it was not until Monday evening he heard of Hess' disappearance – from the German wireless – and not until 10.0 p.m. or so on Monday that he heard from the Prime Minister of his arrival in this country. He told the assembled company that he had not yet seen a transcript of what Hess had said (!), but that his general line was that we were bound to be defeated by starvation if in no other way; that if the Government fled with the Fleet to the U.S.A. or Canada, our starving condition would be used as a weapon to bring peace; that, our prospects being so grim, he had come to see the Duke of Hamilton, as he thought the position of Churchill and his clique so weak that they could be overturned if only the real truth were told.

Clearly this meeting was too big, and should in any case have taken place before any official announcement was put out. Now that the Government has more or less killed the story, we are invited to come and flog the dead horse. The whole thing was a pathetic exhibition – Duff Cooper believing that truth is the best propaganda and yet that there must be some other ingredient somewhere; Beaverbrook wanting to help Duff Cooper, he doesn't quite know how; both hamstrung by the Prime Minister and officialdom generally, but too timid to attempt to break a way through.

June 5, 1941
I have been shown a cutting today from a paper *The Greenock By-election Special*, which contains the report of a speech by McGovern M.P. to a Glasgow study circle on May 25. The definite statement was made that in April 1940 Beaverbrook sent for McGovern and Maxton, and offered to support their peace appeal [for a negotiated peace] by putting a peace candidate into each of the constituencies and fully supporting them financially. He even offered to send special reporters into the constituencies, because he saw no sign of Britain beating Germany.

When I got this story, Campbell and I sent out Condon of the Sunday Pic staff to ascertain from his friends on the [*Daily*] *Express* what they were doing or saying about this very startling development. Condon was evidently pretty clumsy, as this afternoon Robertson, general manager of the *Express*, came round to see Cowley and find out what we were doing about it. Naturally we are doing nothing, as there can be nothing gained by compromising one of the two or three of our leaders who seem to have some guts.

However, in the course of conversation between Campbell, Cowley, and Robertson, it became clear that the story is substantially true. Robertson said Beaverbrook *had* seen Maxton and McGovern at that time, but that anything he may have said was merely a joke! Campbell got the impression that Beaverbrook had made this offer to the Independent Labour Party, but that he had drawn back when offered a place in Churchill's Government a few days later. Meanwhile we hear the story has reached America and, it is also thought, Russia. If there were any choice of leaders in this country this would finish Beaverbrook for ever, as the Prime Minister for peace negotiations would clearly be Lloyd George, not Beaverbrook. But we are in such a leaderless condition that his position may survive even this.

Operation Barbarossa (Hitler's code name for it) was the greatest military operation so far in the history of the world. On June 22, 1941, the Germans invaded Russia with 164 divisions supported by 2,700 aircraft, a force estimated at about three million men. The Red Army in the west of Russia was massacred along a 2,000-mile front. By the end of the year the Germans had reached the outskirts of Leningrad and Moscow, captured Kiev, and driven deep into southern Russia past Kharkov towards the oil wells of the Caucasus.

Whatever past differences, Britain greeted her new ally with enthusiasm, and on July 13 a mutual aid pact was signed by the two countries.

June 22, 1941
When I left the office at 12.30 last night, the rumours about a Russo-German campaign seemed on the wane, but when I listened in to the nine o'clock news the march had already begun. Hitler's successes so far seem to me to be due to the fact that he has been exploiting the underlying realities of contemporary Europe, but in this latest move he seems to me to have these same realities against him. He can doubtless win victories against the Russians, but it is hard to see how he can obliterate Communist Russia as he could and did obliterate Belgium or Yugoslavia. It seems to me, taking a very long view, that Hitler has signed his own political death warrant, and quite likely that of the Nazi Party as well, though it does not follow that what he has done will turn to our advantage.

My main feeling about this whole development is one of misgiving, as I think the war has now got out of anyone's control. Where it will spread to next, what it will involve or when it will end, is now quite unforeseeable. Hitherto, also, one could always get a line on the probable course of events by arguing from what one would try to do in Hitler's place. Now that he has done something which seems to me from his point of view obviously unsound, I feel baffled.

June 25, 1941

In the House of Commons this afternoon the Prime Minister was asked about Beaverbrook and his offer to finance peace candidates. He dismissed the story as 'Communist vapourings'. Challenged by both McGovern and Maxton on the truth of the allegations, he insisted that the whole story was untrue. McGovern and Maxton both said in effect that they were not interested in disputing over Churchill's comment, but insisted that the story was in fact true. Churchill seems to me to have handled this very badly indeed. He should surely have insisted on Beaverbrook bringing a libel action or else resigning. This story, combined with Hess', will leave very many people even more suspicious of the real attitude of those in high places than they are at present.

July 7, 1941

Had lunch with Frank Owen, editor of the *Evening Standard*, at Simpson's. He is a tall dark Welshman with a somewhat American enunciation. He was a Liberal M.P. in the Parliament of 1929–31. He saw Lloyd George the other day, when he and Beaverbrook went down to see the old man. Old Lloyd George was very bitter about being called Pétain by Churchill in the House of Commons. He said the Prime Minister wasted too much time 'looking down the barrels of guns'. Owen said this sort of thing should be done by the Royal Family – or, broke in Lloyd George, one could always appoint a couple more Labour ministers! Lloyd George said Winston's speeches were made with one eye on the House of Commons and the other on posterity. Altogether, Owen said, the old man has a 'mind like a scorpion'. Beaverbrook refers to the Prime Minister as 'old bottleneck'. Churchill apparently insists on making every important decision himself, but wastes much of his time inspecting our defences or sitting up all night drinking, with Harry Hopkins or the like.

We were laughing over various stories of Kemsley (alias Gomer Berry). Apparently Churchill was there to dinner one night, and towards the end of the meal Kemsley asked him to pull up a chair by him at the top of the table. When he did so, Kemsley asked him what intrigues he was carrying on against Chamberlain (this when Churchill was First Lord of the Admiralty!). Churchill rose instantly, and told Kemsley to ring the bell and send his servant for Winston's car. Winston then left. This has led to a vendetta and explains the attacks on Churchill in the *Sketch* [*the Daily Sketch, controlled by Lord Kemsley*]. They are not based on political probabilities, but on mere personal animosity!

From what Owen said, I gather the Prime Minister is rather afraid of Hore-Belisha, and sends nice messages to him via Brendan Bracken just before an important debate when he expects old Horeb to be critical. Horeb wants desperately to be in office and gladly pulls his punches if he thinks there is any chance of getting back, even to the Ministry of Pensions.

July 11, 1941

That American intervention will have to be paid for in one form or another, has escaped the notice apparently of both Churchill and his Cabinet. It is hard to say what price the U.S.A. will exact. We have no money, so it may well be political subservience. All of which is based on the assumption that the Russians hold out. If they collapse, American help may not even be sufficient to prolong the war, as it will not be forthcoming in significant volume till after this critical year.

A further point that impresses me is that however short-sighted and irrational English policy was, American, German, and Russian policies were self-interested but intelligible. But when Germany attacks Russia and America begins to occupy bases in Northern Ireland,[8] the behaviour of the great powers has become so irrational that almost anything may happen next.

The American government could have been very helpful earlier by exerting purely diplomatic pressure. This she did not apply, but she is now gratuitously inviting a war with the whole of Europe, in which she stands to lose a lot and gain nothing. Germany, with the whole of western Europe at her feet, goes off on a crazy expedition into Russia, which must create more problems than it solves. After such developments as these, it is impossible to look into the future except for very long-term developments. The actions of wise men may be foreseen, as in any given set of circumstances the number of sensible things to do is very limited; the actions of fools and lunatics may not, as there is always an unlimited number of possible moves for either.

July 15, 1941
Campbell had lunch with Hore-Belisha today. Hore-Belisha very repentant, and admitting that we were right and he was grievously wrong in the tactics he adopted after his removal from the War Office. He now wants to switch from the *News of the World*, who won't let him write anything critical of Churchill, to the Sunday Pic. He says the position of Churchill's Government in the House is visibly weakening. He thinks events will bring about a complete reconstruction – he can't say when, but thinks in a period of a few months, perhaps two. He thinks he may well be Churchill's successor, and is wondering whether or no he should accept the Ministry of Defence if Churchill offered it to him!

Quite obviously Hore-Belisha could not be Prime Minister under anything like current conditions and his chances are, if anything, fading. Churchill would only relinquish the Ministry of Defence in the teeth of a threat of immediate dismissal and would certainly under no circumstances accept Hore-Belisha in that office. His best hope is to be Minister of Information with a seat in the War Cabinet, but that he seems to think infra dig. He is still obviously and entirely interested in himself and his career, which attitude of mind is a great, and likely to be increasing, handicap. His political judgment seems pretty fantastic, too.

David Walker came into the office yesterday morning after being abroad for two and a half years, mostly in Rumania. He was with our Ambassador at Sarajevo and was captured with him by the Italians. He was two weeks as a prisoner in Yugoslavia, one week at Durazzo in Albania, eight weeks in Italy, ten days in Spain, and so home by Gibraltar.

Walker was in the first air raid on Belgrade, which he described

as a massacre. The first time over, the German bombers flew high
(about 15,000 feet), the second time only at 300 feet. He was also
in the attack some days later on Sarajevo, when the German
bombers flew at seventy feet or less and bombed the house
occupied by the British Ambassador. Walker said it was an
astonishing sight seeing these planes almost touching the tree-tops
and dropping bombs, while elderly members of the legation hid
behind tree-trunks and fired their revolvers at them. I asked him
if the Yugoslav coup d'état was organized by our people or by the
Russians. He has the lowest opinion of our diplomats in the
Balkans and evidently thought them quite incapable of organizing
anything. He said he believed the coup d'état was really spon-
taneous, and actually organized by some young air-force officers.

Italian morale he said was much higher after the occupation
of Athens and Crete, but was still very low. He was given good
food, unlimited wine and cigarettes, but he gathered the ordinary
Italian citizen is not doing too well. His menu included Danish
ham, which suggested to him that the Germans cannot be feeding
badly or they would not be sending hams through to Italy.

July 17, 1941
Had lunch with David Walker. Couldn't get a table at the
Escargot in Greek Street, so repaired to the Gourmet. Walker had
been spending the morning with the B.B.C., talking to some of the
people responsible for broadcasting our news to foreign countries.
He said our stuff for the Balkans was laughable and did us far
more harm than good. These birds from Portland Place ('with
their green trousers and flowing ties', as Bart says) took his
criticisms with a very bad grace indeed, and obviously had no
intention of changing their methods. They apparently think
anything said with feeling is rather vulgar, and so usually give
out a very pansified B.B.C. message translated into (say) Bulgarian
by a friend who knows very little Bulgarian. The effect on the
Bulgars is to confirm all that the Germans say of us.

I asked Walker about the Vichy French and he said he gathers
they have sunk into a state of apathy, and rarely bother to listen
to the news or read the papers. Their interests are bounded by
schemes to win an extra cigarette or glass of wine.

Churchill in a speech this week said that in the last few weeks
we had dropped half as great a weight of bombs on Germany as
she had dropped on us throughout the war. Today the Air
Ministry tells us (not for publication) that Mr Churchill must
have 'misread his script', as these figures are gross exaggerations!
Today we are told that the weight of bombs dropped on Germany
in a recent period of three weeks was 3,500 tons, which seems to
represent the work of about a hundred planes per night – which
is nothing like the German effort for long stretches of last winter.
A lot of stuff is being put out about our growing strength in the
air and how we shall soon overtake the Germans. It seems to me
to be a mixture of wishful thinking and plain lying, but it is
amusing when the Air Ministry is quite so frank about the Prime
Minister's claims.

July 26, 1941

We published a spread in the *Mirror* about idle workers in factories, bad organization, idle machines, and so forth. Such stories
reach any newspaper office – I regret to say – by every post. All
the papers had published them, but Bart, with one eye on the
Production debate on Tuesday [July 29], published a fresh batch
very prominently yesterday. During the day he received calls
from the Deputy Director of Gun Production, ditto of Shell
Production, and an official from the Ministry of Aircraft Production; and a telephone call from the Admiralty. His general line
was that he would not tell them which firms were concerned, but
he would take an accredited official to the factories concerned
and show him. He is tired of giving facts and then having officials
ringing up the firm and announcing their arrival, and duly finding
the factory working like a beehive – for the duration of their visit.

Meanwhile Cowley had had a summons from Beaverbrook,
who said the spread was subversive and was calculated to set
master against man. If this went on, the Government would take
action, though he of course in such a matter would stand aside.
He also made Cowley swear he would not breathe a word of this
interview to anyone. Poor old Cowley, quite dazed by all this,
says it is so hard to distinguish between criticism that is subversive
and criticisms that are a legitimate and necessary part of our war

effort: so will we be careful! We will, but feel the Government must be rather jittery about Tuesday's debate to have thought of bullying Cowley in this way.

July 30, 1941
The main news has been the Production debate yesterday. Churchill delivered a long speech, little rhetoric, few facts, mainly a very glowing and rather wordy account of the work of the Government and a bitter denunciation of his critics. The speeches that followed were all critical (including one by the chairman of the 1922 Committee), some very critical (notably Shinwell's and Wardlaw-Milne's). Bevin wound up with a rather feeble speech, and so it ended.

Our little fuss seems to have died down after a visit from two detectives on Monday, who seemed to be trying to trump up some charge of a breach of defence regulations. They said it could be deduced from our spread last Friday [July 25] that anti-tank guns were being made in Manchester – or something to that sort of effect. This is apparently instigated by Morrison, who feels rather a fool. He recently took the American naval attache round the Sterling telephone factory: and the spread we published revealed that there was no work going on in the factory, and how activity had been faked for the duration of Morrison's visit.

What it all boils down to is that the House and the newspapers are convinced that our production is not what it should be, and that this is due partly to bad organization on the ministerial level and partly to the poor quality of minister responsible for this part of our operations. Churchill will not try and find better men outside his own little circle, and will not alter the arrangement by which his Cabinet is a lot of dummies and he is the one supreme bottleneck. In this debate he finally refused to listen to what was entirely well-meaning criticism, and is forcing his critics into open hostility to himself. This will not result in direct attacks at this stage, but certainly will do so in the future. How far in the future depends on the Russian campaign. If the Germans clean up in Russia, then Churchill will be encountering stormy weather in a matter of weeks. If the Russians hold the Germans up into the winter, then Churchill is probably safe from any real criticism until the spring.

The latest lot of Government appointments had such a bad reception in the House that they did not even give Duncan Sandys the customary cheer, when he got up to answer questions for the first time for the War Office.

August 7, 1941
Churchill is growing increasingly unpopular with his ministers: Hudson and Woolton are both highly critical of him in private. He has ministers out of bed at 2.0 in the morning and engages them in long talks about things that have nothing to do with their departments. He will not listen to any of their problems, and some go so far as to call him an old fool at times.

August 8, 1941
Campbell is told that the 1922 Committee plucked up its courage recently and sent the Prime Minister a message deploring recent appointments in the Government – particularly that of Duncan Sandys [*Churchill's son-in-law*]. The Prime Minister sent back a message to say that from time immemorial the Prime Minister had appointed to public office his friends and those he understood particularly well, and that he intended to continue the practice. The Committee could do nothing about that, except register another nail in Winston Churchill's coffin.

Cowley was at a meeting of the Newspaper Proprietors' Association this morning, where it was revealed that Beaverbrook had asked the N.P.A. to take over the collection of salvage for the whole country. In return he offered to sanction the import of more newsprint. This very discreditable suggestion was turned down, mainly, I suspect, because none of those present felt competent to handle the salvage problem. They are now negotiating on the basis of paper in return for publicity for the salvage campaign.

August 23, 1941
Churchill gave a talk to the editors yesterday afternoon. Campbell said he looked older and more worn, but was more cheerful than

on previous occasions. Churchill said that he and Roosevelt hammered out the eight points [of the Atlantic Charter⁹] in three hours, and that the eighth (a particularly vague one about post-war disarmament) was Roosevelt's own and surprised him by its large scope! He was obviously very impressed by Roosevelt, particularly by the way he had triumphed over his very serious illness, which had wasted the whole of his body below his shoulders.

About the Russians, Churchill said they had amazed him by their resistance, which had proved to him they were not an oppressed people, but had definitely gained something by their revolution. He would venture on a prophecy that whatever was the outcome of the present fighting, the Russians next spring would be putting up a most formidable opposition to the Germans. He was constantly being urged to do more for Russia, but what could we do? We had sent them all the rubber they asked for; we had diverted to them some 300 American fighter planes that had been destined for us. We had actually prepared a force for intervention in Murmansk, but the weather would soon be bad so far north and he was not keen. He preferred an opening into Russia in the warm south, and he implied this would be through Persia and would be taken in hand almost immediately.

We could not effectively land a force on the Channel coast so as to divert German troops from Russia. We could gain mastery of the air from Ostend to Dieppe only very temporarily, and an invasion in that bit of coast and under such circumstances would inevitably lead to a minor Dunkirk.

He was very anxious that America should declare war, owing to its psychological effect. He said he would rather have America in and no American supplies for six months, than double the present level of American shipments while she maintained her present position as a neutral. He had come to the conclusion that this was a psychological war and that much depended on whether the Germans could get the inhabitants of Europe to acquiesce in their New Order before we could convince them of our ability to set them free. In this race for time, American participation in the war would be a great psychological point in our favour. Meanwhile American supplies, particularly of bombers, were very disappointing, and Beaverbrook had gone to Washington to speed things up. Here again Churchill doubted whether it would prove possible to speed things up very much without America entering the war as an actual belligerent.

He was very cheerful about the Battle of the Atlantic, and said at first the German submarines worked close in to our shores, then they were pushed out into the Atlantic, then they went further afield and had much success in American waters. Now that the Americans had started patrolling (he mentioned here that his battleship the *Prince of Wales* had had an escort of two American destroyers), the German submarines had moved off and were now operating from the Bay of Biscay to the Cape Verde Islands. He assumed Hitler did not want to risk a clash with Roosevelt until the Russians were out of the way. In the meantime the figures for our shipping losses were much lower and the German losses much higher than they had been earlier in the year.

About the Japanese, Churchill said we were threatening them with very definite and drastic action jointly with the Americans if they made any further aggressive moves. He thought if they did play the part of the 'Wops of the Pacific', the Americans would declare war first, followed by ourselves. He would venture to prophesy that the Japs would shout and threaten, but would not move.

Asked how he proposed to win the war, Churchill said he had no more idea than he had after two years of the last war. (Obviously-inspired statements by American politicians since Roosevelt's return say that Churchill's plan is to remain on the defensive next year and invade the Continent in 1943. I think this version of Churchill's ideas is authentic.)

Churchill said that whatever we did for Russia must not weaken our effort in the Middle East, where we had built up a great army by prodigious effort. There we now had air parity, or perhaps superiority. We were still sending out 40,000 men there per month, and he was far more confident of holding Cairo twelve months from now than he was six months ago. In fact he thought our position all round had vastly improved. He thought we were now safe from starvation and he could not see how we could be successfully invaded. Our air defences were so formidable he felt we could beat off any attempt the Germans might make

to invade this island. He did not wish us to say so, but that is
what he thought. What a contrast with last year, when the
prospect was of invasion or starvation! If this improvement in
our fortunes could be maintained (and why not?), we should
next year be in the possession of a plan for bringing victory.

Other points were raised in questions at the end of his talk. He
said he had given Bevin instructions that 100,000 more men must
be found for the Army. At present the Army was *shrinking*, not
growing, in size as the loss from illness, casualties, and so forth
exceeded the intake.

September 11, 1941
Campbell had lunch with W.J. Brown yesterday. He was in good
form, just off to America on a lecture tour. He said Churchill explained to a friend of his (unnamed) the principles on which he
conducts his Government. Churchill was very struck in the last
war by the feeling of insecurity engendered among ministers by
Lloyd George's habit of calling into consultation men of all ranks
without reference to their departmental chiefs, and often accepting advice from very junior people in the teeth of contrary
opinion from higher up. He had resolved therefore to give complete trust to the ministers he appointed, and in that way to
create a ministry based on mutual trust and loyalty. He will,
therefore, under no circumstances submit to any important
changes in his Government.

This is all very well, but depends on the quality of the men in
whom he places his confidence. Brown thinks it is this method of
sticking to men who are proven failures which will eventually
bring him down.

September 20, 1941
An item of mild interest is that J.M. Keynes has been elected a
director of the Bank of England and that Montagu Norman,
Lord Kindersley, and Sir Edward Peacock, the three directors
who would normally retire on reaching seventy, are to be recommended for re-election at the court in April next.[10] The grounds
are that it is impossible in wartime to get substitutes of suitable
calibre. This is obviously untrue, and is part of the campaign to

maintain the status quo – in both policy and personnel – as long as possible. Norman, I think, is entirely disinterested and public-spirited and, as a personality, head and shoulders over all his colleagues, but as a governor of the Bank for the longest period in history he has been a lamentable failure. His policy has been for restoration of the gold standard and for deflation to that end. I should have said that twenty years ago it was quite plain that the gold standard was through, and that his policy of deflation was mistaken. It led to much unemployment and distress, and operated to the advantage of the rentier, a particularly worthless class, and to the detriment of the entrepreneur who, in a capitalistic society, is the one positive and active element. Quite clearly, on his record, Norman should have been shunted in 1931 if not earlier.

The Bank's appointment of Keynes is rather like a newspaper which secures G.B. Shaw as a contributor. Because Shaw was revolutionary forty or more years ago, some editors still see him in that light. Keynes was thought revolutionary twenty years ago, but now, at the age of fifty-eight or so, is merely our one really good economist. He will be useful now, but his influence twenty years ago would have been really worth having. His appointment now, I am sure, is a gesture to the critics, showing how modern we are.

October 3, 1941

We have been angling for some articles by Lloyd George for the Sunday Pic. He has been holding back, but invited Campbell and me to tea yesterday. We went down to Churt in a hired car, arriving at 4.0 and leaving at 6.30. The old man looked the same as when I saw him last, but was much older to talk to. He faltered a lot in his conversation, lost the thread of his remarks, fumbled for the right word, and spoke very slowly. As we saw him yesterday, he is incapable of more than a set speech on a set occasion – if that.

He had recently seen Churchill – I think on Tuesday [September 30] – and had some conversation with him about the future. He said Churchill considers himself a great strategic genius (of which Lloyd George sees no signs)! Churchill has no plan for winning the war. He considers that this island cannot now be invaded and that therefore we cannot lose; that in 1944 or 1945 something will turn up to give us our chance. He feels sure we *shall* win, but has no idea how. He is not interested in propaganda or production, and intends to retire immediately on the cessation of hostilities, as he has no interest at all in post-war problems.

Churchill and Lloyd George discussed the possibilities of a landing on the Continent. Lloyd George thinks that on the outbreak of war between Germany and Russia we should have landed a force on the coast of Norway and retaken the country. He selected Norway as the most difficult country for the Germans to reinforce. He thought that with bold handling of the Fleet it should have been possible to recapture the country, even if in the end we were thrown out again. Our part was to occupy one million German soldiers somehow. If we could have done this, the Germans and Russians would have been on equal terms and the German attack would have got nowhere. Churchill said that we lacked the means to make a successful attack at any point on the Continent, and that if Lloyd George would like an expert view on this, he would arrange an appointment between him and either Pound ('Do-nothing Dudley') or Portal, at which the matter could be explained in detail. Lloyd George said this was a military matter, so could he see Dill? Churchill very reluctantly said yes, but has not arranged the meeting. Lloyd George got the impression, and has confirmed it from other sources, that Pound and Portal were against a continental landing, but that Dill was in favour. He also said that in the Cabinet discussions Eden was in favour (I gather Eden told him so).

We asked the old man about the political situation, and he said the House of Commons would do very little. In the last war the House of Commons did not get rid of Asquith: it was the newspapers that did the trick. He said Asquith towards the end played very much the same part that Churchill did now. That he had not the drive or imagination required in a wartime premier, and made up for it by his ability to produce excellent speeches whenever people began to be uneasy. Lloyd George thought Churchill had clearly shown his unsuitability for the premiership, and said he thought that of the possible successors Eden was the most promising. Asked if Eden would be better than Churchill, he said he thought he would: he would be more 'malleable'. Lloyd George thought the collapse of Russia would create a situation in which large political changes would be possible, but doubted whether a German advance to Kharkov, Rostov, and the all-important Donetz basin would sufficiently alarm people. The only towns in Russia they know are Moscow and Leningrad.

October 9, 1941

Ivor Lambe tells me that his impression of the Ministry of Information is that it shows no improvement under Bracken's management. One or two dummies at the top have been moved, but the spirit permeating the whole remains identically the same.

October 11, 1941

I forgot to mention that when waiting for Hugh [Fraser] at the Savoy on Wednesday [October 8], I saw General de Gaulle. He was attended by a French A.D.C. and there were a couple of Czech generals and a French admiral in his party. I didn't see him in the restaurant, so I dare say his party had a private room. He wore a khaki uniform and a khaki képi with a gold-encrusted peak, not at all like an ordinary French general's hat. He wore no medal ribbons, but had a small double cross, which seems to be the emblem of the Free French movement. He is tall and good-looking in a stupid way and has an almost regal manner towards his inferiors. His attitude was at least that of a sovereign in exile. I should imagine he is stupid and vain, and it is curious that though he obviously fancies his appearance he should be so sticky about being photographed, or in fact over any personal publicity.

In Government circles and in Parliament, there was growing dissatisfaction with Churchill and much speculation about a possible change in leadership. It was widely suggested that Beaverbrook had his eye on the position of Prime Minister.

For most of 1941 Beaverbrook, appointed Minister of Supply in June, was at loggerheads with Ernest Bevin, the Minister of Labour. It was a complicated confrontation, a compound of differences – of personality, background, outlook – and the fight between them to control vast areas of the country's war production. This fight continued into 1942.

When Russia entered the war in June, Beaverbrook became an en-
thusiastic protagonist of the Soviet cause, advocating first generous aid to
Russia and eventually the opening of a Second Front in western Europe. In
September he travelled to Moscow to discuss aid to Russia. There, in
A.J.P. Taylor's words, he 'won Stalin's heart by the lavishness of his
promises' on Britain's behalf. He returned home still fervently pro-Soviet.

October 14, 1941
On Sunday night [October 12] Beaverbrook gave a talk at 9.0 –
not after the news, but before it. It was about his trip to Moscow,
and on the line that he had promised much on our behalf and we
must implement these promises. It was a very emotional tub-
thumping speech, but the emotion did not ring true to me. He
gave no facts at all, and I interpreted his speech as part of his
'Beaverbrook for premier' campaign. He seemed to me to be
using his trip to Moscow to get himself publicity, and to be using
his broadcast to cash in on everyone's wish to help the Russians
and to ingratiate himself with the British working man. I am told
the script of this speech was gone over by Beaverbrook and Stuart,
the Conservative Chief Whip, but that Churchill did not see it.
Stuart is said to be no Churchillian.

October 19, 1941
Beaverbrook's intimates are going round and saying that he is
convinced we cannot win this war: our production is in a mess, we
are short of men, and where can we create a front where the
advantage would not rest overwhelmingly with the Germans?
The only answer is peace, and he is visualizing himself as the man
to succeed Winston and give us peace.

I very much doubt whether Beaverbrook can bring that one off.
(a) Would Hitler concede terms that the British people, who are
absolutely unaware of our precarious position, would accept?
(b) Peace at this stage would mean a political revolution, and in
such an upheaval could one rely with any confidence on any of
Churchill's henchmen coming out on top of the pile? I should have
thought that if Beaverbrook plays his cards well, he might be
accepted as a 'win the war' premier, but not as one to carry the
olive branch of peace. Lloyd George is the obvious man for the

job. Anyway, the more I think of it, the more I feel this is not the moment to talk of peace, which could only be on the basis of an abject surrender to Hitler. If we wait and if the worst comes to the worst, it is better for our future that we should be defeated than that the enemy should win on a walk-over.

October 22, 1941

I met Lucius Thompson-McCausland for lunch on Monday [October 20]. He went over to the States on a Government mission with Keynes in April and, though he returned in August, this was the first time I had seen him. He had a very poor opinion of our people at the Washington Embassy. They consisted of men who were posted there before the war, plus a few odds and ends of people who had been stranded in America on the outbreak of war. Not having been home for more than two years they were completely out of touch with current English opinion, not only of the mass of the people but even Foreign Office and Civil Service opinion, which had moved a lot in two years.

Lucius said the New Dealers were very academic and mostly very second-rate – 'wedded to shibboleths'. The non New Dealers said they [the New Dealers] were men who could not get good jobs in private enterprise in the pre-Roosevelt era, and jumped at their chance when Roosevelt began his New Deal. Now, nine years later, they are very cocky, but in Lucius' opinion quite shallow. Lucius did not see Roosevelt, but Keynes did and was very impressed: said that in intelligence, breadth of view, grasp of the situation in all its urgency, and sympathy Roosevelt was head and shoulders over any other figure met in Washington. Even he, though, is very suspicious of us: even if he doesn't think like others that we may rat on him, he does fear that some sudden turn of events in England may leave him high and dry with a rebellious Congress on his hands. To be more precise, I gather many Americans are afraid we may sign a separate peace; while Roosevelt thinks we may, by some tactless move, put him in a false position with Congress.

In general in Washington there is no realization of the need for speed, or of the danger threatening us and ultimately the U.S. Everyone grossly overestimates the military might of the U.S.

and grossly underestimates the strength of Germany. Lucius says
so many Americans emigrated there to avoid European entangle-
ments of different kinds that there is almost a complex about it,
but that this does not apply to the Pacific and Japan. In consequence it would be very much easier to get America into the war
over Japan than over events on the continent of Europe.

October 31, 1941
The main interest in political circles just now is centred on
Beaverbrook and his alleged asthma. K.M. [*Kathleen McColgan,
Cecil King's secretary*] saw Sinclair, who says Beaverbrook is trying
to get all supply into his hands – Ministry of Supply, Ministry of
Aircraft Production, and the supply side of the Admiralty. This
is not going very well, and he is using his retirement on the grounds
of ill-health as a threat. Other stories going round in circles near
Beaverbrook are that he has promised Stalin far more tanks than
we can possibly supply, and that this is causing a good deal of
peevishness in the Cabinet. Another story is that he is picking a
quarrel with Bevin.

Some of the *Mirror* people had dinner with Aneurin Bevan
last night. He says Beaverbrook thinks a major political crisis is
coming in the next few months and means to be out of the Government in the meantime. Bevan thinks Beaverbrook has put off his
withdrawal from the Government too long and that when a
Government crisis comes in a couple of months' time, he will be
too deeply involved in the Government's blunders to make any
effective attack. Anyway, however that may be, the idea is that
Beaverbrook is about to resign. To his colleagues the reason will
be dissatisfaction over the rate of production; to the public the
reason will be asthma; and the real reason will be to be outside
the Government when the storm breaks. In the meantime he will
use his papers to attack the Government for not fulfilling his
promises to Stalin. When the big political rumpus comes, he
hopes to return to the Government either as Prime Minister or
as an overwhelmingly powerful figure in a reconstituted Churchill
administration. There seem to be innumerable possible slips
between that cup and his lip, but he has the enormous advantage
of no serious competition.

November 5, 1941

Campbell saw Michael Foot yesterday, who says Beaverbrook has been the centre of furious rows in the Cabinet, where he is all for a far more complete mobilization of all our resources. He has returned from Russia very pro-Russian and this description does not apply to any of his colleagues. Foot thinks Beaverbrook will not leave the Government, but will be given much wider powers on the home front and will remain. He thinks this will be announced first and a Cabinet reshuffle will come later.

Foot says Churchill accepted Roosevelt's invitation to the Atlantic meeting thinking thereby greatly to enhance his prestige. After he had accepted, the Russian fighting started and he found all interest was transferred from the Americans to the Russians. Since then Churchill has been the protagonist of the Americans in the Cabinet, while Beaverbrook is the protagonist of the much more popular Russians.

Campbell has also seen Byron, just home from the 'Muddle East', as he calls it. He injured his leg and had to go to hospital. He was in a 'hospital train', which was just an ordinary train, and eight men were crammed into a third-class carriage, some of them severely wounded. They travelled for fourteen hours without attention and then had to change. They were then left for five hours unattended waiting for their connection. All the supply arrangements were of similar quality. The impression out there is that things were better under Wavell than Auchinleck.

November 18, 1941

Cudlipp looked in on Saturday evening. He is now a second lieutenant in the Royal Sussex Regiment and is stationed at Ramsgate. He gets on well with his fellow officers and does a good deal of lecturing to the troops, both his own battalion and others. Morale is even lower than he had expected, but he says the men are pathetically eager to accept any leadership that is offered and can easily be enthused.

From time to time they have lectures, and Cudlipp mentioned two: (1) One from a man who had been on a raid on the French coast. He said it was preceded by an hour's bombardment by a destroyer, under cover of which they landed with blackened faces, long knives, knuckledusters, and tommy-guns. They each had a task assigned to them. His was to deal with a cinema where a dance proved to be in progress. A number of German officers were dancing, partnered by French women – he machine-gunned the lot. After an hour they had to swim out to the boats, which were waiting for them, and then the destroyer opened up a second bombardment, under cover of which they withdrew. On an average about half the men are lost on a raid of this kind, often by being caught by our second bombardment before they can complete their task.

(2) The Italian attack on Malta by surface craft was reported on by an officer who was there. Our radio-locator reported the arrival of a ship from Sicily, which had approached within forty miles of Malta and then turned back. Subsequently noises were reported off the coast, but little attention was paid. Then suddenly the big boom across the harbour went up with a roar, and the defences got going. It appeared that the Italian ship had launched fifty very small boats before turning back. They were manned by one Italian each, who sat astride the contrivance. They were propelled by a small and nearly silent motor. The head of the boat was packed with explosives. The pilot was to drive the boat up against the boom, or a ship, press the trigger, and dive off. There was a delayed-action fuse to enable him to get away. One of the boats was early on captured by an R.A.F. speedboat, and the pilot had on him the operation orders for the whole venture. These plans were based on a reconnaissance of four days earlier. Since then the convoy had gone out, but another had come in. Apparently the entrance to the Grand Harbour was floodlit and, what with this and the operations orders, the Italian boats were picked off as they appeared. The men showed superb bravery, but were all killed or captured. The Italian boat came out again to pick up any stragglers and we just missed getting her too.

December 8, 1941
Decided to spend the day at home and slept past the eight o'clock news. Rang up the office about 11.0 to discover war has broken out between America and Japan! Not a whisper had reached me, though I believe it was on the nine o'clock news last night. The

Japs seem to have staged a naval attack on Pearl Harbour (Hawaii), Manila, and Guam.

On Sunday December 7, when Japanese carrier-based aircraft bombed and torpedoed the American Pacific Fleet in Pearl Harbour, the war became truly a world war. Britain's declaration of war on Japan followed next day; and Hitler and Mussolini, not wholly predictably, declared war on the U.S. on December 11.

To the score of four American battleships sunk at Pearl Harbour, the Japanese quickly added two famous British ships: the battleship Prince of Wales *and the battle-cruiser* Repulse. *They were attacked and sunk by torpedo-bombers off the coast of Malaya on December 10. Britain had suffered and was to suffer many more disasters. But none cast more gloom at home than the loss of these two fine ships.*

In February 1942 came what Churchill considered to be 'the worst disaster and largest capitulation in British history', the capture of Singapore by the Japanese and the surrender of its garrison of 60,000 men. The great 16-inch guns of this British naval base could have blasted an invading fleet out of the water; but they were no use against the ill-equipped Japanese troops who came bicycling enthusiastically through the Malayan jungle.

Japan's initial conquests were even more spectacular than those of Germany. By May 1942 Malaya, Hong Kong, Burma, the Philippines, and all the major islands of the East Indies were in Japanese hands.

The Japanese decided not to fight Russia. This was certainly as well for the Russians, who were now involved in a life-or-death struggle on all fronts. Two December victories temporarily eased the pressure: Marshal Zhukov's successful counter-attack outside Moscow and the recapture of Rostov, in the south.

The war in the North African desert offered some temporary consolation to Britain. General Auchinleck, who had replaced Wavell as Commander-in-Chief there, attacked in December and by the middle of January recaptured Cyrenaica. But Rommel had merely made a strategic withdrawal in good order, and when he came to counter-attack in May he drove the British forces back over the borders of Egypt, to El Alamein.

Churchill was undaunted by the disasters in the Far East. With America now in the war he felt certain of victory. But criticism of his leadership was growing in Westminster. Some suggested that he should appoint an in-

dependent Minister of Defence (Churchill held this office as well as that of premier). Others speculated about alternative Prime Ministers. In this context a name soon to be on all lips was that of Sir Stafford Cripps, who early in the new year returned to the political scene from his post as Ambassador in Moscow. Cripps was a left-wing Socialist who had been expelled from the Labour Party. He had made no disastrous mistakes; was high-minded, intelligent, respected, neither loved nor hated, and of sufficient stature to provide an alternative to Churchill's leadership. He also added a complicating factor to the bitter struggle between the two strong men of the War Cabinet, Bevin and Beaverbrook.

Churchill first offered Cripps the Ministry of Supply. Cripps refused it. Then on February 19 he made Cripps Leader of the House, Lord Privy Seal, and a member of the War Cabinet. Earlier that month Beaverbrook had been given increased responsibilities through his appointment as Minister of Production. But he failed to wrest control of the labour force from Ernest Bevin, and after only a few weeks in office resigned: Churchill could not support him against the opposition of both Cripps and Bevin. Beaverbrook was replaced by Oliver Lyttelton.

All in all, it was a very disturbed period politically. And there must have been few Members of Parliament who ruled out the possibility of a new war leader before 1942 was out.

December 16, 1941

Had lunch at Wilfrid Roberts' invitation with Lady Violet Bonham Carter, a daughter of old Asquith. She is very highly thought of in the Liberal Party and is said to be a good public speaker. She is intelligent and obviously expects to be listened to; her mouth has that twisted look of people who were hurt too much long ago. She seemed to me preoccupied with purely academic problems – 18B,[11] the treatment of conscientious objectors, and so forth. At no point did she reveal any understanding of the fact that this is the year of grace 1941, and yet the Liberal Party are trying to find her a seat in the House.

She is a considerable personal friend of the Prime Minister and believes with fervour that, with all his faults, he is the only man to lead the country just now. She thinks his handling of America was brilliant, and would deplore Anderson [as Prime Minister] as much as Beaverbrook. She seems to think the agitation against him was got up largely by the Tory back-benchers, with a view to another premier and a separate peace. Lady Violet is a governor of the B.B.C. – just the sort of elderly, spinsterish, blue-stocking you would expect them to choose. Clearly this type of woman should be firmly in the discard and not be looked upon as a Woman with a Future.

December 28, 1941

Cudlipp looked in at the office last night and told me that as duty officer he had two hours to fill in on Friday night with nothing to do, so he had read through the secret defence plans for the Isle of Thanet, officially regarded as the most likely point for the Germans to invade this country. The plan stresses the essential importance of guarding night and day against parachutists three vital bridges over the Stour. Cudlipp says he knows for a fact these bridges are unguarded. It mentions that the civil administration will be taken over by Colonel ——, but his name has never been filled in. The food, post office, and one other public service are to be taken over by three majors, one of whom is dead and the two others are overseas! Why are we so lax and incompetent?

1942

"The price of petrol has been increased by one penny."—Official.

Sunday Pictorial

October 25
TWOPENCE
No. 1,441

'Get At Their Throats Boys'

GENERAL Bernard Montgomery, 55, commanding, tactical pen of a Bishop, is the Western Desert's Man of the Moment. The troops all love Montgomery as Pop. Go look—and the laugh. You can see it in his tense face and penetrating eyes in the little glare above as he directs operations in the desert.

"ATTSM—even when you're on the defensive," is the fighting slogan flashed by the C.-in-C., General Sir Harold Alexander, to the Eighth Army as they tore into battle.

Alexander, 51, 55—commander-in-chief, Middle East, and he is Britain's most experienced General. He has played a big part in the Eighth Army's thrust into the attack.

Rommel, for bombing of Battle of Germany and hitting with only a handful of tanks.

8TH ARMY SMASHES THROUGH IN EGYPT

SMASHING its way through deep minefields and field fortresses, our Eighth Army in Egypt has launched a new offensive. Fierce fighting has been raging since 10 o'clock on Friday night on land and sea and air.

According to Berlin last night we used "special units" and "shock troops" to swathe a path through their minefields. We also used large numbers of tanks.

The Germans claim to have made a number of counter-attacks, but nowhere do they claim to have repulsed our onslaught.

Our own communiqué gave no details of the land fighting except that it was in the El Alamein area, near the coast. But plenty was happening in the air and at sea.

The RAF's aerial preparation, extending over two weeks, reached an even higher level in the past five days and then rose to a twenty-four hours' non-stop day-and-night blitz on Rommel's advanced landing grounds.

Then, as the troops advanced, the RAF blasted a path for them, using every type of plane.

AT THE SAME TIME THE NAVY SENT SPECIAL TORPEDO-BOATS TO RAID ROMMEL'S BASE AT MERSA MATRUH.

John Nixon, Reuter's special correspondent with the Eastern Mediterranean Fleet, cabled this dramatic story last night:

"The aerial force was ordered to attack the coast at two points with the object of cowing all possible damage ashore. They met with opposition, and a running fight developed lasting three hours.

"Time after time the enemy planes zoomed down on to the ships, blasting away with their cannon and hurling bombs.

"Our force suffered no casualties and no other damage. Despite the air attacks, the torpedo-boats twice swept in close to the shore, according to plan. They met no opposition on either occasion, though they poured in a heavy hail of fire.

Continued on Back Page

MILAN BOMBED IN DAYLIGHT!

THE MOST AMAZING AIR RAID OF THE WAR WAS MADE YESTERDAY. IN DAYLIGHT A LARGE FORCE OF LANCASTER BOMBERS ATTACKED THE GREAT ITALIAN WAR PLANTS AT MILAN, IN ITALY. THE ROUND TRIP FROM ENGLAND TO MILAN IS 1,350 MILES—NEARLY ALL THE WAY ACROSS SKIES CONTROLLED BY THE ENEMY.

The Air Ministry announcement was issued at two o'clock this morning.
— STORY ON BACK PAGE

MOTHER HEARS THE SECRETS OF HER DEAD CHILD—Page 5

January 21, 1942
Yesterday the House met. It gave Churchill a warm but not enthusiastic reception – not one member rose to his feet. He proposed
a three-day debate for next week, and said if necessary he would
interpose a vote of confidence on the second day. He looked tired
and ill, and had a cold. It is reported now that he will under no
circumstances make any changes in his Government: that he will
defy his critics and generally take a very high hand.

He also proposed that his speech should be recorded and broadcast. This roused a great deal of feeling and had to be hurriedly
dropped today at the insistence of the Labour members in the
Government. The proposal had a poor press, except in the *Express*,
but its rejection is the first definite setback Churchill has had
since he became premier. The *Express* is noticeably more sycophantic these last few days, and Bart says it is because Beaverbrook
has after all returned to this country [from America].

January 23, 1942
The political situation is developing. It appears that Churchill's
visit to America[1] ended with a week's holiday at Palm Beach. He
returned home in a very complacent mood ready to receive the
plaudits of the politicians and the country. Last Saturday there
was a Cabinet meeting, at which it was clear to him that the
atmosphere here was very different from what he had expected.
His proposal to have his House of Commons speech next Tuesday

[January 27] recorded and broadcast was turned down almost unanimously by the Cabinet. The 1922 Committee were against this proposal, and also demanded changes in the Government.

Beaverbrook is said now to be against changes in the Government, and to be off the job of Production Minister, which Bevin is reaching for. Greenwood's department of Post-war Reconstruction is being dismantled, and the staff transferred to other departments. The whole venture was on a ludicrously small scale at the start and this latest development shows very clearly the Prime Minister's entire lack of interest in the future. Margesson, K.M. says, is unpopular with the generals, but Churchill will not move him.

Cripps is back in this country, in spite of talk of his return via India. It is thought he will be offered a post, but not in the War Cabinet. He will almost certainly decide to lead the Opposition.

January 25, 1942

Weston saw Beaverbrook just after his return from Moscow, and said Beaverbrook was genuinely and immensely impressed by Stalin. He regarded him as enormously able and having at heart one object only – the welfare of his country. He would strangle his mother or his best friend if he thought the interests of Russia demanded it.

January 27, 1942

Well, the great debate was opened in the House of Commons. The Prime Minister's speech reads quite well, though as usual it lacks facts. His story in general was that we had sent all available material to Libya and Russia, and so were caught short in Malaya. Further, that the decisions on policy were his own and that he refused to make scapegoats – referring specifically to Duff Cooper.[2] Needless to say, all this is no answer to the critics who say (1) that our production is nothing like what it could and should be; (2) that in Malaya there was complacency and complete muddle, as a result of which we made the feeblest use of the material we had got; and (3) the organization and personnel of the Government are not such as to produce good results, that in fact we should have been defeated ere now if the Axis powers had concentrated on us instead of ignoring our puny efforts and attacking Russia and the U.S.A. Subsequent speeches were sycophantic or critical, the critical ones being by Sir Herbert Williams, Henderson Stewart (Liberal), and a few minor Labour men.

Bill Greig of the *Mirror* rang up and said the Prime Minister had the critics in the hollow of his hand. Cunningham-Reid rang up the office, on the other hand, and said the House was pretty angry. K.M. is away ill, but her informants told her that the Prime Minister dropped two tears on the dispatch box, when he said he was no longer the man he had been in the summer of 1940.

January 29, 1942
Bellenger looked in this morning with a pathetic story of Churchill in the smoking room after the debate last night. He was looking round with his thoughts evidently far away, when Bellenger spoke to him. He then said, apropos of nothing: 'He's a fine boy – a grand boy.' This with tears in his eyes, presumably about Randolph [his son], who had been speaking. Bellenger thought he looked a broken old man.

The debate continued its very highly critical way, and then Churchill spoke. He gave no fresh facts except to announce the appointment of a Minister of Production – universally assumed to be Beaverbrook. Churchill's speech had quite a good reception and the debate ended with a vote of 464 to one (Maxton!). Bill Greig thought this indicated the collapse of the critics. The impression I get is that Churchill has promised a Minister of Production and changes in his Cabinet, he has been solemnly warned, and there was no possible object in humiliating him by an adverse vote.

February 4, 1942
Campbell had lunch with Garro-Jones and Bellenger today. Garro-Jones in a state of great excitement over the political situation. He says Cripps was offered the Ministry of Supply and was prepared to take it, but first demanded that his position vis-à-vis Beaverbrook, [appointed today] the Minister of Production,

should be defined. This proved difficult, and it seems that Cripps
has now refused the offer. Meanwhile Bevin had got worked up
and said if Beaverbrook were to get authority over him, he would
resign. Also Alexander put his nose in and said of course production
for the Admiralty must be kept out of all this. Now Beaverbrook,
who according to Garro-Jones wants power without responsibility,
is back-pedalling as fast as possible and wants to be sent on a
spectacular tour of America.

Garro-Jones says conferences between Beaverbrook, Bevin,
Churchill, Cripps, and Alexander are going on night and day
with no result so far. He thinks on the present indications that
Beaverbrook will go to America, Cripps will become Minister of
Production, and Bevin will stay where he is. Garro-Jones thinks
that great political changes are ahead and that this week marks the
beginning of the break-up of the Government. He thinks Cripps,
if he plays his cards well, may easily become our next Prime
Minister.

Garro-Jones had one or two other items. He said our intelligence failed to warn us of the six-pounder guns on the German
tanks in Libya. Their shells tore open our tanks like sardine tins.
He says we are likely to have to retreat to the Egyptian border
again, but that this time it will be more difficult to hold Tobruk.

February 16, 1942
Churchill made his first speech on the wireless last night since
his return from seeing Roosevelt in August. The only fact in his
speech was his admission of the fall of Singapore. The point of
greatest interest was his demand for unity at this grave hour. He
offered no suggestion of new men or new methods, but said that
in the Russians' darkest hour they had supported Stalin, and we
should support our leaders in the same way. Of course there is no
parallel at all between Churchill, his record of failure and his
Government of odds and ends, and Stalin, who has led Russia
with much success for nearly twenty years, who foresaw the war
with Germany and the tactics the Germans would employ, who
prepared the proper weapons for dealing with this menace, and
who has only been defeated by the superior qualities of the
Germans as an organizing and fighting race. The speech has had

a reception in the newspapers this morning varying from chilly
to hostile.

February 18, 1942
K.M. was in the House this afternoon and Stuart, the Tory Chief
Whip, was saying that he thought they could afford to throw over
Ernest Brown and Kingsley Wood. The situation has got far
beyond that, and the demand is now not for a strengthening of the
Government, but the separation of the offices of Prime Minister
and Minister of Defence (there is some talk of Lyttelton getting
this office). At this rate, in another two weeks the cry will be
'Churchill must go.' As it is he has only the *Express* and the
Telegraph on his side, and neither of them has much enthusiasm
today.

K.M. saw Lloyd George yesterday at the House. He was
stamping up and down calling Churchill 'the old fool', and saying
he had burnt all the bridges behind him and stopped up all
possible ways of escape. He would now necessarily fall with his
Government. We are trying to get him to do an article or an
interview for the Pic.

February 19, 1942
We were promised a statement about Cabinet changes for
6.o p.m., so I stood over the tape – the minutes ticking away –
should we or should we not get the news into the Sheffield edition?
At last Greig rang up from the Ministry of Information with the
news: Winston to remain Minister of Defence, Attlee to be
Dominions Secretary and deputy premier, Oliver Lyttelton to be
Production Minister, Eden Foreign Affairs, Bevin Labour, Cripps
Lord Privy Seal and Leader of the House, Anderson to remain
Lord President of the Council. Beaverbrook was offered a seat,
but refused owing to ill-health, and would do a liaison job with
America. Other changes are to be announced in a few days. It is
understood that Greenwood is right out and that Kingsley Wood,
while out of the Cabinet, is still Chancellor of the Exchequer.

The scope of these changes is far wider than anyone had expected
and the Cabinet now includes the three Tory white hopes – Eden,
Anderson, and Lyttelton – as well as the two Labour embryo

premiers – Cripps and Bevin. This will clearly take the sting out of the debate on Tuesday [February 24], and brings forward all the men who may play prominent parts in the next round. Churchill, though eating dirt over the changes in general – they were forced on him at the point of the bayonet – is defiant in the way he keeps the Ministry of Defence. Clearly this is silly: it puts him in the direct line of fire and will ultimately bring him down. How long he gets away with this set-up depends on (a) the progress of the war, (b) the number of the real duds he gets out in the next few days.

Sinclair told K.M. yesterday that Churchill was in a towering passion on Monday over the criticisms of his administration, and said he 'hated the newspapers worse than the Nazis'!

February 24, 1942

The main interest of the day has been Churchill's speech in the House. It was a bad speech to a critical House. K.M. thought on Thursday [February 19] the Government would get by for ten weeks without serious trouble. After today she thinks eight is about its limit. She says it is clear the Prime Minister has no idea he is under fire personally: he supposes that all the dissatisfaction is with some members of his team.

He is very angry with the newspapers and proposed in Cabinet last week that the papers should all be suppressed and replaced by a 'British Gazette'. This proposal did not go down well!

February 25, 1942

The debate continues with a good speech by Hore-Belisha for a change. Most of the speeches are critical and no one thinks the Government has any future.

K.M. had tea at the House of Commons with Margesson, who is out – right out. He said that reports that he was going to Cairo were quite wide of the mark. Churchill asked him to recommend for promotion someone outside the parliamentary machine, so he suggested Grigg [*who replaced him as War Minister on February 22*]! He says it is the last time he recommends anyone for anything.

K.M. says Margesson is quite clearly getting ready to snipe at

'The old menace'

When Neville Chamberlain resigned the prime ministership on May 10, 1940, Cecil King commented: 'So at last my campaign to get rid of the old menace has come off. I consider this is the best bit of news since war was declared'

'To him war is a vast pageant

with himself in a scarlet uniform on
a white horse, baton in hand, leading the British forces forward
through the smoke of battle.' Cecil
King on Winston Churchill, September
2, 1945

'A man head and shoulders over any
other politician I have met

—including Churchill . . . he was
witty, he was eloquent, he had a
great sense of the value of men, and
he really wanted to help the underdog.' Thus Cecil King described
David Lloyd George after his death
in March 1945. During the Second
World War Lloyd George, though aged
seventy-six in 1939, ran a model
scientific farm at his home at Churt
in Surrey, where he is shown here
among his kale

The City of London on the night of Sunday December 29, 1940

photographed from the dome of St Paul's Cathedral during
one of the worst raids of the Blitz. Churchill called it 'an
incendiary classic . . . timed to meet the dead-low-water
hour. The water mains were broken at the outset by very
heavy high-explosive parachute-mines. Nearly 1,500 fires had
to be fought.' St Paul's Cathedral itself was 'only saved
by heroic exertions'

'He's really not as bad as all that'

said Morrison and Bellenger of Clement Attlee, hotly defend-
ing their leader against Cecil King's disparaging 'I
wouldn't employ him as a lift attendant.' This was in September 1944. Cecil King was consistent. He had remarked of
Attlee on October 12, 1940: 'If one heard he was getting £6
a week in the service of the East Ham Corporation, one would
be surprised he was earning so much'

Sir Stafford Cripps, just back from Russia in January 1942. At this time Churchill's authority and political popularity were at their lowest ebb, and Cripps was widely thought of as the next Prime Minister. Cecil King wrote of him in February as 'embryo premier', and one rumour had it that there was speculation among the Tories as to what office Churchill should hold in Cripps' Government

'Explosive qualities' and 'demoniac energy'

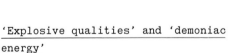

Lord Beaverbrook described himself as having 'explosive qualities'. Churchill spoke of him to Cecil King in June 1940 as a man of 'demoniac energy'. Cecil King two weeks later thought him 'past his best, but still full of vigour and drive'. Looking back in 1970, he considers Beaverbrook's strength to have been in backstairs intrigue, by means of which he wielded, through two Prime Ministers, an evil and a malevolent influence on public life

Fleet Street on Friday June 30, 1944

during the flying-bomb assault on Britain. The smoke in the background is from a V1 that fell outside Bush House, in Aldwych. Cecil King ran to the scene, and describes the aftermath of this explosion. One woman said: 'Hitler'll get hisself disliked if he goes on like this!'

the Government, and is apparently keeping in touch with Beaver-brook. Before Beaverbrook had his crashing row with Churchill and left, he was saying to the critics of the Government that it was no use being like a nagging housewife, always bullying the maid. This sort of treatment usually ended by the maid dropping a tray laden with crockery at a critical moment. It was not clear what particular application this story had.

February 26, 1942
Lucius Thompson-McCausland had a story which, he said, from its source ought to be all right. This was that in the representations made to the Prime Minister by the Tories last week, they requested that Beaverbrook should be played down a bit. Churchill told them the Government was fortunate to have such a minister at such a time, and the country fortunate to have such an alternative Prime Minister. The Tory deputation was not impressed, so Churchill told Beaverbrook that he would have to accept a rather minor position in the War Cabinet. Beaverbrook flared up and said he had broken one Prime Minister, and could break another, and that any attempt to put him in a back seat would lead him to 'harry Churchill both in the House and outside it'. Churchill said that there could now clearly be no position for him in the administration. I think this story sounds phoney, except the bit about the Tory deputation: they are known to be pushing Ander-son and Lyttelton, and what more likely than that they would like to see Beaverbrook played down?

Meanwhile Weston went to see Beaverbrook, who felt he had been very badly treated by the Prime Minister. Weston thereupon returned and delivered a maiden speech deploring Beaverbrook's departure from the Government. This support of one Canadian by another struck me as bad tactics.

February 28, 1942
Talking of America calls to my mind some points Lucius Thomp-son-McCausland made when I saw him on Thursday. He said the raw materials division of the American ministry of supply employed *800* expert economists! These men had to show some-thing for their salaries and produced the most elaborate literature.

The prize brochure to date was one of thirty-two pages on 'Red Squills', whatever that may be. Copper took 140 pages. The Americans were very mystified by our reluctance to engage in competition with this literary output. When in Washington, Keynes was asked to meet the leading economists in the U.S. treasury and talk to them. He said he would be glad to, but that his programme was very full and he had had other requests from other government departments to do the same sort of thing: could he talk to all these important economists at the same time? I gather he expected the result would be a largish lunch party. In fact he found himself addressing an audience of 600 men.

March 2, 1942

Frank Owen says Beaverbrook is still livid with rage at being dropped from the Government and that his papers are to veer leftwards. K.M. was listening in to Radio Salamanca the other night, when it was commenting on our Government changes. The Spanish spokesman expressed the view that the Germans would regret the departure of Beaverbrook from the Cabinet, as there was now no one for them to negotiate peace with if the moment, from the German point of view, seemed opportune. I had no idea the Germans knew so well that Beaverbrook had leanings towards appeasement.

March 5, 1942

The main interest seems to be in the political situation, which from all accounts is rapidly breaking up. W.J. Brown saw Brendan Bracken and Grigg, and was talking of his interviews to Campbell. Campbell also had a talk with Winster, who had dined with Harvie Watt. The general impression is that Churchill has now no authority in his own party. He thought his recent reshuffle would satisfy the House and, now it hasn't, he has no idea what to do.

Bracken says the Government is very disturbed about the low morale in the country, and particularly in the Army, but has no idea what to do about this either. Grigg [the new War Minister], according to Brown, is full of zeal: said he had met the Civil Service caste, the Indian Civil Service caste, and the Army caste, and that of these the last was the worst. It had nearly broken his heart, but he was going to break it before he had finished. At Brown's suggestion he is toying with the idea of real democratization of the Army with something almost equivalent to the Russian system of political commissars!

According to Bower the Tories are wondering what office Churchill should hold in Cripps' Government. On the whole they think Foreign Secretary, so that we should retain his valuable influence in America.

March 11, 1942
Churchill made his statement today on India. It did not prove to be, as was expected, a full statement of Government policy, followed by a debate. Instead the Prime Minister announced that Cripps was to go to India for the War Cabinet, with a full knowledge of their views on the future government of the country. It was felt that no good could come of a Government statement of policy unless it was known that it would meet with general agreement in India. Cripps was going to India to secure that agreement.

This seems to me to make nonsense of the whole existing political set-up, as I do not see how any really satisfactory solution of Indian problems can be expected to arise from Cripps' visit. In the meantime he will be out of touch with both England and Russia. It is quite likely that the next political crisis will boil up here with Cripps in India. In any case his intelligence is no longer available in the War Cabinet.

Cripps departed for India to deal with the Nationalist demands, made more pressing by the proximity of Japanese forces and America's uneasiness about British imperialism. Gandhi, Nehru, and the other Congress leaders wanted immediate independence. Cripps offered it after the war. 'A post-dated cheque', said Gandhi during his talks with Cripps. 'On a crashing bank', added a bystander. Congress refused the offer, the talks broke down, and Cripps returned, his image tarnished, his position in Parliament weakened.

While Cripps was away in India the Daily Mirror *again ran into trouble. On March 6 the* Mirror *published what was to become a very famous cartoon. It was drawn by Philip Zec and the wording of the caption was Cassandra's. It showed a shipwrecked, dying sailor, adrift on a raft in a stormy sea. Underneath were the words: '"The price of petrol has been increased by one penny." – Official.'*

Most people took the cartoon to mean what the cartoonist meant it to mean: that petrol should not be wasted as its import cost so much in human lives. But not Churchill and the Government. The cartoon was passed around the Cabinet, whose conclusion about its meaning was very different: that sailors were losing their lives for the petrol companies to increase their profits. They also concluded that the cartoon was likely to undermine national morale.

The cartoon brought to the surface other, longer-standing grievances against the Mirror, its criticisms of the Army and the political leadership.

The Mirror had by this time become the paper of the forces, because, more than any other paper, it reflected the views and preoccupations of the rank and file. In mirroring these views it was often highly critical of the administration of the Army and its officers. The Mirror poured scorn on the many meaningless military rituals and military preoccupation with such minutiae as the length of Wrens' skirts. Cassandra told how ardent patriotic young men were reduced to apathetic cynicism after a few months' experience of a military machine which was out-of-date, inflexible, and often actually opposed to reform. He described the typical product of the officer class as 'a hideous, moustachioed little twerp, with an impeccable record of club ties, high-class bars, and the ability to talk minced drivel'.

Moreover, the Mirror and Pictorial were just as forthright about the political leadership. And the loss of Malaya gave them plenty of ammunition. In January 1942 the Pictorial stated: ' There are too many ministers definitely not of the stuff of which war-winners are made. And the country cannot afford political passengers.'

By March, when the Philip Zec cartoon was published, Churchill had become increasingly irritated by the Mirror's and Pictorial's jaunty criticisms of the conduct of the war and irreverent attitude towards the military authorities. He wanted action, and suggested to Morrison, the Home Secretary, that Morrison should shut down the Mirror under Regulation 2D, 'providing for instantaneous suppression of a newspaper on the edict of the Home Secretary'. Morrison, backed by Beaverbrook and Bracken, resisted this and suggested that the Mirror should be given a final warning.

A summons went out to John Cowley, the Mirror chairman, and Cecil

*Thomas, the editor, to appear before Morrison on March 19. Cowley did
not go; instead Bartholomew, the Mirror editorial director, accompanied
Thomas.*

*For over half an hour Morrison harangued them. He thought that the
cartoon was 'worthy of Goebbels at his best'. To Thomas he suggested:
'Only a very unpatriotic editor could pass that for publication.' To
Bartholomew, that only someone 'with a diseased mind could be responsible
for the Daily Mirror policy'.*

*The grave warning was delivered, and as the two Mirror men departed,
they heard Herbert Morrison whistling a little tune to himself.*

*Morrison arranged later that day to answer a parliamentary question
about the Philip Zec cartoon. He told the House:*

*'The cartoon in question is only one example, but a particularly evil
example, of the policy and methods of a newspaper which, intent on exploiting
an appetite for sensation and with a reckless indifference to the national
interest and to the prejudicial effect on the war effort, has repeatedly published scurrilous misrepresentations, distorted and exaggerated statements,
and irresponsible generalizations. In the same issue the leading article
stated: "The accepted tip for Army leadership would, in plain truth, be
this: All who aspire to mislead others in war should be brass-buttoned
boneheads, socially prejudiced, arrogant, and fussy. A tendency to heart
disease, apoplexy, diabetes, and high blood pressure is desirable in the
highest posts. . . ." Reasonable criticism on specific points and persons
is one thing; general, violent denunciation, manifestly tending to undermine
the Army and depress the whole population, is quite another. Such insidious
attacks are not to be excused by calls in other parts of the paper for more
vigorous action.'*

*He went on to say that he had warned the Mirror that it would be
suppressed if it did not mend its ways.*

*The end of Morrison's speech was greeted with cheers; but Emanuel
Shinwell was quick to protest that the Home Secretary was endangering
the right of public expression of opinion. He asked Morrison if there
would be a debate. Morrison said there would.*

*The question of the Mirror's ownership was also raised. Morrison's
reply was not reassuring: 'It is one of those mixed financial controls in
which you cannot trace a single directing financial influence, so far as I
can see at present.' Morrison had in fact investigated the Mirror's
ownership at the request of Churchill, who still suspected that sinister*

financial interests might be controlling its policies.

The promised debate came on March 26. In the meantime a core of support for the Mirror had hardened in the House. Wilfrid Roberts, a Liberal M.P., opened with a convincing speech in favour of the Mirror. He pointed out that the Mirror's criticisms and advice had in the past been justified by later events, that it was striking at the roots of democracy to suppress the paper because it did not agree with the Government, and he effectively quoted the Government Information Minister Brendan Bracken, who had said: 'A blindfolded democracy is more likely to fall than to fight.' He also dismissed most effectively the question of the sinister financial interests.

There followed a heated debate, ranging over the whole field of Mirror criticisms but concentrating mainly on those directed at the Army. The highlight of the debate was the confrontation of Aneurin Bevan and Herbert Morrison. Bevan pointed out that if what the Mirror said about the administration of the Army was not confirmed in the daily experience of soldiers, they would not take any notice of it; anyway most of the criticisms made by the Daily Mirror about the leadership of the British Army had 'been confirmed by many military events'. Bevan quoted Morrison's own writings against him. He reminded the House that Morrison himself had used the pages of the Mirror to criticize the Government during time of war. He had also used its pages to defend this right of criticism. 'Public criticism', Morrison had written, 'is one of the essentials of good government. . . . Beware of the foes of democracy using the excuse of war for its suppression.'

The Government had many sincere and passionate supporters including A.P. Herbert, a former Sunday Pictorial contributor, who declared about the Mirror's criticism of the Army: 'By God, I say that it is a damned disgusting, blackguardly thing; a disgrace to the honourable craft to which I belong.'

Morrison defended himself ably, and returned to the familiar line that if a Fascist organization had been trying to undermine a country's morale, it could not have done it more successfully than by copying the Daily Mirror, which in the guise of encouraging the vigorous prosecution of the war was carrying out a vicious attack on the civil and military leadership. He argued that if people became convinced that everything was done wrong and everyone was incompetent, they would see no reason to go on fighting. He made it clear that this was the Mirror's last chance.

But Morrison's ordeal through his own writings was not quite over. For Captain F. Bellenger, who was contributing to the Pictorial *as 'The Voice of the Services', quoted to the House Morrison's own pacifist writings during the First World War: 'Go forth little soldier. . . . Though you have no grievance against your German brother – go forth and kill him!' Here was something not merely likely to but* designed *to undermine the troops' morale.*

The debate ended without a division. It was not a triumph for the Government, who had hoped to make this a show trial of the Mirror. *It was clear in fact that the Government had overplayed its hand. But after this warning, the* Mirror *did tone down its criticisms. A few days after the* Mirror *debate Cassandra left to join the Army. 'I cannot and will not change my policy,' he wrote. 'I am still a comparatively young man and I propose to see whether the rifle is a better weapon than the printed word.'*

March 12, 1942
Bart says Brendan Bracken called the lobby correspondents to-gether yesterday. He was very gloomy: said we might well lose the war and, if we did, it would be the fault of the newspapers, which had caused disunity in the nation! The meeting appeared to have been called to ask the correspondents not to report the speeches of critical M.P.s quite so fully, but to report those of Government supporters more generously. He got a very unfriendly reception and eventually had to bring the meeting to an abrupt close. He was full of sneers at Cripps, which was thought un-suitable.

March 19, 1942
Reached the office to find that Bart was out; would be back at 11.30. It appeared that Thomas and the Chairman had been summoned to the Home Office to hear the riot act read by Morri-son. Cowley was at home, so Bart deputized for him. The principal complaint was a cartoon of some weeks ago of a seaman on a raft, where he had struggled from a sinking tanker. The intended suggestion was that people should not merely have to pay a penny more for petrol imported with such difficulty: private motoring should be stopped. It was, however, interpreted to mean that sailors were dying to make bigger profits for the oil companies. A

piece of a leader was also quoted as calculated to depress the morale of the Army. It was in fact a flight of editorial irony over Lord Croft's announcement about the issue of pikes to the Home Guard.

March 21, 1942

Have been busy and harassed, quite unable to find time to write up this diary.

The main subject of interest at home has been Morrison's threat to suppress the *Daily Mirror*. The Press has been very favourable: *News Chronicle, Star, Herald, Standard, Manchester Guardian,* and *Glasgow Herald* group whole-heartedly for us; the *Express* and *Times* against us as a paper, but against any proposal to squash us; the *Daily Mail* crowd and the *Sketch* say nothing; the *Telegraph,* as always, ardently supports the Government. The question to Morrison which precipitated all this was received with cheers in the House, but as the day wore on opinion veered round more and more to our side. Bevin is said to have been in favour of suppression without warning – presumably because of our support of Cripps. The Government idea was to see how this goes and, if well, to bring in a measure in the House next week for the censorship of views, as well as of news.

It seems likely there will be a debate on the subject in both Houses anyway. The storm has apparently been greater than was expected, and it is not unlikely that if the Government presses for the censorship of views it will be defeated. It is hard to say what will happen: the Government is weak, Churchill is sore and may act rashly. My view is that the *Mirror* has had more support than the Government expected and all will blow over.

Last week, on hearing that Brendan Bracken had spoken to the lobby correspondents about the damage done by quoting at length speeches by M.P.s such as Keyes, I asked for an interview. An hour was fixed, but Bracken could not keep it. On Thursday morning [March 19] he rang up and suggested 6.30 in the evening, so along I went. He seemed less aggressive than when I saw him last.

I explained that I had asked to see him to suggest that even now it was not too late for the newspapers and the Government to get together more. He said in effect that the Army's morale was low, that the newspapers were largely to blame, that he thought we had been irresponsible, and that obviously no co-operation could be discussed till after the debate next week. I said it was a fact that the Government had only one supporting newspaper, the *Telegraph*, and that this was an astonishing, even alarming fact; that I felt sure that if the Government and the newspapers would work more closely together a very much more favourable press would result. It was surely in the country's interest that the newspapers should really understand the Government's difficulties. It was also a fact that the newspapers could help the Government in the formulation of policy by their knowledge of, and influence on, public opinion. I had come to see Bracken's predecessors one by one. They had been polite, but had made no move of any kind. After about half an hour's chat on these lines, I departed. I wonder shall I hear from him next week.

March 22, 1942
The papers today are disappointing about the Morrison–*Mirror* affair. *The Sunday Times* is pro-Government in a second leader, the *Observer* sits on the fence (I hadn't thought it possible), *The People* is weakly for us, the *News of the World* even more weakly, and only *Reynolds'* [*News*] comes down whole-heartedly on our side. Last night I had some of the provincial papers gone through and find that the *Yorkshire Post* was strongly pro-Government, the *Yorkshire Evening News* strongly in our favour; the *Birmingham Post* violently and the *Birmingham Mail* faintly pro-Government; the *Ipswich Evening Star* (another independent) strongly in our favour. All in all we have done better than I should have expected. I cannot believe the Government would have acted as they did if they had anticipated such a hullabaloo. I should think censorship of views is now out of the question: it remains to be seen how the debate will go.

March 23, 1942
Bart tells me that over our spot of bother 644 letters have been read and classified: 614 are for us, thirty for the Government; but of the latter nearly all are anonymous (one from the Guards'

12

Club!). There are others still to count, perhaps seven or eight hundred all told. I am struck by the fact that this Government denunciation has had such little effect. I have received three letters from friends upholding our policy, but in general it seems to be regarded as an unnecessary squabble between Morrison and the *Mirror*. That there should be any substance in the Government's case does not seem to occur to anyone.

K.M. says that in the Prime Minister's address to the Under-Secretaries the other day, he said the fall of Singapore was the most shameful moment of his life. We had been expelled by the Japs, who had less than half as many troops as we had; the casualties were under five per cent; the Australians had refused to counter-attack. From every point of view it was a shocking episode in the history of the British Empire. The fiasco was clearly due to low morale and so something must be done about morale. For a start, he hoped criticism in future would be very much more moderate in tone.

March 25, 1942

Our attention was concentrated on the debate for tomorrow, which seems to be developing into something pretty fruity. The Government over the weekend wished to drop the debate – evidently realizing that they had put their feet into a hornets' nest. But the Liberals have persisted and now Wilfrid Roberts is to open the debate, which will be on the adjournment. It is unlikely to be pressed to a division. All sorts of people are uniting for the debate: the M.P.s who hate Morrison, the M.P.s who want the *Daily Worker* reinstated, the M.P.s who seriously believe in the freedom of the Press, and, finally, those who support the *Daily Mirror*. This last group is not numerous in the House; the first is an undesirable group of allies, but there is no means of preventing them having their say.

I had some talk with Garfield Weston, who said he had seen a good deal of Beaverbrook before he went away, and that he (Weston) thinks this move against the *Mirror* was with a view to political censorship, which, in its turn, was aimed at Beaverbrook. Beaverbrook apparently did not think they would dare to try and muzzle him.

March 26, 1942

Today was the day of the great *Daily Mirror* debate. At first the Government welcomed the idea of a debate and of a division, but as opinion hardened in our favour they (a) tried to call the debate off, (b) called off the division, and (c) made it as short as possible. In fact the feeling of the House was clearly against the Government. There were many would-be speakers in our favour, who had no chance of catching the Speaker's eye in the time.

Wilfrid Roberts opened with a good speech for us; Irving Albery did likewise; Aneurin Bevan made an excellent speech against Morrison, quoting his articles in the *Mirror*. Then there was another Labour man for us; another one against us; A.P. Herbert, who was against the *Mirror* but all for liberty of the Press; and another Labour man [*Lawson*] who talked about miners.[3] The points made in our favour scored far more applause than what was said on the other side. The Government front bench was full most of the time, with Anderson, and of course Morrison, present all the while. After over two hours of this, Weston took me off to tea and I heard no more. It seems that Glyn made a speech against us and then Morrison wound up: naturally not excusing himself but saying we had been more restrained since our warning, and we should have nothing to fear if we stayed like that – as we shall.

The interest in the debate was somewhat diminished by the fact that news came in in the middle that the Independent had got in at Grantham. This is the first time since the electoral truce that an Independent has been returned. The Conservatives were very glum about this, and clearly regarded it as a very serious blow to the prestige of the Government.

The House of Commons is now sitting in what is normally the House of Lords. I had not been to a sitting of the House of Commons for about twenty years. The place, the formalities, and the people all give an impression of complete unreality. Here we are in the middle of a great war, in which we are doing very badly, and yet the House of Commons gave no impression of any sense of purpose or of any sense of urgency. Its members are very elderly and quite unimpressive. This afternoon Eden stood out from all the others by his looks, his charm, and his grace, but he too looks quite ineffectual.

Weston took me to tea and eventually drove me home. He was in a most expansive mood and said he had had much talk with Beaverbrook before he went abroad: he is now in Miami. Beaverbrook told him that he had resigned because Bevin's and Attlee's policy was so anti-Russian that either *they* had to resign or he had to. They even compelled Churchill to go back on a protocol Beaverbrook had signed in Moscow, assigning Estonia, Latvia, Lithuania, and Bessarabia to Russia after the war. Beaverbrook was supported by Eden, but Attlee's resignation would have meant the withdrawal of Labour from the Government, which Churchill could not face.

Beaverbrook said he suffered from such a sense of frustration it was making him ill. On the morning the three German battleships were reported in the Channel,[4] he was in the Defence Committee with the three chiefs of staff. The meeting lasted for three hours, but in all that time not one of the three went to the telephone to find out if the battleships had been hit! He said he would have fired the lot. Pound is so old and tired he often falls asleep at Defence Committee meetings and only wakes up when spoken to.

Beaverbrook has serious doubts of Churchill's sanity: says that he was all for Stalin while the Germans were advancing, but became very jealous of Uncle Joe since the Russians had had some success. He would hold forth at night to Beaverbrook and say how this war was Winston Churchill v. Adolf Hitler, and what was Stalin doing, butting in and dividing the laurels? For two years he, Winston Spencer Churchill, had held Hitler off with 'a broom, the broom of speech', and now that he was buckling on his armour he was not going to have Stalin sharing the glory of his victory. Another time some talk arose over the death of Capablanca, the chess champion, and Churchill, who is a very moderate player, said he would have liked to match his skill against Capablanca, whom he would of course have defeated, being the greatest chess master of all time.

March 28, 1942

The *Daily Mirror* debate on Thursday [March 26] went on and on.

Originally due to end at 5.0, it was continued till nearly 8.0. It seems to be thought that Morrison got such a plastering that he is through. A lot of the comment was unfavourable to the *Mirror*, but hardly any of it was favourable to the Government.

As far as we are concerned, we got over 900 letters from readers, of which only thirty-five, mostly anonymous, were against us. We lost three advertisers: Heath and Heather (the herbalists), the Prudential Assurance, and Odol. Odol are cutting down their advertising all round, but we gather we are being cut right out because of our politics. The shares, which were down to 4s. 6d. last year, were 9s. and steady as a rock throughout. The *World's Press News* came out heavily in our favour, as did the *New Statesman*, which rather obscurely recalls the fact that it is odd that I should get into this spot of bother, when my uncle Northcliffe got into trouble in the last war for attacking Kitchener.

In the House of Lords there were very few speakers, but we had no supporters. Camrose was very rude about us, but did one good job in pointing out that it would take fifty of our shareholders to establish anything that could be called a controlling interest.

Our circulation is of course pegged by our paper ration, but instead of being sold out at 9.0 it is now sold out at 8.0. We have today heard from Walters [Mirror *correspondent in America*] that he has already had cuttings from 300 American papers commenting on Morrison's threat, and he expects many more when it becomes known that Cassandra's column is to stop. Cass says he obviously can't now say what he thinks. He has had seven wonderful years; he had to join the Army in three months' time anyway; so he has decided to retain his journalistic integrity and join the Army now. This will cause rejoicing in the Government ranks as will the calling up of Frank Owen of the *Evening Standard*.

April 10, 1942
I had lunch yesterday with Hore-Belisha at his house in Stafford Place. He had no news of the war and little political information. He said Cripps was clearly a right-wing nominee in the Government and, he agreed, the most likely future Prime Minister. He thought the alternative was Eden; brushed aside the very possibility of Beaverbrook. He said Churchill was flattering Cripps into much

the same position Churchill occupied with Chamberlain – by asking him down to Chequers and admitting in tears (according to Hore-Belisha a familiar state for Churchill) that it was they two who must pull the country through. Hore-Belisha says Cripps falls for this kind of thing. If he does, he will find it hard to be sufficiently ruthless with Churchill and Churchill's friends when the time comes.

Hore-Belisha went on to talk about himself. I said I thought he had not stated his case strongly enough in public, and his enemies had had too clear a run. After all, his record at the War Office was a good one: he did bring in conscription, he did fire Deverell and Knox, he did promote promising men like Wavell over the heads of many officers senior to him. He did not only talk about giving the younger men a chance, he gave it them; and strong ruthless action was more needed now, and more appreciated now, than ever before.

He asked should he speak in the country or in the House? I said, clearly in the House. He asked should it be on India or on Singapore? I said clearly neither: one is of little interest to the British public and the other is stale. Wait for the next serious setback and go for the Prime Minister himself on that. There have been many attacks on the Government, so it is of no use doing that again. But make a flaming speech to the effect that it is no use blaming ministers, they are only puppets, and it is the Prime Minister who makes all the decisions and all the blunders. His battle honours now include not only Antwerp and the Dardanelles, but Norway, Dunkirk, Greece, Crete, Malaya, and Java. Must we lose London before we rid ourselves of this old man of the sea? Hore-Belisha says he will take this line, but I shall only believe it when I see it.

April 18, 1942
K.M. met Eden at dinner one day this week. He waxed confidential and said the future of this country depended on three men: Lyttelton, Cripps – and himself!

I noticed in the Aberdeen paper this week a real wartime note in patent medicine advertising: 'Is your stomach wasting food?'

Yesterday evening, at her request, I called on Lady Cripps at her flat in Whitehall Court. She is tall, dowdy, intelligent, nice, and a bit of a crank. Her flat is comfortable, though nondescript. When I arrived, she launched straight into the troubles we had been having with the Government. So I went through our history with Churchill, Bart's and my call on Attlee, and all the rest. I was there an hour and a quarter and we talked general politics, the Press and the Government, the *Mirror* and the Government, the morale of the Army, and so on.

She obviously wanted to get an impression of what sort of person I was; and then asked me to suggest (1) what to do about the relations of the Press and the Government, (2) what to do about the Army's morale. Would I send her a memorandum on each, and also a list of the papers and the important person on each from the editorial point of view?[5] Lady Cripps also said would I come and see her and Stafford some time soon, when he had had time to settle down after his return – say in ten days' time? I said I would do all this. She explained that she can often help her husband by sifting through a lot of stuff and only showing Stafford the material that will really help him.

I said she was a crank because at one point she referred to her husband's Indian trip, and said that when she was returning from Moscow she *knew* he would have to make this attempt. He might possibly have to go to India again – she didn't know. She spoke as if she believed herself to possess something like clair-voyant properties.

April 30, 1942
Went last night at Lady Cripps' invitation to see her and Sir Stafford. Was bidden at 8.50 and arrived to find Cripps had just completed his evening meal – in their only sitting room. There were still a cup and two tins on a table with a dark cloth. Cripps, who opened the door to me, is tallish and nice; obviously upright and obviously intelligent, I should say.

He started by asking how we were getting on; and I said apparently the Government was burying the hatchet, as at the weekend Bracken, Woolton, and even Herbert Morrison had come to our photographic exhibition. He went on to ask about public opinion and morale. I said I thought morale was generally low, and that the Navy and R.A.F. were to be regarded as islands of high in a sea of much lower morale. Hence Singapore, absenteeism in factories, and much else. I said I thought the main causes were political (the constitution of the Government; graft in high places, of a political kind such as Attlee's appointment as deputy premier, and of a personal kind such as Randolph [Churchill]'s safe seat) and military (bad leaders, no propaganda for the Army, and so on). He said one thing was certain and that was that Churchill would not substantially alter his existing Government: he said Churchill had fought for days before he would agree to exclude the few he had dismissed. This was the first I had heard that Margesson's and Moore-Brabazon's departure was due to Cripps' refusal to join the Government until they were removed.

He said that Churchill was the best war horse in the Cabinet, ready to take risks and aggressive. I objected that he always seemed to underestimate the air factor. Cripps said this was not so; rather the opposite. He was inclined to think – for example in Libya – that air power was everything and tank power did not matter. Of Wavell, Cripps said he suffered from one terrible fault: inability to get rid of the incompetent. It had been in his power to remove Percival [*the commander at Singapore*], when it was quite obvious he was no good – but he just could not bring himself to do it. Personally Cripps thought both Auchinleck and Alexander bigger men.

In a general way, he clearly did not expect the Russians to collapse this summer and he clearly did believe we should win the war. He said it might be that we should lose India, Persia, Iraq, Egypt, and our hold in the Mediterranean, but that even if disasters of this magnitude fell on us, we could withdraw our ships and many of our troops to this country and withstand all attacks until the Russians, Americans, and Chinese finally defeated the Axis powers. I said I thought far smaller disasters would break the people's heart and lead to an irresistible demand for peace. The people had been so deceived – by the Government, by the Press, the B.B.C., and everything else – that they had become invincibly cynical. Any campaign to improve morale would have to start by giving people here something to have faith in: they had lost their religious faith and had nothing to cling to. He agreed with some of this and appears to intend doing something about it. He appeared to believe that the best course was to try and jolly Churchill into making the right decisions. He clearly does not want to get Churchill out or to push himself in. He seems to me to underestimate Churchill's loss of prestige, and hardly to contemplate his almost inevitable departure.

May 16, 1942
Professor Goodhart in Oxford told me he was hearing the other day what a good man Halifax is – such a good type and such a good Ambassador – 'the only thing is the Americans don't like him'! Another of Goodhart's quips was of the avenue of limes in Christ Church meadow, now to be known as the Unter den Lindemann.

May 23, 1942
I have just been spending two days in Birmingham. I was very struck by the atmosphere of the place and the people – busy and prosperous. They are all working so hard that there is little discussion of the actual course of the war. I had a lot of talk with the personnel manager of Hercules Cycle, now making mostly primers for shells (the part that screws into the bottom); and with Morley, the manager of Wolseley Motors, whose factory I went over. These men had no complaints of lack of raw materials; their main interest seems to lie in labour problems: training unskilled labour, making use of women part time, and so on.

McLachlan of Hercules says the women become very highly skilled, but have their particular views on work. They like to have one job and one machine: this machine they soon come to regard as their baby. They work well and work fast, like a lot of noise – particularly radio – and like to talk the whole time. They are incredibly improvident. Single girls earning £6 to £7 per week are flat broke after a week's illness, in spite of the insurance money. They send a good bit home in most cases. They cannot understand income tax at all and no explanation seems to get across.

An item of what seemed to me first-class interest was Morley's information about raids. In April last year they had a raid at Ward End, and forty-two 500-pound bombs fell in their twenty-two-acre factory area. Thirty-nine of these fell through roofs, and 150 incendiaries fell on one shop. In the main machine shop five bombs fell through the roof, but the damage amounted only to eleven machines destroyed and one person killed (the others were all in shelters). The incendiaries burned one shop out, but the other damage was taken in hand at once and in a month production was back to normal: the very next day 80% of their work-people were busy. For a fortnight their employees worked at their lathes in the rain in overcoats.

From this definite information emerges (1) the astonishingly good spirit of our people in an emergency; (2) what very little permanent damage bombing does; (3) if forty-two 500-pound bombs and 150 incendiaries cannot knock out a twenty-two-acre factory for good and all, our R.A.F. policy of bombing Germany is just meaningless; (4) it is fire bombs that do the real damage. We heard in the office next to nothing of this very devastating blitz.

May 26, 1942

Bart had an amusing story today. Our Newcastle man rang up last week to say there was something big on in Leeds. We rang up our Leeds man, who said there *was* something big. We asked what it was: he said a distinguished visitor, but no names on the telephone. We asked if he had a black moustache: yes; if his name began with M: yes; what train would he catch? The Leeds man gave the train, but said he would get off at Brookmans Park, where the train was to be specially stopped. So, well in time, our photographer was at Brookmans Park – fortunately, because the train was forty minutes early – and there were Eden and all the big shots to greet Molotov. Our man asked Eden if he had any statement to make. Eden asked who he was and was horrified to discover it was the much feared *Daily Mirror* on the spot again – the only paper present. Meanwhile any suggestion of Molotov's presence in this country has been censored – at his request, we believe.[6]

May 27, 1942

Today was the Annual General Meeting of *Daily Mirror* share-holders, and it seemed to me interesting that only one shareholder

turned up to make any comment on our brush with the Government – and he afterwards proposed the vote of thanks to the
chairman and directors!

*By midsummer the worst was over for Britain. The last great disaster
occurred on June 21 with the fall of Tobruk and the surrender of its
garrison of 33,000. Although by the end of June Rommel had again recaptured all of Cyrenaica, Auchinleck established a strong defensive
position at El Alamein, and when Rommel attacked in July the British line
held. In August Auchinleck was replaced by Generals Alexander and
Montgomery, the pair who were to win in November the decisive battle of
El Alamein.*

*In the air Britain was hitting back at the German homeland. The great
bomber offensives began in 1942: on May 30, 1,000 bombers attacked
Cologne. But the effect of these raids on Germany was much less devastating
than was thought at the time, and German war production hardly faltered.*

*The Americans were hitting back too. Two great naval victories – in
May, the Coral Sea, and in June, Midway Island – stemmed the tide of
Japanese conquest. In August, a relentless reconquest of the huge areas
lost in the eight months after Pearl Harbour began with the landing of U.S.
marines in the Solomon Islands.*

*Throughout the summer the agony of Soviet Russia continued. In a
colossal summer offensive, the Germans penetrated almost to the Caspian Sea,
looked like capturing the whole of the Caucasian oil-fields, and reached the
Volga at Stalingrad.*

*The Russian clamour for a Second Front in Europe increased. The
American high command favoured an attack in Europe in 1942. Churchill
and the British generals were opposed to this. Roosevelt agreed with them,
and on July 25 the decision was made instead to invade North Africa from
the west, leaving Europe until 1943. In August Churchill travelled to
Moscow to inform Stalin of this.*

*At home, Churchill's position was no stronger than at the beginning of
the year. The January vote of confidence had not silenced the opposition.
On July 1, shortly after the fall of Tobruk, Churchill faced a vote of
of censure tabled by a leading Conservative, Sir John Wardlaw-Milne.*

July 1, 1942
There is little war news today. The main interest was centred on

the vote of censure – and what a flop it was. Wardlaw-Milne teed
off and made quite a good speech with one fatal blunder: he
suggested as an impartial chairman of the Chiefs of Staff Committee the Duke of Gloucester! This fantastic suggestion drew a
chorus of boos and jeers which nullified the effect of what he said
before and after. This reception, strangely enough, seemed to
surprise and shake Wardlaw-Milne a lot. Various speakers made
various points, but they were all pulling their punches. Lyttelton
spoke for the Government so badly that Clem Davies, after his
speech, asked if the vote of censure could be converted to a
measure of impeachment against the men responsible for the
disastrous situation that had been outlined. He was ruled out of
order.

It is now thought the vote of censure may get thirty-five votes,
but that there will be a number of abstentions. My thought today
is that the House is really playing politics and is not interested
in the course of the war. Members regard Churchill as the only
Tory, or indeed parliamentary, asset, and they are therefore
extremely reluctant to damage his value by a vote of censure. They
are all very critical of him in private and certainly have no confidence in him as a war-winner. At the present moment the
country is heading straight for military and, in a different way
and at a different pace, for political disaster, and yet there is
Parliament playing noughts and crosses with itself in a corner.
It seems to be thought that the House will demand another debate
if we lose Egypt, but after this week's showing it seems clear to
me that we shall have to sink a good deal lower before there are
any constructive military or political developments of any
consequence.

July 2, 1942
The debate went on last night till 2.45 a.m., and the vote of
censure was defeated by 475 to twenty-five. This is such a large
number it leaves little room for any substantial number of abstentions. So Churchill wins one more meaningless parliamentary
victory. Meanwhile the Germans claim the capture of El Alamein
– the last fortified post in the desert – and say they are pursuing
our forces towards the Nile valley. It is clearly these events in

Egypt and not processions of turnip-headed M.P.s into the Government lobby that are going to decide the political future of this country.

July 8, 1942

Had Hore-Belisha to lunch yesterday. Physically he *is* repulsive, and he is so obviously and entirely interested in the effect of public affairs on him, not in their effect on the country. He anticipates that the same men (in the Government) will produce the same results; that therefore further disasters lie ahead, and probably the fall of Egypt.

I went at him and said, if his group were in opposition, why did they not get on with it? Yesterday was devoted to the Ministry of Information: why was not a weighty attack being delivered against the Government on its mishandling of our propaganda? And so on – each subject for debate, whether it be health, finance, shipping, or what have you, being used as a text to expose the inadequacy of the Government. Hore-Belisha seemed to think this might be a good idea, but obviously had not thought of any such sustained campaign.

He said Wardlaw-Milne gave him no indication he was going to introduce the name of the Duke of Gloucester. K.M. was dining last night inter alios with one of the Buck House equerries, who admitted quite frankly that the proposal was made with royal approval. They may not realize with what derision the suggestion was treated, but they are by no means set back by the reception given Wardlaw-Milne. They think the seed has been planted and can be allowed to germinate in due course.

July 9, 1942

Bellenger had tea with Cripps yesterday evening. There were about six more or less rebel Labour M.P.s there. Cripps, in the course of conversation, expressed his dissatisfaction with the Government and with Churchill and said he did not think the Government would last much longer, nor would he stay in it much longer. He said the only members of the Cabinet who stand up to the Prime Minister are Bevin, of whom Churchill is rather jealous, and himself. He expressed complete certainty on one issue, that Churchill would not resign without a General Election. Cripps is clearly looking round for supporters – as is Eden, but not Bevin. Cripps said he thought the next Prime Minister would be Eden and, after Eden, himself.

Campbell reports that Churchill wanted to make Randolph [Churchill] an Under-Secretary – hence his presence in London these last few weeks – but the Whips objected so strongly that Churchill has dropped the idea.

July 14, 1942

K.M. was at the Air Ministry this afternoon talking to Sir Louis Greig, Sinclair's social secretary. Greig is very well in at Court and volunteered his enthusiasm for making 'Gloggins' [*the Duke of Gloucester*] chairman of the Chiefs of Staff Committee. The idea seems to be to break the Prime Minister's power by introducing between him and the services a royal personage with sufficient standing to support the services successfully against the politicians. I don't think this is worth doing, and anyway doubt whether Gloggins could do it.

The Air Ministry is getting very tired of the Americans: says their aircraft output is ridiculously low, their planes are bad, and they are entirely non-co-operative. Their Airocobras [*American fighter planes*] are a complete flop; and they now reveal why they want to take over day bombing from us, but not night bombing: their planes have no flame shutters and their exhaust would show up clearly at night. Even though they have been at war seven months, their bombers are still being *made* without these shutters. In formulating war plans the American command is arrogant, ignorant, and non-co-operative.

K.M. had rather a funny story about the Airocobras and Churchill tanks. We offered these to the Russians, explaining that they were no good but saying they could have them if they could find a use for them. The Russians, after twenty-five years of very well justified suspicion of our motives, thought this a cunning way of putting them off our best stuff, and pressed to have it. We sent it with pleasure – and it proved useless.

July 15, 1942
Grant Davidson, an ex-rep on the *Mirror*, came in this afternoon.
He is now rear gunner on a Stirling and has made thirty-three
trips over Germany. He said the German defences are fantastically
good, in particular the co-ordination of their radio-location with
A.A. guns and searchlights. Unless a bomber alters course and
height at least every half minute, it will be shot down for certain
by the first A.A. battery within range. There are also a lot of
night fighters: one of his squadron's bombers had five after it the
other night. He said that for every plane lost about ten are
damaged, in many cases so badly as to be complete write-offs.
Most of their bombing is done from 17,000 feet, at which height
German flak has the accuracy I have mentioned. The constant
jinking, which has to start thirty miles out in the North Sea and
which is necessary to avoid the flak, makes accurate bombing
impossible.

July 17, 1942
On the 15th at 5.30 the Prime Minister saw the editors for the
first time since last September. He was in his blue siren-suit, and
there were more editors than usual – about forty, including
Kingsley Martin of the *New Statesman* and Lady Rhondda of
Time and Tide. I have heard four versions of what took place and I
should say that the two very general impressions were (1) that
Churchill evidently thought his position as Prime Minister was so
completely unassailable that the critics could be regarded as rather
eccentric than dangerous (this was an astonishing attitude to take
up to the editors, so many of whom are highly critical); (2) that
as America is on our side we are bound to win whatever happens.
The Prime Minister is clearly not shaken in any way by our
disasters in the field nor by any criticism in the Press, in Parliament, or elsewhere. His vanity and conceit are evidently quite
impenetrable.

July 20, 1942
Campbell tells me that the decision to press the recent vote of
censure to a division was taken by the 'rebels' on Lloyd George's
advice. Lloyd George won't take any strong line himself, because

he does not want to damage Gwilym [his son]'s political career – surely an ignoble reason for not doing his duty at a time like this.

July 22, 1942

Campbell says the Americans have moved into a big aerodrome at Aldermaston, near Newbury. Within three days one of the Yanks went into the local pub and asked the girl for a pint 'just as quick as your men moved out of Dunkirk'. There were three wounded Gordon Highlanders present, one of whom had lost a brother killed at Dunkirk. There was naturally a fight in which the offending Yank was beaten up, but the pub was wrecked.

July 24, 1942

Had lunch with Esmond Rothermere at his suite in the Dorchester. He says Churchill is a 'muddler'. Churchill is very emotional and, while he is usually up, he has appalling periods of black depression. That is when he summons Beaverbrook, who is the only man able to cheer him when he is in the depths. He recently offered Beaverbrook a job in the Cabinet, but Beaverbrook finally refused when it became known that it would lead to the resignation of Anderson, as well as of Cripps and Bevin.

Esmond thinks the big political crash will come in September, when Russia is collapsing and the British public realizes that there was no Second Front. He assumes Eden would succeed Churchill, with a very similar Government, but doesn't suppose this would last long. He says Churchill has told Eden that if necessary he will serve under him – the same tale he told Cripps!

July 27, 1942

K.M. is now back from her holiday and met Stephen Early, Roosevelt's secretary, at dinner last night. He said the Americans are very fed up about the absence of a Second Front, and the higher-ups are exasperated by the 'non possumus' attitude of our generals. He said that in America there is no enthusiasm for the war and an absolute refusal to sacrifice anything for it. There is a lot of hostility to England mixed up with hostility to the war, and this is compounded of very various elements. For example, the Liberal Left think we have let down all our, and their, friends in

Europe, while the Isolationists are still Isolationist. Without a Second Front, the Americans will soon tire of paying for the war and may well sign a separate peace with Hitler, though not with Japan.

Later

K.M. just back, as she said, from two lunches and three coffees. Firstly with news from the Russian Embassy. The Russians are this time in despair, far more so than when Moscow was only saved by a severe and unexpected frost. Their main worry is famine – the actual word was used – and they are disgusted and appalled by our complete lack of help. The First Counsellor had a talk with Brendan Bracken, who pointed out that no Second Front had been promised in 1942. Apparently Maisky [*the Soviet Ambassador*] suggested this to Molotov, who ticked him off for being so suspicious. The Russians, who have definitely been counting on a real Second Front, hear that all that is now intended is a raid by *one* division, which is obviously neither here nor there. They themselves expect to be attacked by the Japs at any time now. They are asking what is the point of fighting on, if they are to be deserted by their allies, and talk of signing a separate peace. K.M. said surely Stalin would never do that, and they admitted *he* wouldn't. They are well aware of the attitude of the Americans and their lack of enthusiasm for the war.

July 31, 1942

Campbell just back from a talk Maisky gave the editors. In the office, too, was Bevan, who had heard him speak to M.P.s yesterday. Maisky's story was very gloomy. He said the Russians had lost five million trained and equipped soldiers, killed, wounded, and missing. They had lost vast natural resources, including four-fifths of their aluminium. This was the peak of their military effort. The most they could hope to do this year was to keep the Germans off the Volga and off the Caucasian oil. Next year their effort would of necessity be on an altogether smaller scale. The Russian government asked for a Second Front last July, and only accepted Beaverbrook's offer of material as a second best.

   Maisky made it clear that this talk of his had been arranged

13

because of an acute difference between the heads of our respective governments on this important issue. In fact he almost said that as he could get no sense out of our Government, he was appealing over their heads to M.P.s and to newspaper editors. He said Litvinov [*Soviet Ambassador in the U.S.A.*] was making similar moves in Washington, where he did not find any enthusiasm for the Second Front either.

August 1, 1942
K.M. tells me that Cripps gave a dinner this week – not his usual tea – and invited a number of Liberals: Vernon Bartlett, Driberg, Wilfrid Roberts, Horabin, Mander, and so on. She got impressions from three of the guests. Cripps expressed no interest in a Second Front one way or the other, but was entirely taken up with post-war reconstruction – not in so far as it affects current policy, but because he is confident he will be Prime Minister at that time and is thinking now what he will do then. He was particularly insistent that as Prime Minister under such circumstances, he would need wider powers than those possessed by the Prime Minister now. He impressed those present with having a very slight knowledge of what is going on in the country. The party ended by being stuck in the lift for an hour and a quarter on the way down.

Geoffrey Parsons, editor of the *New York Herald Tribune*, is in London just now and saw the Prime Minister yesterday. The Prime Minister expressed some impatience with the 'noisy clamour of the Communists' for a Second Front. He was apparently unaware that the demand was anything more than a Red stunt.   Even Parsons was struck by the degree to which he is out of touch with popular opinion in this country. He neither seemed to know nor *care* what the country was thinking. It was his war, he was in charge, he was winning(!) it, and what did anyone else matter? He showed Parsons a long range of cutting books in which was pasted every reference to him in the national papers. It is really hard to believe that even Churchill's vanity can go so far.

August 3, 1942
Had lunch with Michael Foot, now editor of the *Evening Standard*,

Derek Tangye, now at the War Office, and Ronald Hyde, also of the *Standard*.

Tangye had some stories about Ironside and Norway, as he was on duty when the news came in from Oslo, and it was he who told Ironside, then C.I.G.S., that German ships were at that moment heading up Oslo Fiord. He said Ironside, whom he described as the worst general we ever had, was cock-a-hoop: he kept on saying what a disastrous mistake Hitler had made, 'like Napoleon and Spain'. When they came to discuss what should be done, it transpired that there were no maps showing the navigable passages through the fiords and no knowledge anywhere of whether the railway to Lillehammer was single- or double-track! On investigation they found there were only two battalions ready to sail. These were accordingly sent, and as a touch of genius– Ironside's own – they sent round to the gunsmiths, collected the only thirty tommy-guns in the whole country, and sent them too. Tangye was appalled by the nonchalance with which hundreds of men were sent to their deaths – for no possible good reason.

August 6, 1942
K.M. just in from lunch with her Russian Embassy friends. They are pleased about the Prime Minister's trip [to Moscow[7]]. They quite frankly agreed that his main motive in making the trip was to strengthen his own political position in view of the strong feeling in the country for Russia and a Second Front. The Russians are quite prepared to help him out in this – as are the Communists here – because they think Churchill is the most likely premier to keep us in the war. They dislike him personally and ridicule his war-winning capacity, but consider that any successor would be a stopgap leading very shortly to appeasement and a separate peace.

August 24, 1942
I hear from a friend at Lewes [Sussex] that there could have been no question of secrecy about the Dieppe expedition.[8] The invasion barges were assembled at Newhaven for all to see; for three or four nights before the attack, trains were roaring through all night, while German planes kept the place lighted up with flares

and incendiary bombs. She says the Canadian soldiers she has met were very gloomy about the show.

I am reading Churchill's *Great Contemporaries*, a pot-boiling book of essays published in 1937. The essays are not good, but give a good many sidelights on Churchill's own attitude. He is impressed most by the traditional, the charming, the aristocratic, and above all by men who can express themselves well. Mere administrative capacity or brains (let alone genius) do not interest him. He is obviously very anti-Lloyd George (which I did not realize), not even including him among the 'great' contemporaries, very anti-Irish, and *very* anti-Socialist. He seems to possess no real political sense at all and to have very little sympathy with the mass of the people. Politics are mostly a social game, in which the prizes are gained by charm and by fine speeches. That there are problems to be solved which cannot be solved by either charm or eloquence hardly seems to occur to him. It is to me altogether strange that anyone with such an interest in at least some aspects of history should be so insensitive to the political trends of his day. To him Rosebery, Balfour, Asquith, and F.E. Smith were great men, while Marx, De Valera, Hitler, and even Lloyd George are vulgar upstarts who would be ignored if only people were more sensible. He makes one rather good crack about the pedestals of the great Victorian statesmen being vacant for long, and how even the pedestals themselves have now been swept away.

September 8, 1942
Had a couple of drinks with an Air Force friend yesterday. He was expatiating on the lack of interest in the war shown by the mechanics at his aerodrome. They have no interest in the war or in politics. He also had a curious, though deplorable, story of a group captain at the next station to his own. He went up in a Whitley with his wife and a crew of six, took off with his flaps down, crashed, and the whole party was burnt. On investigation it appeared that the woman was not his wife, but that her real husband was bringing divorce proceedings citing the group captain as co-respondent; it also came to light that he was in debt to the tune of £3,000 and that he had left a letter announcing his

intention of committing suicide. To do so with a crew of six was quite like a return to the burial rites of Viking chieftains.

In the evening yesterday I saw Cripps. He seemed more perky than when I saw him last and had changed his flat. His wife was there wearing sandals, but without stockings. We talked of this and that and I mentioned how slight was the interest in the war in Aberdeenshire, as elsewhere. This struck quite the right note. It was this that was worrying Cripps.

I said I thought people were cynical not only about the Government, but about Parliament, the Press, the law, and everything else – a state of cynicism which would continue past any change of Government. Cripps said he quite agreed, and took a very serious view of the situation. He said Dieppe had had a momentary effect in some quarters. In one colliery (I believe Betteshanger in Kent) output had doubled, but only for twenty-four hours, when it went straight back to normal. He thought people were in need of a spiritual incentive and with this in mind he is appearing himself on the platform with the Archbishops of Canterbury and York at the Albert Hall on the 26th, in an attempt to bring home to people the importance of religion in their daily lives. He thought that without some sort of a religious revival we should get nowhere in this war. His invitation to me was partly to find out if I would help him over this quasi-religious campaign.

In the second place he is obviously feeling very uneasy in the Cabinet, feels his resignation is inevitable sooner or later, and wants to know what support he would get if he did resign. He seemed to have moved a long way since I met him last time. He had to select the right occasion for his resignation. I said it was important not to wait too long. Lady Cripps at this said: 'He mustn't get so covered with tar that it won't melt off.'

Cripps expressed a shuddering loathing of Beaverbrook. Said that Beaverbrook had him to dinner alone and for two hours did his utmost to get Cripps to accept the Ministry of Supply under him. He thinks Beaverbrook is playing a very deep game and that he passionately wants power – supreme power: in a mildly drunken mood he had told a friend of Cripps' as much. He said that Beaverbrook's blunders with tanks were only now working through to the battlefield, hence our setback in Libya; that Beaverbrook was intriguing for supreme power, had a hold over the Prime Minister, and if he achieved his aim – probably behind a façade such as Eden (his words) – would endeavour to sign a peace with all possible speed. When I saw Cripps last he pooh-poohed the idea of Beaverbrook getting the premiership or any-thing equivalent, but this time both he and his wife said that more and more of the insiders were worried about this possibility, which, they thought, might arise if the Government fell leaving the political direction of the war in a state of chaos for perhaps twenty-four hours. I said I thought the main danger of Beaver-brook was that he was fundamentally mischievous. He quite agreed, and said that the way he turned his bright young men into drunkards was done out of sheer sadism. Beaverbrook has cer-tainly had an intentionally demoralizing effect on his young men and young women.

About the selection of generals, Cripps rather horrified me by saying that few of the Cabinet knew Alexander when they appointed him Commander-in-Chief Middle East, and none of them knew Montgomery (though Commander-in-Chief South-eastern Command for some time!!). They took their military recommendations from Brooke [C.I.G.S.] without any cross-check or interview.

Churchill, he said, was afraid of two things: (1) the Press, and (2) that someone should become a more popular broadcaster than himself. His fears are due to his realization that only from these two quarters can his power be challenged. Of one thing Cripps said he was quite sure, that if Churchill had to go he would certainly not go quietly. My whole interview lasted one and a half hours, but Cripps was really only warming up as I had to leave for my last train.

September 11, 1942

A spy story going round concerns the advertising of 'Sylvan Flakes'. On August 15 in the *Daily Telegraph* there was an ad-vertisement for Sylvan Flakes referring to a Dieppe beach coat and saying that, now such things were unprocurable, women should preserve them by washing them in Sylvan Flakes. This was four days before the Dieppe raid, and the woman in the picture is pruning a tree whose branches are said to bear a striking resemblance to the railway and canal system round the Dieppe coastline. Further investigation showed that the same series of advertisements had copy dealing with Malta, India and, I believe, Bute – the last just before an important American convoy got into Glasgow. The whole business is being sifted, but it would seem to me that it can hardly be anything but pure, though startling, coincidence.

September 16, 1942
Bart tells me that we have appointed a correspondent in Ankara! It appears that we had an appeal from the Government in some round-about way to appoint a man in Ankara. He was there acting I suppose as an agent of sorts, but it was felt his continued existence in Turkey needed more explanation. His appointment by the *Daily Mirror* as our special correspondent, particularly in view of our known hostility to the Government, was considered a suitable blind. Our rulers seem to be slowly learning a little sense from the enemy.

September 17, 1942
I am reading Greville's *Memoirs* for 1842, and have come upon a passage quoted by Churchill – though without its source – when I had lunch with him at 10 Downing Street [February 19, 1941]. 'In Pitt's (Lord Chatham's) administration, when Wolfe was going out to take the command of the army in America, at that time a post of the greatest importance, Mr Pitt had him to dinner with no other person present but Lord Temple (Mr Grenville's uncle). After dinner Wolfe got greatly excited, drew his sword, flourished it about, and boasted of the great things he would do with it in a wonderfully braggart style. Lord Temple and Mr Pitt were horror-struck, and when the General was gone, they lifted up their hands and eyes, and said what an awful thing it was to think that they were about to trust interests so vital to the discretion of a man who could talk and bluster in such a way.'

This anecdote was told by Mr Grenville to Greville, and quoted by Churchill as an example of what queer people it takes to win wars. I wish we saw more queer ones and fewer of the case-hardened conventional kind!

September 24, 1942

We have been discussing future *Mirror* & Pic policy, and feel that criticism is now futile and merely boring. The war no longer rouses interest and therefore the only possible line – until things start moving – is great preoccupation with the young, both in services and factories – this with the minimum about the war and politics. Bart will try and get closer to the War Office, Admiralty, and Air Ministry, to be of service in any possible way to the troops.

September 26, 1942

Went to a meeting in the Albert Hall organized by the Christian Industrial Fellowship, whatever that may be: principal speakers the Archbishops of York and Canterbury, and Stafford Cripps. The audience was elderly and obviously churchy, with many nuns and scores of parsons. The seats had been applied for many times over weeks ago, so I rolled up to see what it would be like.

The Archbishop of Canterbury [*William Temple*] made an excellent speech, in substance and in manner. In general he claimed that land and money, which are essential to the life of any community today, should be used for the benefit of the community as a whole and not for the private profit of a few. This would strike me as pure socialism, and coming from the Archbishop was startling. His toughest phrases brought the loudest applause, and this from an audience which appeared to be overweighted by the more reactionary elements.

Then the Archbishop of York [*Cyril Forster Garbett*] spoke, mostly about housing. He had not the authoritative voice and manner of Canterbury, but the substance of his remarks was excellent. He was the first public figure who has given me the impression of realizing what an immense and daunting problem lies before us in rehousing the people after this war. This is obviously a subject which will be very much in the public eye for years, and it is interesting to note this, the first authoritative statement on the subject. Both Archbishops were emphatic that we must have planning, and that the interests of the community must come first. There was much conventional religion mixed in with this, but to an extent that in no way obscured the main message.

Cripps then spoke. He has a pleasant voice and was the most easily audible of them all. He has no frills when speaking but gives the impression of great sincerity. His speech was more specifically religious than the Archbishops' and was very well received.

My own reflection on the meeting is that the British people are very ready to listen to someone who will teach them the elements of religion. On the text 'Man shall not live by bread alone' a good speaker could hold almost any audience enthralled. But I doubt whether this will bring them back to conventional Christianity.

September 28, 1942
The story going round the pubs of Fleet Street is that Churchill, Stalin, and Hitler all met. Hitler asked Stalin what he was fighting for: Stalin said Communism, and what are you fighting for? Hitler said Nazi principles and Lebensraum. They both turned to Churchill and said: 'And what are you fighting for?' Churchill said: 'Who said I was fighting?'

October 1, 1942
K.M. saw Sinclair at his request yesterday and had considerable talk about the future of the Liberal Party. From that he went on to describe a dinner party given a few days ago by the Prime Minister to Beaverbrook, Sinclair, and three other Cabinet ministers, none of whom was Labour. The conversation turned on newspapers and in particular on the *Daily Mirror*, about which the Prime Minister was very bitter. He said he thought its policy was to break down the party boundaries and so lead to anarchy; that its policy had been cleverly pursued before the warning and even more cleverly since. Beaverbrook (very unexpectedly!) spoke up for the *Mirror*, and said that though he did not agree with its policy or its methods, it undoubtedly reflected the views of a large mass of people – particularly young people.

Sinclair very clearly (and apparently sincerely) said he had not summoned K.M. to pass all this on and would rather it were not, but let the *Daily Mirror* beware: it had a lot of powerful enemies who would gladly catch hold of anything to bring it down. I gather suppression under 2D is not now regarded as practical politics.

October 5, 1942

K.M. tells me Churchill in private conversation with one of her acquaintances at the House the other day referred to Hore-Belisha as 'discarded trash'. Whatever one may think of Horeb, this is surprisingly bitter and quite unfair.

October 6, 1942

In the train on the way home last night were two American soldiers, very drunk. One was a railway foreman from Indiana, the other a cement construction foreman from Palm Beach, Florida. They expressed some admiration for Hitler, contempt and dislike for England. They grumbled about the low rate of their pay; were very bitter about their officers, whom they wanted to shoot; but the only subject on which they got very animated was negroes. If they could have a chance of shooting their own American negroes over here, then their journey would indeed have been well worth while. They may have been a particularly poor pair, but they didn't look it, and on their performance yesterday I should say their morale was at zero and their military value very near nil.

October 10, 1942

Had Shinwell to lunch yesterday. I had not met him for some considerable time and then only once. I had a good look at him. He is shrewd, bitter, capable, emotional and, I should say, sincere. He is commonly represented as ruthlessly self-interested, but I should not say that was true. He is to face his executive on Monday [October 12], and get a caning, with Laski and Bevan, for criticizing the Labour Party leaders. He does not suppose any of them will be expelled.

He is very agitated by the failure of the Churchill tanks at

Dieppe.[8] Apparently they were designed for two-pounder guns, but were fitted with six-pounders. The six-pounders had not enough room for the recoil and the tanks blew up. He thinks attacking these tanks is good tactics, as their failure will rebound on Churchill, after whom they are named.

I asked him what he thinks of the political future. He is very gloomy. He thinks the only hope is either a real Opposition or a rejuvenated Labour Party. He says the rebels in the House are quite incapable of working together, and that the mandarins of Transport House are at present an insuperable obstacle to any reinvigoration of the Labour Party. His present idea is to go on going on and to hope that something will some day emerge.

October 21, 1942
Went to see Cripps this evening at 8.30 in his flat at Whitehall Court. Conversation tended to flag and I wondered why I had been summoned. Cripps was very emphatic – apropos of nothing in particular – that you must take the Prime Minister as he is or leave him; that recently he had tried so hard to be different, but could only keep it up for twenty-four hours and then slipped back into the old ways. 'The old ways' seemed to mean running the war on his own without reference to his Cabinet. I said surely if he *knew* his tenure of office depended on his mending his ways, he would mend them. Cripps said no. He might have been capable of this even two years ago, but not now. For one thing he was too worn out and tired. These last two years had taken a lot out of him. Cripps said that by (say) January 1 the fate of the Government would be sealed: either it would have a new lease of life or it would have crashed. I said I didn't see why.

I asked him if there were any line he thought we could usefully adopt in the paper. He said the Beveridge Report on social security would soon be out and he laid great stress on the importance of pushing it with all possible vigour, as this was the only way of forcing its adoption on the Government.

He then expressed alarm and despondency over the Americans; said they had fallen down on their promises in every way, particularly in planes and ships. This not only deprives us of badly needed material but lands us in serious difficulties, as we have disposed our material on the supposition that the President's written word would be honoured. Cripps said much of the American stuff was going to the Pacific. In particular, at one Pacific port there were thirty-one American ships, although there was only one lighter by which they could be unloaded: and many of these were ships that had been promised to us! In the case of planes, the Americans had let us down by not supplying promised material to the Middle East. They gave no warning and made no excuses – the stuff just didn't turn up.

Cripps wants to recall Halifax [*British Ambassador in the U.S.A.*] and appoint someone really good, who would press our case to some effect. In any case he thought Halifax could do a good job in India as Viceroy: he and Gandhi had established a relationship quite different in kind from anything Gandhi had established with any other official, Gandhi having an immense admiration for Halifax's brand of mystical religion. I said I thought Eden would go down well in America. Evidently he had been considered, as Cripps immediately said there were two schools of thought about Eden. I said that anyway he was very popular in the U.S.; and Cripps said, in the country generally, yes, but that in Washington he was afraid he would be ineffective, and it was in Washington that his work would have to be done.

He then went on to talk of military appointments, and spoke highly of Montgomery. He said when Alexander's appointment as Commander-in-Chief Middle East came up, he had wanted Pile (a tank expert, therefore Commander-in-Chief A.A. defences!), but Brooke, C.I.G.S., had raised objections. Brooke is an infantry officer and therefore tends to make recommendations to important appointments along certain stereotyped lines. Obviously Cripps had little confidence in some of these recommendations, but does not know how to avoid accepting them. The same point came up last time I met Cripps, so it is evidently worrying him.

This all seems to me an interesting sidelight on the chaotic lack of organization at the top. Important naval and military appointments are evidently partly in the gift of Cripps, who has no qualifications either for choosing military commanders or in fact for choosing any kind of staff. In the discussions on the subject,

Cripps made it clear that neither Alexander nor Grigg, the ministers constitutionally responsible, had any serious say at all.

October 29, 1942

Had Hore-Belisha to lunch, among others, and stayed to tea with him. We talked of the political situation: the absence of any Opposition, the lack of any cohesion among the critics, and so on. I maintained that (a) any parliamentary opposition is a waste of breath unless Hore-Belisha can get on his side some worth-while Tories, this being a Tory House of Commons; (b) the alternative is a campaign in the country. If this has any real success, it will compel attention in the House. Such a campaign to get anywhere now must be constructive, rather than critical: did anyone know what Hore-Belisha stood for? Privately I came to the conclusion that he is a pure opportunist with poor political judgment, and that he has no idea what to do.

Church bells rang out all over Britain to celebrate the victory at El Alamein. It was Britain's first major land victory against German forces in the Second World War. Rommel had been beaten by a stronger enemy (well supplied through the Suez Canal) and first-rate generalship. From November 4 he was in full retreat.

The British-American landings in French North Africa, in Morocco and Algeria, took place successfully on November 8. In Algiers at the time was the Vichy politician Admiral Darlan. The Americans settled on him as head of the French government in North Africa, thus certainly facilitating the Allied take-over of these countries. But such dealings with a man of Vichy aroused fury in Britain. 'Thanks, Admiral,' said the Pictorial. *'Now scuttle yourself!' Much embarrassment was saved when Darlan was assassinated on December 24. After this, the leadership of the Free French was disputed by Generals Giraud and de Gaulle, the latter's superior political skills bringing him out on top.*

Between January 14 and 25 Roosevelt, Churchill, and their advisers met at Casablanca, Morocco, to discuss future strategy. It was agreed that war would end only with the unconditional surrender of the Axis powers.

Stalin was invited to Casablanca but refused. At this vital moment he could not leave Russia. January and February 1943 were the turning point in the war on the eastern front: a whole German army was destroyed around Stalingrad and the remnants forced to surrender; and Russia's winter offensive undid most of Germany's summer gains.

In Britain Cripps announced his resignation from the War Cabinet. He had become increasingly disillusioned with Churchill, who had anyway now no need for his support. The biggest domestic news before the New Year was the publication of the Beveridge Report, a remarkable document, the basis of the present Welfare State. 'The Beveridge Report', commented the Pictorial, *'will so much break the old order that it will rank as little short of a Magna Carta for the toiling masses in Britain.'*

November 5, 1942

At last things have taken a more definite turn in Egypt. There was a special Cairo communiqué at 10.0 last night announcing that Rommel was in full retreat, battered by our Air Force. Not satisfied with what is, after all, the very successful completion of the first round in the Battle of North Africa, the B.B.C. and the newspapers have gone quite mad. The *Daily Mirror*, I am sorry to say, leads the paper with 'ROMMEL ROUTED', 'HUNS FLEEING IN DISORDER' – all of which may come to pass in the fullness of time, but hasn't happened yet. The King has cabled congratulations to the forces and the general reception of the news suggests that the war is over.

November 8, 1942

This morning I turned on the nine o'clock news and found that once more in this war the big news had come in in the early morning leaving the poor *Sunday Pictorial* high and dry. The news was put out from Washington between 2.0 and 3.0 that American troops protected by British aircraft and naval vessels had landed in North Africa; that General Eisenhower was in command; and the usual blah about our coming to help the French, not to take their colonies.

November 21, 1942

I had a message this morning that David Owen, Cripps' secretary, wanted to see me. So he came round about lunchtime and blurted out this deplorable story: that Cripps was asked if he would

accept the Ministry of Aircraft Production and the chairmanship
of the Radio Board (mainly concerned with radio telegraphy and
radio-location), together with the chairmanship of a committee to
deal with U-boats. This jumble of jobs is not to include a seat in the
War Cabinet, where he will be replaced by Morrison. Owen said
he spoke strongly against acceptance of this proposal, but Cripps
had accepted.

The move is apparently quite cynically the result of our
victories in Egypt: the Prime Minister now feels himself strong
enough to discard a colleague who, on India and on post-war
reconstruction (among other things), had views of his own. The
Cabinet now contains no one who will argue with the Prime
Minister except perhaps Bevin, who will only stand out on
industrial and trade-union matters. Morrison's promotion is
quite undeserved. He was a failure at the Ministry of Supply and
by no stretch of the imagination could be called a success at
the Home Office.

I suggested to Owen that Cripps was being jettisoned by
Churchill before the publication of the Beveridge Report, due on
the 26th. This had not occurred to Owen, but he thought it was
very probably correct. It is clear that Churchill wants to get
Cripps off any contact with domestic policy. Cripps has fallen into
the very crude trap set by the Prime Minister, and is now en-
tangled in three very technical jobs from none of which can he
derive any great kudos. If the war goes well he will be dropped;
otherwise he will linger on. Cripps himself does not think it
possible that the Prime Minister should drop him, but Owen is not
so confident. So ends the Cripps myth. The field is so barren of
talent he may have a comeback, but no newspaper will support
him with any confidence in the future: it is impossible to stand up
for a man who won't or can't stand up for himself.

Owen said that the Beveridge Report, which he had read, is a
good piece of work, but that its essential value is as a comprehensive whole. He says it will be cut up in pieces and some parts
will be adopted. Kingsley Wood is already mobilizing the
Treasury against it. Kingsley Wood, according to Owen, is
gaining in influence – partly as the result of some discreet little
lunches. I cannot take this ridiculous little puppet seriously, but

so low is the standard of realism in the Tory Party and the House generally, that they really think he might matter.

November 25, 1942

Davidson, a former *Mirror* advertisement rep, came in to see me. He has now earned a period of rest and a commission after a run of thirty-four operational flights over Germany. For most of this time he was the rear gunner in a Stirling. He said that in the early days the missing aircraft usually came to grief because of slight damage or engine trouble, and a large proportion of their crews baled out and were captured. Now the proportion of their crews shot down in flames is much larger, and of the men missing only about ten per cent turn up as prisoners. Most of the remainder disappear – either lost at sea or so burnt up that their identity discs go. He had himself seen several of our bombers shot down by both night fighters and A.A. guns, and he said there is suddenly an immense ball of fire hurtling to the ground. No one could have a chance of getting out.

He had himself been attacked by five night fighters at once, but when they saw they were spotted they sheered off. Night fighters are shy of an exchange of fire as, if they are damaged, they have little hope of landing safely in the dark. Casualties are high. Of the air crews at his aerodrome in Norfolk only two survived at the end of six months.

Some of their most severe losses were in mine laying: these losses are not given by the Air Ministry. The Germans have established flak boats about five to ten miles off their coast. These boats are impossible to pick out in the dark and often open up unexpectedly. Apart from hindering mine-laying operations, they prevent our planes flying home just above the surface of the sea where they are fairly immune from attacks by night fighters.

A fair number of damaged bombers come down in the sea, and there is now an arrangement by which a self-inflating dinghy is released automatically when the plane touches the water. Even if the plane lands gently on the surface it may sink in thirty seconds, so it is a real problem getting out in time. One of Davidson's squadron radioed home that they were coming down in the North Sea and gave their position. Their dinghy was found, but

none of the crew: the aircraft must have gone down too rapidly
for any of the men to escape. They never bale out over the sea, as
to do so would give them an even smaller chance of survival.

December 2, 1942

The big news today is the publication of the Beveridge Report.
His scheme is a comprehensive social security plan: embracing
health and unemployment insurance in one scheme with old-age
pensions, and adding allowances for all children after the first;
also maternity and burial benefits. Its acceptance would mean a
heavy blow at the industrial assurance business, whether in the
hands of companies or societies. By and large it is an admirable
scheme, but I did not anticipate such a press.

The volume of Press support is so great that it seems to be
assumed in the House that it will be politically impossible to drop
the Report, and so it may well be adopted by the Tories as their
best way out. It is to be debated in January, so we are holding
most of our fire till then. Bart is planning to give it a big burst of
publicity prior to the debate. He agrees with me that our preliminary booming of the Report did much to secure the favourable
Press reaction this morning. Our constant harping on it made
everyone very conscious of its importance long before they knew
what was in it.

December 4, 1942

Had lunch with David Owen, Cripps' secretary, just off to
Sweden to explain the Beveridge Report to university groups (so
at least he said). Owen says Churchill does not understand the
Beveridge Report but 'likes it'. He also says that Churchill has
been stricken with remorse since demoting Cripps, that he has
personally invited him to every meeting of the War Cabinet since
his nominal departure, and consults him more than ever! When
Cripps accepted the new job there was a meeting at which
Churchill wept, and said Cripps' acceptance of the Ministry of
Aircraft Production was the noblest act of self-abnegation in
public life that he had encountered – or words to that effect. As
for the Ministry of Aircraft Production, where Owen has been for

14

a fortnight, he said he is struck by the amount of hard lying he is encountering.

Owen thinks the Indians should have accepted Cripps' proposals and is certain that Gandhi wrecked the scheme. While Cripps was in India he was the recipient of a very large fan mail, which Owen handled. He said many of the letters had a very sexual tinge (this to Cripps!) and cited one from a station master on the South India Railway, who asked Cripps to lift a spell someone had laid on his wife, as a result of which she was frigid in bed!

December 8, 1942

Had lunch today with Professor Blackett among others. A most intelligent and interesting person, in peacetime Professor of Physics at Manchester University, specializing in cosmic rays, but now Scientific Adviser to the Admiralty. He has a poor opinion of the intellectual powers of admirals. He was himself for eight years in the Navy, including Osborne, Dartmouth, and the last war, but says it is desperately hidebound and professionalized. The Navy, he considers, has fallen down on its job and is now clutching at the Coastal Command and expecting it to do most of the Navy's work. Our bomb design, Blackett said, was frightfully bad. Dingle Foot, who was also there, confirmed this and said that our Secret Service reports used to reveal that as many as seventy per cent of our bombs did not explode in some raids early in the war! Things are now much better and our bombs, like the German, are pretty good, though we are still using up our stocks of poor material.

December 19, 1942

K.M. reports hearing from Lady Violet Bonham Carter that the latter met Mrs Churchill at the Dorchester, at the lunch to celebrate the Beveridge wedding.[9] Lady Violet talked of this and that – and of Darlan, and said how the Grenadier Guards (her son being in that regiment) hated the pictures of the march past of their regiment at Algiers with Darlan, among others, at the saluting base.

Mrs Churchill protested against this; she said the Prime Minister was sore about Darlan but resented having the whole matter kept on the boil like this: the newspapers had published pictures very unnecessarily of this march past, and 'that horrid newspaper, the *Sunday Pictorial*' had gone too far and actually used a sentence, slightly misquoted, from an important speech in the secret debate! The sentence being that Darlan 'should be squeezed dry like an orange and then flung away'. Actually we had been given a D-notice weeks before that we must not say Darlan should not be used; so all we could say was that he should be used, but discarded immediately he ceased to be useful. On November 22 we had had an article about squeezing him like a *lemon* (as in the secret session) and throwing him away, and it was made into an orange last Sunday – not to avoid a straight quote from the secret session (of which we had no verbatim account) but to avoid repetition of a cliché of three weeks earlier. But the incident, trivial in itself, does show how jumpy the Government is. The pictures we used were official hand-outs – issued presumably because the Government wanted us to use them.

1943

Did They Really Die?

FAMOUS AIR CHIEF SIR HUGH DOWDING DECLARES: "I CAN PROVE THEY LIVE ON."

TODAY THE "SUN-DAY PICTORIAL" BEGINS PUBLICATION OF AN EXTRAORDINARY TESTAMENT OF FAITH. AIR CHIEF - MARSHAL SIR HUGH DOWDING, THE MAN WHO LED OUR FIGHTER PILOTS IN THE BATTLE OF BRITAIN, DECLARES THAT HIS BOYS WHO DIED IN THE GLORIOUS EPIC ARE LIVING ON IN A FUTURE WORLD.

Sir Hugh writes: "I believe it because I have in my possession messages from men who have died in this war. And they are messages that could only have come from them . . .".

Sir Hugh supports his astonishing declaration by printing two of these letters. They are incredible documents: intimate, fresh and lively.

"My sole object in giving these messages to the public is so that the bereaved may avoid the black load of grief which is so harmful to themselves and so infinitely distressing to those whom they mourn," he writes.

The "Sunday Pictorial" considers that so distinguished a person as Sir Hugh Dowding is entitled to have his views on this engrossing subject made public. He does not ask you to believe him but merely to read his stories and to form your own opinion. With this we wholeheartedly agree, and so today

ONE OF THE MOST RE-MARKABLE DOCUMENTS THIS NEWSPAPER HAS EVER PUBLISHED BEGINS TODAY ON PAGES 12 & 13

January 1, 1943

Now that we are embarking on a New Year I shall try and sum up the situation as I see it. In the last year we had a series of disasters in the Far East, in Russia, and in Africa, with a turn of the tide some two months ago which certainly leaves the situation looking a great deal more healthy that it did in the summer.

The effect of these various operations is that the importance of this country as a belligerent has greatly decreased. We are now in essence an American bridgehead into Europe. Victory in the Far East will depend on American production of ships and planes, and in Europe on the combination of Russian spirit and American material. Churchill's policy commits us to trailing at America's heels instead of acting, at least, as the balance between Russia and the U.S.

On no view are Russia's strength and Germany's on the increase, but the opposite is true of America, which is getting into action in very leisurely fashion and may well not be all out until 1945. If any serious use of American strength is deferred until then, the Germans and Japs will have had time to develop the enormous potentialities of their occupied territories. For myself, I cannot see how – barring bad accidents or miracles – decisive results can be reached on the eastern front. Surely on some line not very far removed from the present one a state of stalemate will be reached. This should leave the Germans with enough men to police occupied Europe and to ward off any attempted invasion. The enemy is apparently going to try and hold Tunis and Bizerta. If he fails, I expect him to occupy Spain and achieve the same result – command of the Mediterranean – by other means. At sea I don't see how the Germans can starve us out or how we can sink all their submarines.

In fact on the military side it looks to me like a stalemate, in positions roughly similar to the present. If this diagnosis is correct, then the war turns into a trial of moral strength, in which we are not free agents, because of America, while the Germans are liable to be pulled down by the stresses and strains of occupied Europe. The breaking strain of the Americans is lowest, but they are a long way away and won't feel the war directly. The Russian breaking strain is very high, but then from now on they may well have to contend with famine. All in all it seems hardly possible that a result could be looked for till autumn 1944, and the issue is still much more likely than not to be some sort of draw. Unfortunately, under existing circumstances the draw is more likely to suit American views than ours: we have mortgaged so much of our position to America and shall doubtless be made to feel it.

Politically the situation in this country is obscure. The Government enjoys no prestige. Churchill's position is more and more based, not on his merits, but on the lack of an alternative. A House of Commons that let Churchill get away with the loss of Singapore and Burma is unlikely to quibble over the less spectacular events of the months ahead. The situation gradually developing is not one of hostility to him and his party, but one of cynicism and contempt for the whole constitutional bag of tricks. This cynicism cannot come to a head at all quickly at a time when money is good, casualties are low, and rations are ample. It simply means a weakening of the underlying position, which will be revealed whenever a crisis may develop in the future. The House of Commons has lost all confidence in its constitutional position and has become a body of placemen, or at least placehunters. The Opposition group is ineffective as it lacks cohesion, through absence of any very convincing sense of public service.

Miracles may happen, but I see in the developments of the last year a continuance of the steady drift towards a revolutionary situation which has been noticeable for the last fifteen years or so.

It did seem that the greater talents of a Churchill and the compulsion of a war would lead to a reversal of this trend, but to this possibility 1942 has returned a decisive and negative answer. At this rate the revolution will be of the Right and will not come in time to save this country from a catastrophic decline in its world position compared, shall we say, with what it enjoyed in 1925. Politically, in fact, we are in much the same position as France: all existing political personalities and parties are utterly discredited, but nothing is appearing to take their place. The future must be along totalitarian lines; but the Communists, who have the greatest sense of political realism, of self-sacrifice, and of organization, are irremediably committed to a policy subservient to Russia.

In fact politically as well as militarily I should expect a rather inconclusive year, in which the various forces operating beneath the surface will be sorting themselves out. I should not be surprised if a year from now the ostensible position were very much what it now is, but looking ahead had become a good deal easier.

From the beginning of the war both the Mirror *and* Pictorial *stressed that victory must result not only in the defeat of Hitler but in a new Britain, in which the evils of poverty and ignorance would be swept away and there would equal opportunities for all. It was a policy expressed in their slogan: 'We believe in tomorrow.' And they hailed the Beveridge Report as a blueprint for their vision of 'tomorrow'.*

After his conversation with Cripps in October 1942, Cecil King determined that both papers should give the Beveridge Report their full support. And they did. They also became suspicious, with some justification, of the Government's attitude towards it. They warned their readers that the Government was paying nothing more than lip service to the virtues of the Report and would whittle away the scheme if they could, to leave the mere pittance that hard-headed Conservative economists thought the country could afford.

A three-day debate on Beveridge took place in February. An Amendment was moved by which more enthusiastic support for the scheme was demanded from the Government. The Amendment was defeated. But all except two of the Labour Members of Parliament who were not in office voted for it – though the Labour ministers in the Government voted against.

Churchill could not ignore the problem of post-war reconstruction. The Beveridge Report had captured the imagination of the public, and on the day it was published a queue a mile long formed outside the Stationery Office. A committee of civil servants was formed to draft legislation based on the Beveridge plan. In September 1944 two White Papers closely following Beveridge were produced on the social services. In November 1943 Churchill appointed a Minister of Reconstruction, Lord Woolton, who spoke favourably on the scheme. But not all this could banish suspicions that the Conservatives were opposed to the Beveridge Report. This was to be a decisive factor in the Labour landslide of 1945.

January 21, 1943

Had Shinwell to lunch today, a very shrewd little man and a great fighter. On political matters, he thinks there will be a real flare-up if the Beveridge Report is not accepted substantially as it stands. There is to be a three-day debate in the House in mid-February, and a lot of the Tories are already recruiting opposition to it.

Shinwell had recently had some talk with Cripps, and asked him what he made of the Herbert Morrison appointment to the War Cabinet. Cripps said Churchill now had the War Cabinet where he had always wanted it. Every member of it except Anderson is now so cluttered up with departmental responsibilities that policy and the conduct of the war are left entirely to Churchill. This is an amusing sequel to the campaign which has been running ever since he took office as Prime Minister, to urge on him the necessity of a small War Cabinet of members without departments. He now has a large War Cabinet of men of straw, all too busy to bother him.

February 2, 1943

The most important news is the surrender in Stalingrad of General, now Field Marshal, Paulus and about a dozen other generals. There are still a few pockets of resistance in the town, but the German army at Stalingrad has been destroyed. The Russians say that it totalled 330,000 men. Without taking these figures too seriously, we can say that the Germans have sustained their greatest defeat since 1918. It has been a triumph of endurance by the Russians, backed up by good generalship.

February 18, 1943
The political scene has indeed livened up these last few days. I am writing in the middle of the last of three days' debate on Beveridge. The first Government spokesman was Anderson, who said the Government accepted most of the Report in principle, and then proceeded to make it quite clear that no legislation was to be passed till the end of the war and that what he had said about Government intentions would have to be revised in the light of financial possibilities at that time. This struck Bill Greig, who was in the House, as going further than had been expected! However, it did not satisfy the Socialists, who were insistent that Anderson had only promised to do something (if possible) some time. With this Government's reputation for procrastination and broken pledges, that was not good enough. Then yesterday the Government spokesman was Kingsley Wood, who made a silly speech which satisfied no one.

It was then concluded that unless the Prime Minister intervened today with a conciliatory speech promising at least the appointment of a Minister of Social Reconstruction as a first step, there would be a revolt by the Socialists and a major political crisis. However, Churchill this morning is said to be in bed with a 'feverish cold', which is widely taken to mean that he is not going to budge an inch, and has not got the courage to come down to the House and say so.

Meanwhile, the Parliamentary Labour Party had a very stormy meeting this morning. They were addressed by Bevin, who made an astonishingly reactionary speech. He said he was not in favour of a lot of the Beveridge Report anyway. In particular he didn't like the children's allowances or the workmen's compensation provisions, and saw no reason for disturbing doctors' private practices. This speech whipped up the Party to a state of real indignation, and when it came to a vote to decide whether or no to vote against the Government on this issue, only ten hands were raised (in a very full meeting) against opposing the Government.

Later

Campbell is just back from the House, where the vote on the Amendment (demanding the immediate preparation of legislation implementing the Beveridge Report) went 335–119 in favour of the Government. The vote was about as expected in favour of the Amendment, but the Government got many more votes than was anticipated. It appears that the Labour vote was stronger than was expected – about a hundred – but few Liberals and no Tories went with them. In spite of the fact that many Tories spoke against the Government in the debate, they did not even abstain, let alone vote against the Government, when it came to a division.

Shinwell was delighted with the turn of events: thinks most of the Labour leaders will rat on the Party, and that there will soon be the great bulk of the Labour Party, in opposition, winning most of the by-elections. On the other hand I think this division of the House on old-fashioned party lines is unfortunate. I would much rather see a young progressive group formed from members of all parties. Shinwell thinks that the present storm will blow itself out, but that a split – with most of the leaders in the Government, and most of the Socialists in opposition – is a question of months, if not weeks.

In the lobby it was said that Herbert Morrison had really fought for Beveridge; Attlee and Bevin did not. Morrison made a clever winding-up speech addressed entirely to the Tories. It is not thought on the figures for the voting that the Government will make any concessions. Churchill is said now to be quite seriously ill, and to have had doctors to and fro quite frequently for a whole week.

February 21, 1943

Aneurin Bevan told Campbell that he is well aware that he and his wife, Jennie Lee, will be 'on the run' one day, and that with this in mind they have hidden five £100 notes in the garden of their Berkshire cottage, so as to be prepared if the moment arises unexpectedly. Of course Nye has an active imagination, and in any case the story may be untrue, but it gives some idea of the prevailing feeling of political uncertainty among the more progressive figures in public life.

February 23, 1943

I met Lord Leathers [*Minister of War Transport*] at lunch. Afterwards I walked with him back to his Ministry (it was then 3.30
and he said he had a meeting at 3.0!), and he started talking
about his trip to Casablanca, which he wouldn't have missed for
worlds, in spite of an appalling journey there and back. I asked
him if the President, when conducting business, had made a
favourable impression comparable with that which he made on
the world in general as a politician. He said definitely no; Roosevelt is extremely friendly and buoyant, and this coupled with his
flair for American politics has got him where he is. He has nothing
like the grip of Churchill on the problems that confronted them
all. And then there were the odd people the President had around
him, notably Harry Hopkins, whose influence on every aspect of
American affairs except the army and navy seemed to be considerable. Leathers evidently regarded Hopkins as a lamentable
little man. He volunteered the information that while he liked
Averell Harriman, whom he had to deal with every day, he
couldn't say that he had any high opinion of his capacity.

February 26, 1943

I bought a lunch today for David Owen, Cripps' secretary. He is
not an impressive man, but evidently reads all the Government
papers and knows what is going on. He says Morrison really did
fight for Beveridge in the Cabinet and that, but for him, the
Treasury would have had it all its own way. Owen thinks that if
the pressure on the Government is maintained, legislation will
be put before the House of Commons this year. He says Bevin is
against the appointment of a Minister for Social Security as he
feels this would encroach on his own position as Minister of
Labour.

Cripps feels that he is dissociated in the public mind from any
domestic legislation, and to strengthen his position in this respect
refused to attend any Cabinet meeting at which the Beveridge
Report was under discussion. If he resigns now, it will be on a
question of principle affecting his department. This is not, in my
opinion, very likely to arise.

I cross-examined Owen on what is Cripps' view of his political future. He said that Cripps now considers himself detached; and that when the Government breaks down over some issue, the country and the King cannot very well turn to someone outside the Government as the critics do not carry sufficient weight, so they will try someone in the Government who has stood aloof from controversial issues – that is, Cripps. I said that if by chance the Government had been defeated in the Beveridge debate, it would have resigned; the King would then have sent for Churchill, who would have dropped Attlee and Kingsley Wood, admitted a few of the rebels, and gone on as before. If the Prime Minister's pneumonia had been fatal the King would have sent for Eden, or just possibly Hudson, but I didn't see how, either way, Cripps came into the picture. In any case, 'aloof' or not, Cripps voted with the Government on Beveridge (Owen admitted this), and that fact puts him in a ridiculous position. Owen indicated that though he agreed with this statement of the case, he had only been reporting Cripps' view.

March 10, 1943

On Sunday [March 7] I did my first spell of fire watching, 6.0 p.m. to 6.0 a.m. I was told my beat would be Raymond Buildings in Gray's Inn, and the fire watcher's post would be at No 6. I turned up at the air-raid warden's post in Bedford Row about 6.10 to find a woman in charge. We chatted away. None of the other fire watchers had turned up, so I stayed till 6.30, when the first man strolled in. I then moved off to Raymond Buildings, where I expected to spend the night with my two fellows.

I found a rather ill-looking man of middle age with a white face, red nose, and Irish accent, stoking up the fire. His main interest was in football pools. He started denouncing the income tax and I eventually discovered that he was a whole-time fire watcher, for which he got £4 a week. He slept there six nights a week. In the daytime he had 'a little job' which is apparently somewhat shady. At least he gave me the impression he is not paying income tax on both his wages. Some time after 7.0 his mate came in, a man with tattooed hands and a strong Glasgow accent. He, too, fire-watched for six nights and had a 'little job'. After a time they disappeared, I thought for a drink. But apparently it was for a consultation. The Scot came back and pointed out that there were only two bunks – theirs – and that it was usual ('mind you, I am not telling you!') to go home, emerging if there was an air-raid alarm, or in any case at 6.0 a.m. So off I went and slept on the sofa till 1.0 a.m., when there was an alarm. I flew off and got to the top of the basement staircase at No 6 as soon as they did, and just as the shrapnel started dropping. It was nothing of a raid – only one plane got over London – so I soon went back again home, waking at 5.45 in time to return to No 6 to clock off, and subsequently to the warden's post. At neither place was anyone awake.

Of course London has had only three night alerts since May 10, 1941, so it is to be expected that there would be a lack of interest and efficiency. In my particular case, I am asked to protect a block of buildings with the aid of two others: (a) they are horrible old buildings in the grimmest 19th-century manner and would be much better burnt; (b) if a shower of incendiaries fell on the block we could certainly not cope with the situation; (c) why should we risk our lives guarding a building which we don't own and where we neither work nor live? It is moreover entirely surrounded by gardens, so a fire there could not extend to more important premises.

For the Allies in North Africa there was one more major battle to fight. Rommel had retreated to Tunisia, where he joined up with Axis forces already there. He was faced with an enemy advancing from east and west and now under the supreme command of an American, General Eisenhower; with Alexander, his deputy, commanding all land forces; Tedder the air; Cunningham the sea; and Montgomery the victorious Eighth Army.

The Germans showed enterprise and fight. They beat off an attack from the west, but when Montgomery advanced rapidly from the east and linked up with the western forces the situation altered. By April, after heavy fighting, the Axis forces were driven into northern Tunisia and concentrated around Tunis and Bizerta. Meanwhile heavy German reinforcements poured in, for Hitler was determined not to lose his foothold in North Africa. But it only meant he had more to lose, so that when at the beginning of May Tunis fell to the British and Bizerta to the Americans, 250,000 Axis prisoners were taken. It was a great victory, and again the church bells rang out in Britain.

March 19, 1943

Campbell had lunch today with a War Office friend of his, and some talk with a lieutenant-colonel just back from Algiers. From his Tunisian experience this man said the Americans are at present useless, rather like the Italians. They can organize transport well and repair tanks well, but as fighters they just don't compete. The soldiers are bad material badly trained, and the officers give a most unfavourable impression – with the single exception of Eisenhower.

April 2, 1943

Cudlipp arrived in the office today. I hadn't seen him for quite a year, since when he has been in Rommel's final thrust at Alexandria from El Alamein and in our advance to Tripoli, a lot of the time with the general commanding our Seventh Armoured Division. He arrived by air yesterday from Marrakesh, direct to Scotland and so to Hendon. His first impression is that people here look tired and have very white faces. He is filled with admiration for Montgomery, and considers that his austerity and devotion to his job have had a tonic effect on the troops under his command.

In Egypt, Cudlipp says, the government is pro-Italian and the place is crawling with fifth columnists. In Algiers he was appalled by the utter indifference of the French people. The administration is full of Fascists; there is no goodwill towards the Americans or ourselves; the restaurants are full of young loungers doing nothing; Giraud is an old man quite incapable of dealing with the situation. People out there told Cudlipp that Algiers is really an outlying part of France. He thought this looked true and that in that case the French are utterly demoralized.

The Americans have no sort of idea of what they are up against, and seem to imagine that when we have taken Bizerta they will all be able to go home. The concern of their senior officers is with 'welfare', which seems to cover food, drink, games, and whores, but fighting hardly enters their heads. The villages of North Africa are full of American soldiers dancing in the streets or sitting in cafés with tarts on their knees. Cudlipp does not see how

they can ever be made into good soldiers, and contempt for
everything to do with them is universal in our Army out there.

April 14, 1943
Back in Aberdeenshire for a few days, where I met an old friend
just back from India. She went to Durban from Bombay in a
troopship, spent two and a half weeks there, subsequently two
and a half months in Capetown, and so home in an Orient liner
which stopped en route in South America. She said the sinkings
round the Cape were very bad when she was there; and she had
to go to Durban to the Cape by sea, because the trains are so
crowded you have to book your seat a month in advance if you
want to go anywhere by rail. Her steward on the Orient liner had
been torpedoed three times and spent a fortnight in an open boat,
so she asked him whether the contents of her emergency bag were
sensible. He approved generally but urged her to take a mirror,
comb, toothbrush, and book, as these had been immensely sought
after in the lifeboat!

Apparently the English in India, in spite of all the shocks they
have had, are very complacent and not appreciably war-minded
even now!

April 18, 1943
Cudlipp had an article on the Eighth Army in last Sunday's
Sunday Pictorial and was rung up by Beaverbrook with a message
from the Prime Minister congratulating him.

Cudlipp had lunch with his brother and others at the Savage
Club and met A.V. Alexander. Alexander struck him as being a
sound little man wafted up far and away above the utmost limits
of his capacity. He will therefore cling to office with both hands
and both feet, as he can have no hope that a series of happy
chances could so exalt him a second time. Anyway, at 4.0 p.m.
Percy Cudlipp, editor of the *Herald*, A.V. Alexander, First Lord of
the Admiralty, and Hugh Cudlipp were all singing Baptist hymns
(A.V. Alexander at the piano) at the Savage Club – all of them
being at least slightly drunk.

Cudlipp also met Quintin Hogg, who is trying to get his
15

committee of progressive Conservatives going. Cudlipp thought
him intelligent and amusing but too small a personality to get
away with anything much.

*March 1943 was a losing month in the Battle of the Atlantic, with nearly
500,000 tons of shipping lost and only twelve sunken U-boats to show for it.
The following interview which Stuart Campbell, editor of the* Sunday
Pictorial, *had with Lord Woolton, Minister of Food, reflects the gravity
of the situation. After April, however, things improved. America provided
hundreds of destroyers for escort duties, and Coastal Command attacked
U-boats in the Bay of Biscay with great success. By the end of the year
British shipping losses had decreased dramatically.*

April 29, 1943
Campbell saw Woolton last night to ask him about the food
position. It appears that a couple of months ago or so, our wheat
stocks were down to four and a half weeks' supply. Since then
they have been built up to eighteen months' supply, and with the
increasing quantities of adulterants (oats and barley mainly) he
hoped to get through till next spring. He hoped he would not have
to mix potato with the flour, but would certainly do so if necessary.
Last month, when shipping losses were high, he had a run of
luck and few food ships were touched. His sugar stocks are not so
good as those of wheat – say about twelve weeks – but meat is his
chief worry. He does not propose to cut the meat ration, but
more of it will consist of bully beef. Butter may fizzle out, but
margarine rations will be increased to make up.

His scientists advise him (a) that only a small minority of people
feed out, and (b) that for those who feed at home present rations
are only barely adequate. He thinks he can see ahead to next
spring (even allowing for having all his shipping taken for six
weeks for the next military operation) without any cut in the basic
ration. 'Points' may be trimmed a bit, but all foods on points are
semi-luxuries. To keep up the supply of fats for margarine in *1945*
he is having a special crop of oil beans grown in West Africa now.
It was his scientists who worked out the production of dried eggs,
and they have done great work on dehydrated meat. This last
will be distributed only to restaurants, as its preparation involves

too great difficulty for the housewife. This story strikes me as convincing and cheering.

May 7, 1943
Horabin, M.P. for Cornwall, came in this morning to discuss a possible article in the Pic. He had one or two good stories. He said that early in 1939 he was campaigning for Churchill as premier – but Churchill asked him not to, as he didn't feel up to the job! When Horabin told Admiral Keyes this, Keyes said Churchill and he had had their great defeat at Gallipoli, but whereas he, Keyes, had had a chance to regain his self-confidence over Zeebrugge, Churchill had had no Zeebrugge: and his failure to deal with vermin like Simon and Kingsley Wood was fundamentally a lack of self-confidence stemming from Gallipoli.

Another good remark of Horabin's was that people say they are willing to *die* for their ideas, but what we want are some people prepared to *kill* for their ideals. He thought a large part of the population had contracted spiritually out of the war, and regarded this as a very bad sign from any point of view. This development was most conspicuous among the miners – where 5,000 more miners are producing substantially less coal than at this time last year – but the tendency was widespread.

May 8, 1943
Tunis and Bizerta have fallen! You could have knocked me down with a feather! Apparently the First Army attacked at dawn on Thursday [May 6] and captured both towns yesterday at about four o'clock. The War Office last night seemed as surprised as anyone else.

May 19, 1943
I saw Geoff [*Captain Geoffrey Norman*] again for the first time since the autumn of 1940. He has been Chief of Staff in the Mediterranean all this time and he now has a command at home. The man who impressed him most in that time – far more than Churchill – was Smuts. He said Smuts arrived and summed the position up very quickly. At that time nothing very much was happening, and he urged on Churchill, and through him on

Roosevelt, the absolute necessity of clearing the Germans out of North Africa before anything else was undertaken. He assembled the generals and other brass hats and lectured them like schoolboys – producing a marvellous effect.

Geoff saw a lot of Auchinleck: spent three days with him in the desert when the Germans were threatening Alexandria. At no time did the Auk waver in his conviction that the Germans would not reach Alex. He was apparently almost forced to take the job, which he didn't want and didn't consider himself fitted for, and Geoff felt that he has had less than his due. Wavell was thought out there to be quite first class but rather past his best. Montgomery is known as 'Monty the Mountebank' and is rated very, very high as a general, but his publicity-seeking antics are not liked. He is said to be supremely ambitious and only to be kept in bounds when soundly kicked every month. Alexander has not made much of an impression; is thought to be a bit wrapped up in punctilio.

There is little co-operation between the services. Geoff himself was at one conference at which Cunningham (quite correctly as it turned out) said that in his opinion the situation at Malta would continue to deteriorate until they got some Spitfires. Tedder sprang to his feet and took the strongest possible exception to this remark: he never interfered with the Navy, why should Cunningham criticize his service, and so on.

The Americans know nothing and will not learn from us. The French Admiral told Geoff that when the Americans landed at one town in North Africa, they overcame what little opposition there was on the beaches and then marched towards the town four abreast. They came to a crossroads where there was one Frenchman with one machine gun. He waited till they came near and mowed them down. They withdrew, reformed, and came on again in column four abreast: they were again mown down by this one Frenchman. They actually did it a third time and had some hundreds of casualties before someone thought of a tank, and even then they ran down the machine gun and squashed it, but the Froggie escaped!

Winster had lunch with Lloyd George yesterday, who said that

Winston was like an elephant – an elephant pulling a load of teak through the jungle: he doesn't know where or why, but he is going on pulling his load all the same! Lloyd George says the cards are stacked all wrong and he doesn't see how we can pick a winning hand. In any case he is quite sure Winston can't. He flatly denies that we have any grand strategy or that we have any idea what to do with our victory in Tunis.

May 26, 1943

We had a strange visit in the office this afternoon. Sir Hugh ('Stuffy') Dowding is to publish three articles in the *Sunday Pictorial* about spirit messages from dead R.A.F. men, communicated by automatic writing to a Mrs Hill, daughter of a Colonel Gascoyne, an old friend of his!

Dowding is most unimpressive to meet, a slow man with a dull eye who looks much older than he is; Mrs Hill a nice woman, very 'county'; and both obviously quite sincere. The spirit messages they have taken down are to me quite unimpressive, and they are unable to identify any of the senders. In fact the story is the most usual spiritualistic stuff, but the fact that it was brought to us by Dowding, who sponsors it, makes it sensational. From a casual meeting it would be hard to imagine anyone less suitable for the post of Commander-in-Chief Fighter Command in time of war!

May 31, 1943

I am now getting the annual reports for 1942 of various insurance companies in which I am interested. They all tell the same story – abnormally low death claims, even when one includes all deaths from enemy action. Of course the young men in the services cannot insure, so the youngest groups of war deaths are excluded, but whatever way one looks at it the number of deaths, war or no war, is well below average. This result is attributed (a) to the better standard of nutrition due to rationing, and (b) to the sulphonamide group of drugs, which have virtually extinguished some very lethal diseases. The idea of a war with *lowered* mortality seems to me to be a sensational one!

June 3, 1943

London is now blossoming with coloured posters of heroes of the past: Drake and William Pitt spring to my mind. Whenever they appear there is placed alongside a similar print of Churchill! Only yesterday R.A. Butler spoke of our 'immortal premier', so evidently the old man's vanity is in no sort of decline.

Bishop Barnes of Birmingham, whom I regard as an able and saintly man, though no diplomatist, has been having a crack at the morals of the present day, laying particular stress on the increasing amount of lying prevalent everywhere. Other bishops at the same meeting stressed (as they would) the growing sexual laxity, and all expressed considerable alarm about the future.

Why I take such a poor view of Churchill and his colleagues is that amid all the boasting no attempt is being made really to rebuild the moral greatness of this country, and that in all essentials the situation is getting worse, not better. Supine appeals for American help are no way out of our difficulties. In whatever role we eventually find ourselves we must stand on our own feet, and our rulers must be men whose character commands respect and whose policy is sound. I see at present no force in politics making for this highly desirable result. Graft and incompetence in politics are on the increase; sectional interests are growing more, not less, powerful; private morality is disappearing and the public interest is a cause which is hardly worth lip service.

June 12, 1943

On Thursday evening I found myself at a loose end in Leicester Square with M., and saw *The Life and Death of Colonel Blimp* was advertised. I knew this was a new film and asked if it was being shown yet. This was, it appeared, the world première and there were some seats available, so we got a couple of tickets and found ourselves sitting near Major Astor of *The Times* at the back of the dress circle. When the show was over (good colour, indifferent film), being at the back, we got out quickly and found ourselves in the front of the theatre in the centre of a big space kept clear by police. At that moment out of the main door popped Mrs Churchill, as good-looking as ever, and the Prime Minister

looking balder and more bent. I didn't see who were in the other
cars as the crowd was too thick. Suddenly I turned round and
there was Londonderry, the biggest B.F. you ever saw, followed by
Wavell, obviously his guest, and both slinking out of the door we
had used. Wavell in mufti with regimental tie, without monocle or
glass eye, looked a good man and strong, but old and worn –
obviously quite beyond his present job (Commander-in-Chief
India). M. said to him: 'It's you they want to see, not the politicians.' He seemed disturbed at being recognized and made off
to his car, but no one else recognized him in spite of all the
photographs that have been published!

June 15, 1943
Campbell has had some talk at lunch with 'Stuffy' Dowding. He
was full of talk about his spirits, but also at the end of lunchtime
held forth about the Air Ministry. He says he was responsible for
the Spitfire, for its armament of eight machine guns, and for the
preliminary plans of the Typhoon [*rocket-firing fighter plane*]. He
attributes his retirement to Lindemann, who has his knife into
him.

Apparently, shortly before the war Dowding was chairman of
the Aeronautical Research Council, of which Lindemann was a
member, but so spiteful and so troublesome was he that he was
dropped by Dowding from the Council when he came up for re-
election about 1937. Disgruntled Lindemann got together with
disgruntled Churchill, and that is how Churchill got a lot of his
information. Then, in 1940, Lindemann had Churchill's ear and
it was only a matter of time before Dowding was out.

Dowding thought nothing of our Air Ministers, from the last
war to Sinclair – except Swinton. He said Swinton was ousted by
Nuffield (I heard this at the time) and Kingsley Wood, and that
is why Kingsley Wood got Swinton's job.

Dowding thinks we are doing far too little research, and that
the delays attending the production of the Typhoon were quite
inexcusable. He is under the impression that the Germans are
lying low in the air this year and allowing their output to fall
behind, with a view to a smashing technical superiority next year.
If the war goes on long enough, he does think there is anyway a

serious danger of the Germans wresting technical superiority from us.

He said that the Germans in the Battle of Britain threw everything they had at us, and that there was a riot on one Belgian station when German fighter pilots were asked to go on their fourth sortie in twenty-four hours. In his view the decisive factor was his eight-machine-gun fighter against German planes which at that period were unarmoured.

I put these forward as Dowding's ideas and opinions. To me he is so unimpressive that I feel convinced there is another (and very different) side to most of this, even where, as in the technical points, I have no information of my own.

The tide of war had turned. In the Far East the American General MacArthur's forces were busy recapturing the islands of the South Pacific. The Russians had gone over to the offensive. Although in March the Germans recaptured Kharkov, the Red Army's summer offensive brought colossal gains. By August the Russians were back in Kharkov, and in September Smolensk fell. By October the Russians had reached the Dnieper, and in November they entered Kiev, capital of the Ukraine. It had been a gigantic battle, involving over 500 divisions. The Pictorial, *an ardent supporter of the Red Army, labelled the fighting around the Dnieper 'the greatest battle in the history of the world'.*

The Russians were anxious to see the British and Americans involved as soon as possible in northern France. But the much longed-for Second Front did not open in 1943. Instead the Allies invaded Sicily in July and captured it in a month, the direct result being the overthrow of Mussolini by his own Fascist party and the setting up of a new government under Marshal Badoglio, which opened secret negotiations for peace.

From August 14 to 24 Churchill and Roosevelt met in Quebec to discuss future strategy. Churchill wanted to invade the Italian mainland, and was still reluctant to proceed immediately with the Second Front in the north, perhaps because of his belief, already shown by his enthusiastic backing of the Dardanelles campaign (1915), that an indirect blow could be as decisive as and less costly than a major confrontation of land forces. Roosevelt authorized the invasion of the Italian mainland, but only on the condition that plans for the invasion of northern France in 1944, Operation Overlord, were put into action immediately.

At the beginning of September the Allies landed in southern Italy, shortly before an armistice with Italy was announced. The Germans reacted quickly, and managed to occupy most of the country, so presenting the Allies with the painful and costly task described by Alexander (commander of the land forces) as 'slogging up Italy'.

July 3, 1943

Walters (our New York correspondent) has an Australian wife and has met a lot of the Australian editors now in London. Their pro-American feeling has entirely evaporated. They refer to General MacArthur as 'Chocko', short for 'Chocolate Soldier'. He apparently gives long press conferences criticizing British generalship in North Africa! He went to New Guinea at the end of the campaign from Port Moresby. He was put up in the Governor's house, while the Governor made do with a grass hut. He didn't consider the sanitation adequate, so had a bath and lavatory bowl, with necessary plumbing, flown from Australia!

An American division in New Guinea was so cowardly that it had to be sent home to California, and it was only thanks to the Australians that the situation was saved. In America these soldiers were told by a general to thank God for the censorship, which would conceal their shame. The whole division had to be disbanded and the men dispersed to other units.

The *Daily Express* today excelled itself with a leader ridiculing the importance of damage to architectural monuments in Europe and referring to Cologne cathedral and similar treasures as 'picture-postcard stuff'. *Reynolds'* in their leader for tomorrow take up an equally philistine attitude. All this is apropos of a speech by Dean Inge who mildly said that if we destroyed the architectural treasures of Europe we should be sorry, as they were our heritage as well as that of Italy and Germany.

July 10, 1943

Campbell had a sudden call from Bracken at 4.10 yesterday afternoon to come and see him at 6.0. There was a good deal of talk and then Bracken said if Campbell came back later he would meet a couple of generals, who would tell him about the big attack which was planned for last night. Soon after 8.0 Campbell met the generals, who told him that our paratroops would land at midnight (our time) on Sicily. They said the night would be dark with a good deal of cloud and they could not be sure of equally favourable conditions in August. They said the Germans had just sent two army corps to Sicily, bringing up the total forces on the island to at least 300,000; that they had strongly reinforced the Luftwaffe in that area and had formidable beach defences at every possible landing point. The generals implied plainly that the rapidity with which the Germans and Italians were improving their defences had hastened the hour of attack. They said we should know on Tuesday [July 13] how it was all going and that if all went well, further attacks on Sardinia and on the mainland of Italy would follow.

11.0 p.m.

We have just had an unexpected communiqué saying our landings extend over a hundred miles of the south-east Sicilian coast, and are going according to plan. Already by 8.0 a.m. this morning artillery was being landed. The Axis powers have said little enough all day and that very cautiously. I interpret this latest pronouncement as *good* news, though of course we are not even half way through the wood yet. The enemy claims to have wiped out all our parachutists, of whom there is no news at all from our end. It is significant of Anglo-American relations that this latest communiqué, the only news of our great venture, is put out at an hour primarily to suit the convenience of the American, not our, newspapers.

July 26, 1943

Got back to London last night after a long day in Winchester, in which I had been out of touch with the news. I listened in at midnight rather sleepily to learn that Mussolini's resignation had just been announced over the Italian wireless and that Badoglio had taken his place!

Badoglio is primarily a soldier, the only good one the Italians appear to possess. It may be that with the loss of most of Sicily the higher-ups in Italy are insisting on better military leadership than Musso has provided. He has constantly changed the military and naval commanders, but so far without finding one winner. At the same time it must be dangerous at a critical moment to sling out of office a man who has been the government of Italy for twenty-one years. Hitler must feel it very much, as from the days of *Mein Kampf* he has always spoken of Mussolini in terms of respect, and almost of affection. There have been stories for a long time past of Mussolini and a succession of young mistresses; of Musso boosting his failing vitality with aphrodisiacs; and he may of course just be failing.

There is no news of Mussolini today, but this presumably marks the end of his career – a few days short of his sixtieth birthday. At present he is a figure of fun in the English newspapers but I doubt whether he will go down to history in that light. In the development of the totalitarian state, his Fascist party played a part, uniting the experience of the Russian Communists and the Roman Catholic Church in the development of what may be called either 'Order' or 'Right-wing Politics'. What got him down in the end was the administrative incompetence of his government, better though it was than its predecessors, and his inability to instil any self-respect into the Italian people, at any rate in the time he had at his disposal.

Bart has just returned from a visit to the main submarine base near Dunoon. Apparently some Russian naval units, including submarines, recently came on a visit. This was not a success: our men were horrified by the severity of Russian punishments; the Russians thought our men lacked discipline – were too democratic! They didn't approve of the mixed dances for officers and men.

Among the boats up there was a French one. Recently the captain had six months to fill in while his ship was being repaired, so he decided to spend some time with his wife in Paris. He was dropped by parachute, spent two months with his wife, and returned via Spain!

Yesterday I went to Winchester College chapel for the first time since 1919. What struck me very forcibly was the immense power that lay in these 450 boys. When they sang they put more punch into it than ten times the number of people in St Paul's would do. This vigour properly directed could indeed move mountains. How foolish we are not to use the force of our youth, but to leave so much to the logic-chopping and hair-splitting of a lot of impotent old men.

July 31, 1943

It is officially announced in Algiers that Giraud is to be Commander-in-Chief of all Free French troops and that de Gaulle is to be permanent president of the French Committee of Defence. De Gaulle also seems to have strengthened his position on the main French Committee of Liberation. This seems a common-sense solution, but as it strengthens de Gaulle's hand it is unlikely to be popular in Washington. A document has recently been published in the U.S., which Churchill admitted in the House was authentic. This document is a statement of the Prime Minister's views and is for the guidance of British officials in America. The paper states that de Gaulle has left behind him, wherever he has gone, a 'trail of Anglophobia', that he shows signs of acting out of personal ambition, and that he is to be supported only with great caution.

August 4, 1943

Had lunch with Wilfrid Roberts today. He tells me he was recently invited to a very confidential meeting of M.P.s and peers to consider a negotiated peace with Germany. He said the gathering was very funny – like a nudist party, in which each man came out very frankly in his true colours. Stokes wanted to stop the war to prevent the bombing of Rome (he is a Catholic); the Duke of Bedford was just pacifist; while Maxton took the rather unexpected line that it was difficult to come to terms with a country that had no social philosophy, but that the Nazis had such a philosophy, so a deal could be done.

My view about a negotiated peace is (and always has been) that it is highly desirable if a favourable moment presents itself. Such a moment has not come yet, but it is far more to our advantage that a reasonable peace should be established by negotiation than that we should dictate terms to a crushed Germany. If this takes place, Germany (and subsequently Japan) will be undervalued in the subsequent international set-up, America and Russia will be overvalued, and the seeds of another world war will be well and truly planted.

August 19, 1943
Have not written up this diary for some days as I have been in Scotland coping with the very wet opening of the grouse season. When one is right away from London one realizes how hard it is to form any opinion of what is happening from the newspapers.

The idea is now prevalent that the war will be over by Christmas. This is based partly on our occupation of Sicily and partly on our bombing; also, but to a much less extent, partly on the Russian successes. I would put it the other way round. The Russian attack on the eastern front may so wear down the Germans as to achieve decisive success, either now or in the winter. Our victory in Sicily is mainly of naval importance, as it partly frees the Mediterranean route to the east and gives us a greater degree of control of the central area of the Mediterranean. Bombing will reduce German production and cause much hardship and dislocation, but I have not seen any evidence that it will produce decisive results, or anything like them.

August 23, 1943
With the Prime Minister in Quebec is Mary Churchill [*his daughter*], nominally on duty. This has caused great resentment here. We have made no comment in the papers, but have received a lot of letters. Why does the Prime Minister do these things?

September 12, 1943
The terms of the Italian armistice were announced today, with some facts about the negotiations, which began about a fortnight after Badoglio became Prime Minister and lasted a *whole* month, mostly in Lisbon. Eisenhower in an interview today made a rather apologetic statement, saying that the surrender of the Italian fleet was worth the time lost in negotiating the armistice, and that when the terms were agreed Badoglio was in a position

to carry them out (though this had now been modified by the latest German movements). One of the astonishing things about this war has been the immense overvaluation by our admirals of the French and Italian fleets, which from first to last have proved complete white elephants.

September 23, 1943
Cecilia [Sempill] came to lunch very concerned at the increasingly hostile feelings of the man in the street towards the Americans. One of Cecilia's friends, an A.T. [*member of the women's Auxiliary Territorial Service: the A.T.S.*], was walking in the park when she saw one of our generals and two very sloppy American soldiers approaching each other. She watched to see whether the soldiers would salute, but was taken aback when one soldier said to the general: 'Well, skirty-pants, who's winning the war now?' The fact that no hint of this feeling is allowed to appear in the papers does not reduce the intensity of the feelings involved.

September 25, 1943
The Cabinet changes consequent on Kingsley Wood's death are out this morning. Anderson goes to the Exchequer, there is a general shuffle, and Beaverbrook, of late an active critic of much of the Government's policy, returns to the Government – but not to the War Cabinet – as Lord Privy Seal!

October 6, 1943
Had lunch today with David Owen, Cripps' secretary. He is very cautious but I gleaned the following bits: (1) Cripps is thinking of resigning over our lack of an Indian policy. Has probably been headed off this, but will look round for a sharper issue nearer home. Would like to lead a political group composed of the progressives of all parties. (2) Together with several other ministers he was dismayed by the inclusion of Beaverbrook in the Government. Bitter complaints to the Prime Minister were made by more than one minister. So far Beaverbrook has been assigned only civil aviation, but as he says himself: 'I have certain explosive qualities.' Bevin thinks that he will be the cause of inner friction

in the Government which will lead to important resignations in the course of the next two or three months. At the moment both Beaverbrook and the Prime Minister are at pains to avoid giving offence. (3) Owen had read in the Cabinet papers all about the rocket threat. The Government's scientific advisers say the rockets cannot be radio-controlled at ranges of a hundred miles, and the Government's present attitude is to warn the civil defence authorities but in general to pooh-pooh the whole thing. (4) Bevin's plan for boys for the coalmines is to seek for volunteers, and he hopes to get twenty per cent of the public-school boys to take on this work. Surely this is an optimistic estimate?

Disturbing reports of secret weapons which Hitler was planning to unleash against Britain had been finding their way to the Government. These statements were not at first believed, but though they had exaggerated the destructive properties of the mysterious weapons, they were proved in the event to have been very near the truth. For the weapons in question were the flying bombs and rockets – the V1s and V2s (V: Vergeltungswaffe: revenge weapon) – which were to fall with alarming effect on southern England in 1944.

October 12, 1943
Campbell has just returned from a Ministry of Information editors' conference, at which Bracken presided and Herbert Morrison spoke; the theme – rockets. Morrison said that reports have been reaching the Government for some time of the elaboration of a new German weapon based on the rocket principle. On the one hand a wealth of information, even of detail, had been received. On the other hand the Government's scientific advisers, for the first time unanimous, had considered the construction of such a weapon to be impracticable.

The very wealth of detail coming from our Secret Service and from neutral sources made us wonder whether we were not having a fake planted on us. We have a drawing of the weapon, which seems to be a kind of gun. It has a barrel, but in other respects is more like our Z-guns in the Park. It is said to fire a projectile which at the start of its flight is thirty-eight feet long and seven to eight feet in diameter. It is loaded with ten tons of an explosive more powerful than any we possess, and has a range of 120 to 150 miles. Our 8,000-pound bombs devastate 320 acres, but it is not known how much greater the area would be in the case of these very much larger projectiles. It is not a very accurate weapon, so would presumably be used in the first place against London or Birmingham.

The Government has called for a considered report on the whole question of these rockets and expects one from its scientists in three weeks. In the meantime they are sceptical, though inclined to think there may be something in the reports. The rockets would take but three minutes en route, and so no system of air-raid warnings would do. It is assumed that they would be released from somewhere on the French coast, but it is not known where from. Original reports spoke of an attack in August; it had been deferred and deferred and now there was talk of the spring.

Morrison asked the assembled editors as experts on public opinion what they think the Government should do. He did not, however, wait for their reply, but said the Government thought the whole story might have been fabricated as a Nazi morale-raiser, and that we should only be playing their game by giving any publicity to it. They therefore proposed to do nothing until the first rocket arrived, and they would then cope with the situation as it arose. They thought that if the stories about this weapon proved approximately true, these rockets would arrive at the rate of one an hour night and day. It had been reckoned on the basis of English and German air-raid experience that this would cause 3,600 deaths in the twenty-four hours, and a further 3,600 hospital cases. If this went on for a month (Morrison's own calculation), deaths and figures of seriously injured would both rise to 108,000.

In my opinion it is quite clear from German pronouncements to their own people that they have some secret weapon up their sleeve. They will not save it up for some military purpose: they will be compelled by conditions on their own home front to use it as soon as it has been perfected. If one of these terrible bombs lands on London or Birmingham unexpectedly, there will be a most frightful panic. If these things are really discharged at the rate of one an hour for a month, a large part of the south of England will be evacuated and its inhabitants will be living in the open somewhere up north. In this connection I don't understand Morrison's reference to Birmingham, which is quite 200 miles from the nearest bit of French coast.

The war, under these conditions and as far as this country is concerned, will largely be brought to a standstill. And the Government's policy of doing nothing will aggravate things badly. The size of the rockets seems exaggerated, though of course a good deal of the thirty-eight feet drops off during the flight, as the propelling material burns up. But even diminishing the size very much and assuming the operation of the gun is much interfered with by air attacks, you still have something which will change the whole appearance of the war.

October 22, 1943

Had some chat with Fred Bellenger, who was talking to Nye Bevan and Greenwood in the House yesterday. They say that the coalition is spiritually dead and that no one expects a National Government on present lines in peacetime. They say that Churchill has lost a lot of ground in the House, not in his conduct of the war (why not?), but in his handling of home affairs. He is considered to have overplayed his hand in stamping on all plans for post-war reconstruction, and it is believed that the coalition may well break up before the end of the war.

November 2, 1943

In contrast to the paeans in all the papers this morning over the Russian news,[1] I find everyone in the office particularly cynical. And not only cynical themselves, but appalled by the cynicism they meet in very ordinary people in everyday life. Some of them had seen a newsreel of the wounded and repatriated prisoners of war. The pictures were put over with a lot of blurb about our gratitude to these men being eternal. This led to widespread calls of 'Oh, yeah!' in the cinema. No one believes any longer in any statement by any minister, nor do they believe their newspapers, the B.B.C., or anyone else. The B.B.C. is regarded as official and therefore slightly more authentic than the papers; professional men

16

from doctors and parsons to judges have lost their prestige; even millionaires have lost their glamour.

Unfortunately all this has been growing for some years and now attaches to everyone in authority. It would be a long time before any new regime acquired any real confidence from public opinion. Unfortunately attacks on the powers that be do not stir people to anger and action, but rather add to the current attitude of cynicism – a lesson I have learnt in the last eight years from the reaction to the politics of the *Mirror* and Pic.

November 13, 1943

De Gaulle is really beginning to throw his weight about. He has ordered the arrest of the Lebanese government,[2] and the whole place is in an uproar. We have stated that we will not allow our strategic position to be jeopardized by events in the Lebanon; the French Committee is more or less saying that it is French territory and has nothing to do with us. De Gaulle is playing for very high stakes and I wonder shall we let him get away with it. French friendship or hostility is worth so little that I wonder we treat them with so much ceremony. I should make it quite clear to de Gaulle that his only hope of getting anywhere is by being useful to us. If he ceases to be useful, he will be removed from the scene. As it is, I expect we shall be firm enough to make a bitter enemy of de Gaulle, but not firm enough to deprive him of his power to hurt us.

November 24, 1943

M. met Slessor of Coastal Command over the weekend. His points were (1) that in the last six months Coastal Command had sunk more submarines than the British and American navies combined; (2) that the output of planes was falling off badly: but for the bad weather of the past three weeks Bomber Command would have had to slow down for lack of planes, and his own operations were seriously curtailed for the same reason; (3) that the High Command looked with dismay on Beaverbrook's return to the Government. Slessor said that Beaverbrook acts as court jester to the Prime Minister, but has a baneful effect on our military operations by his mischievous irresponsibility.

November 26, 1943

Campbell has been hearing more about the system of Government as organized by Churchill. The War Cabinet seldom meets – and receives none of the papers on strategy. It is informed of any major decisions and is given the benefit of a speech on the war situation by Churchill about once a month. Most of the meetings of the Cabinet that one hears spoken about are meetings of committees of the Cabinet called together for specific purposes. Churchill sees the chiefs of staff every day and at these meetings Beaverbrook is now usually present. The session is liable to degenerate into wisecracking between the Prime Minister and Beaverbrook, in which the rather tongue-tied chiefs of staff have no say.

This one-man Government is justified by Churchill on the grounds that every move in the war has to be agreed with Roosevelt, and this is impossible if at every step he has also to consult his Cabinet. The Prime Minister is careful to inform Attlee of almost everything. Attlee can be relied on to have no views of his own, and his connivance rather spikes the guns of the other Labour ministers, if they get restive.

Anti-American feeling is still a burning subject. It appears that though we see Americans at every street corner, this is nothing to what is in store. If there are to be three times as many Americans, I reckon we can look to an increase of nine times in the intensity of anti-American feeling. A nurse from St George's Hospital told me yesterday that she was nursing a man stabbed through the liver by an American. He didn't know the American, had not even spoken to him; the attack was quite unprovoked and it was too dark for him afterwards to identify his assailant. An advertising agent I was lunching with today said he had had similar stories from his daughter, a Wren in Londonderry. There they set on single British sailors. One was kicked to death by a gang of eight; another was stabbed by a gang of four.

Roosevelt met Stalin for the first time at Teheran at the end of November. He travelled there with Churchill from Cairo, where they had had discussions with Chiang Kai-shek, the Chinese Nationalist leader (who had been fighting the Japanese since 1937).

The Teheran conference was the first meeting of the 'Big Three' – though this designation was already obsolete: 'Big Two' would have been more accurate. For Stalin and Roosevelt were now unquestionably the two most powerful men in the world. Churchill's reservations about Operation Overlord were brushed aside, and it was agreed at Teheran definitely to proceed with the invasion of France by May 1944.

December 1, 1943

We have just had an advance copy of the communiqué issued from Cairo. It appears that Churchill, Roosevelt, and Chiang Kai-shek have been meeting outside Cairo at Mena, and have agreed that Japan shall go back not only to where she was in 1914, but further: that Formosa shall return to China and Korea gain its independence. This sort of declaration seems to me unnecessary and silly. It cannot help, may tie your hands in the future, and in any case stiffens Japanese resistance.

It is rumoured that the party has now moved on to Tiflis³ to see Stalin. How the President of the U.S., and a cripple at that, could swallow his pride and go to see Stalin in Persia passes my comprehension, but Tiflis sounds too much altogether.

A funny point about the censorship on tomorrow's communiqué is that we can say the party visited the Pyramids and that the communiqué was issued from Cairo, but not that the meeting took place at Cairo – all of which seems to me the merest mumbo-jumbo.

December 8, 1943

Met John North [*the author*] for the first time for a long while. He was in North Africa in the summer, but has been laid up with tummy trouble since September. He had some talk with Murphy, who told him that if there had been the slightest opposition to our landing in North Africa, there would have been a catastrophe. Therefore Darlan's help in the initial stages was of priceless value. This explains why Darlan was used, but not why he was not ditched immediately his usefulness ceased. The decision to attack Sicily was a political one, North thought, based on a desire to keep the Americans interested in the war against Germany.

North said the Americans were pouring money into North

Africa for the French – every local official now has a Chrysler –
but that opinion is becoming more pro-British all the time.
Macmillan says the French don't know the meaning of the word
gratitude, and he is prepared to let the Americans go on trying
unsuccessfully to curry favour with them. The Germans were very
clever in their dealings with the French and, though not liked,
were respected.

December 18, 1943

No change in the news from the war fronts, but dramatic news of
Churchill since my last entry. He is down again with pneumonia[4]
and has obviously been very ill. He was to have returned for the
war debate this week, but it was not until Thursday [December 16]
that the announcement about his illness was made. The suggestion
is that he is seriously ill, but is now recovering, though the latest
bulletin mentions an 'irregular pulse'. There are rumours that
penicillin has been flown out to him, and certainly Mrs Churchill
has gone.

The political reaction was first: 'What if he dies?' and the
reflection that this is the worst possible moment for a change of
leadership. The second and more realistic reaction is: 'Assuming
he recovers from his second attack of pneumonia in ten months, it
will be clear to all that his days as Prime Minister are numbered,
or at least that his days as sole political and military dictator are
over. Who will now share his throne?' At the time of writing
speculation is going on on these lines, with no outcome. The most
popular Minister of Defence would be Montgomery, but what
people are afraid of is that as Churchill's vitality decreases,
Beaverbrook's influence will grow. On the other hand this
tendency could not go very far without some important resignations from the Government, which might well bring it down. In
the event of Churchill's death, the only possible successor, in my
opinion, would be Eden, though the Tories are trying to build up
Anderson!

December 21, 1943

Churchill is evidently better, though his heart is still causing
some concern. There is talk of his going to South Africa to recoup.

I don't see how he can be out of this country just when we are planning to launch a continental invasion. In any case it seems to be recognized that he will have to delegate very much more authority. The only possible man for him to lean on is Eden, but Eden is quite incapable of weathering the storms in front of us. The general result is likely to be a quickening of the political tempo, with less authority and more dissension being displayed in the military conduct of the war.

1944

Sunday Pictorial

June 11, 1944
TWOPENCE
No. 1,556

WE'RE ADVANCING ON THE WHOLE FRONT—AND MONTY'S THERE

LAST NIGHT'S LATE NEWS FROM THE INVASION BEACHHEAD WAS THAT WE ARE ADVANCING ALL ALONG THE FRONT, WITH OUR TROOPS STORMING INLAND AGAINST STIFF GERMAN RESISTANCE AND STRONG TANK FORMATIONS.

General Montgomery, who has already paid several flying visits, has now landed in France—to stay—with his advanced H.Q. Among the first things he saw in our booty was a group of British-made cars captured at Dunkirk and now back with their rightful owners.

It is revealed that our air forces are now based on French airfields. Spitfire fighters are operating from landing strips.

Yesterday only fifty enemy aircraft were sighted over the battlefield. But many hundreds of Allied aircraft took advantage of the improvement in the weather to rain tons of bombs down on German tanks, supply convoys, road and railways.

To try to stop the steady surge forward of our troops, the Germans are flooding low-lying areas near Cherbourg.

Last night, experts surveying the invasion front reported: "So far, so good." But the next three or four days will be vital. It's an urgent race against time, to carry across the Channel and land in France a fighting force, fully equipped, which will be mighty enough to counter any surprise.

300,000 Troops Landed, Says Berlin

MORE than 300,000 Allied troops have been landed on the beachheads according to enemy estimates—300,000 of them are said to have been put ashore in the forty-eight hours.

Indications are that the Germans are about to open an all-out attempt to drive us back into the sea.

It looks likely to come in the Caen area, where the British tank warfare of the week is now in progress.

Our Brown miles beyond Caen the roads are jammed as German convoys of ammunition, petrol and equipment

Already there is heavy fighting for Caen. Twenty-three barrages preceded the tank battle. Smoke-clouds, three-quarters of a mile burst over the heights which masked the advance of water where our men are advancing

Any account now for whole of the Allied line to Normandy will be passed up throughout its fifty-mile length. the belief of the 21st Army Group H.Q. The capture yesterday of Isigny and Trévières, both lying east of Caen, has strengthened our grip on the roads leading Carentan, a key town now the scene of sharp battle toward battles.

Around this centre of roads and railways the Germans have let the Bondo loose. Pouring out of ruand twice and ditches, the waters have flooded a huge area in front of the American troops.

At the Bamard has thrown at all the reserves immediately available The Germans are fighting with hard
fierce quickness fighting time.

5 Questions and the Answers

Here are the answers to five questions everyone is asking about the Battle of France today. They are given by Vernon Bloid "Sunday Pictorial" Air expert.

1 Can the Luftwaffe now seriously challenge our Air Forces over the invasion area?

But now, but there are signs that they are bringing up their reserves. Even so, I doubt whether they could ever put up more than a fraction of the 15,000 aircraft we have available. The Germans need fighters, and it will take a great number to equal our air power.

I'd it would be dangerous to believe that the Luftwaffe is knocked. I still feel that they are wasting until they can bring out a sufficient number of new types

2 Why doesn't Hitler bomb the invasion ports on this side?

It would be a waste of machines and effort. The ports are already defended; it is doubtful whether he could to raid. This he cannot do, because he hasn't the machines.

3 Can our bombers hold up the German concentrations now massing towards the beach-head?

It depends just on the weather. In cloudy weather the enemy forces are hidden from both reconnaissance and bomber aircraft. When we have got to concentration, where the Germans are unlikely to run. In any case it is now more a job for the light bombers and fighter-bombers than the heavies. They are more accurate. The "break-through" will depend largely on the fighters. The day of a heavy bombers is over.

4 Have our Airborne Forces now served their purpose in this operation?

So soon as they have established a secure bridgehead into which sufficient forces have been brought by direct air, the Airborne Forces should be withdrawn. They are special troops and are not expendable.

The Germans report, according to their own reports, that we shall use Airborne Forces for more strategic landings in the rear. It would be a miracle if such a force could unload at many places and times. These unloaded in direct air strike and fighting: the Germans must expect us to be able to carry at least the sort of force carried by air.

As far, apparently, only Horsa and Waco gliders, able a carry large, light tanks and light artillery, have been used. They report seen to have no striking bigger, I believe we still have some surprises up our sleeve.

5 Have we seen the maximum possible use of the Allied Air Forces in the last few days?

I doubt it. As we get airfields in France and open up landing areas on the other side, the number of aircraft will increase several times. There will be greater demand for air transport than ever before, because we need more than ever.

GENERAL FULLER: PAGE FOUR

GREAT PICTURES TODAY INSIDE

January 1, 1944
While in Scotland I met a captain in the Black Watch, double
M.C., just back from Italy. He said one of the difficulties in
dealing with the Americans is that they refuse to do any menial
work and wait for their black troops to do it. At Salerno one of the
reasons for their setback was that they had no ammunition: they
wouldn't unload it themselves, and the black troops had not
turned up. Similarly they would rather get typhoid and dysentery
from dirty latrines than clean them themselves.

January 2, 1944
The home political situation is to me infinitely depressing. Since
about 1920 I have been looking for a seriously constructive
development in English politics. For years I thought it would
inevitably come with the war. For a moment at the time of
Dunkirk it looked as if it were coming, but then we relapsed into
our political coma and the chance was missed.

Churchill, in my opinion, plays the part here that Pétain does
in France. He stands for our glorious past. That is why he, quite
rightly, is seriously afraid only of Lloyd George, who also represents
that past. That is why Singapore can fall, but he stands untouched.
He has found no new talent, and in fact the political scene was
never so bare of even second-rate ability. I regard this as evidence
that the parliamentary system is failing, and therefore dread the
alternatives of either some sort of Fascist regime, perhaps under a

successful general, or the decline of this country to the status of a
Portugal. In a development of this magnitude, Churchill is a mere
fly on the wheel.

I see no salvation from the Labour Party; the Liberals will not,
in my opinion, bestir themselves and deliver the goods; and if we
are to be saved it must be by some neo-Disraelian movement
inside the Tory Party. One can visualize the programme and
the supporters for such a party, but I cannot see a leader, and in
politics leadership is more than half the battle. We have been
without a leader for a generation, and without a great leader
since Gladstone's day, so tend to deride the very idea. Churchill
is a great character, but neither a great strategist nor a great
statesman. In fact I should say he was a miserably poor strategist
and doesn't know what statesmanship is about. And all this is
particularly important because not only is the future of England
at stake, but also the future of western Europe, which for the past
500 years has been the dominating civilizing influence in the
world.

It is possible that we are ripening for a religious revival. If this
is so, things will have to get much worse before they are better. I
think the important lesson to be learnt by the peoples today is
that man does not live by bread alone. I cannot see him being
brought back to the old sects and I don't think that at present
the ground is prepared for a new faith. The Roman Catholics
seem to me to be politically too reactionary – I cannot see them
entirely filling the need – and the other sects just don't compete.
I should say that Christianity will have to be restated in fresh
terms, which can indeed be done as early Christianity was highly
socialistic; but such a restatement calls for a religious leader of
the first class, of whom at present we see no sign.

A rule I have made so far in writing up this diary is that I
never read what I have written. This diary thus remains a statement of my news and views at the time, uncoloured by any attempt
at consistency. I have no idea what I wrote at the beginning of
1943, nor of whether my views then agree or conflict with the
views I am expressing now. They most probably agree, as for
years I have contended that we are heading for a revolution,

very slowly – but at any moment the tempo may quicken. A prolongation of the tendencies at present operating in British politics can lead only to a continuation of the national decline, which has been pretty continuous since something like the eighties of the last century. At the same time I cannot see any fresh development except as the result of a break with present tendencies: a revolution in fact. Such a break can only come as the result of serious dissatisfaction with the status quo. It may be that the rocket guns will serve this purpose, or the general dislocation of trade after the war. But I have been looking and hoping now for twenty-five years and it doesn't seem appreciably nearer now than it was then.

January 4, 1944

Had lunch with Geoffrey Crowther, editor of the *Economist*. He opened by saying he thought we were in a bad way politically: five per cent of us had been to a public school and were inhibited by the fear of showing bad form; the other ninety-five per cent were inhibited through not having been to a public school! As a result we all suffer from an inferiority complex.

Crowther has a theory that the great moment will come when those born in the 20th century will take over. He said that only one Cabinet minister in England, Germany, or France had been born since January 1, 1900 (and he was Malcolm Macdonald!). The point being that hitherto we have been ruled by the men who were over military age in 1914. Those who served in the war were either killed or, with their vitality sapped, have lost their way. Now we can look to a revolution under younger men who never knew the security before the last war, and have grown up in the insecurity of the years between the wars. A further point Crowther made was that in the 19th century most technical discoveries applied to processes in factories: since 1900 so many of them affect our daily lives. Those of us born since 1900 are completely familiar with bicycles, cars, aeroplanes, telephones, radio, and birth control. As a result, he said, he thought the distinction was no longer between Right and Left, but between the New and the Old.

Rex North tells me that the price of a tart in Piccadilly is now

£4 to £5, as against 10s. to £1 before the war. In Algiers, however, the figure has soared to £10 or even £12 10s. a time!

January 21, 1944

Fuller wrote a piece for the Pic this week that was censored, and the War Office even wrote across it in red ink that on no account must any part of it appear! It was very vague general stuff saying (1) that the main objective of our invasion armies must be Paris, because it is the communications centre of France; (2) that if the coastal fortifications are in fact five miles thick, as is reported, then our breakthrough must be a pyramid with at least a ten-mile base. This necessitates two landings, linked up. To achieve two successful landings, quite four must be launched. The *Pictorial* reporter who went down to the Ministry of Information to discuss the matter was convinced that their alarm at Fuller's article was due to the fact that it correctly forecast our plan.

January 30, 1944

We were dining with the Wrights, who have been in civil defence since the outbreak of war. Mrs Wright said when war broke out she had at her air-raid warden's post 260 coffins, some shrouds done up in packets of 150, a jack-knife, a long surgeon's knife (purpose unknown), and some gas masks – not one bandage of any kind. It is curious how before the war the Home Office was preoccupied with corpses and with gas. The far more important problems of helping the injured and housing the homeless escaped their attention.

February 2, 1944

Met Wilfrid Roberts last night, who had little news. He says the generals are filled with alarm and despondency at the idea of a Second Front. He thinks that if the venture fails the prestige of Churchill and his Government will go; that there would have to be an election fairly soon, when entirely new faces would emerge.

The alarm in official circles over the secret weapon is now subsiding and ministers' wives are returning to London. Wilfrid Roberts was talking to one member of the Secret Weapon Committee, who said it is very difficult to judge the value of such evidence as we possess, as so many groups, both here and in Germany, are interested in proving that a dangerous attack by some new weapon is imminent. I continue to think that in the course of this year the Germans are bound to bring off some counter-stroke, and this counter-stroke will probably be either a rocket gun or a pilotless plane.

February 5, 1944
On Wednesday night [February 2] the delegation representative of the British Press, home from Australia, gave a dinner to the editors and others. The delegation consisted of Walter Layton, Sam Storey, and Neville Pearson. It was chosen by Brendan Bracken and not considered representative by Fleet Street generally. So most of the big shots boycotted the dinner. Our only representative was Stuart Campbell.

Apparently Walter Layton got up and gave the assembled company a most sensational picture of what they had seen and heard. To start with, he said that the Australians are violently anti-American and more pro-British than they have ever been. He said the Americans were 'the greatest British Empire builders in history'! The Australians loathe the Americans, regard MacArthur with derision, but have no idea how to get rid of him. Layton said that the Australian government is grateful to the Americans for coming to their rescue after the fall of Singapore, and particularly grateful to MacArthur, who carried sufficient weight in the States to get material which, but for him, would have gone elsewhere. But they feel he has now more than out-stayed his welcome.

Layton and his party saw MacArthur, who received them in a large room which made him think of a film star's boudoir. There was in it no hint of war, not even a map. MacArthur talked the whole time – mainly about himself. The interview lasted one and a half hours, of which only the last ten minutes touched lightly and vaguely on the war.

MacArthur has around him a staff of officers who for some reason are ecstatic admirers. While Layton's delegation were in Darwin they were visited at night by some senior officers from New Guinea, who begged them to do something about MacArthur.

He is apparently not interested in the war, but is quite frankly electioneering. All hint of difficulties in the fighting in his area is eliminated from correspondents' dispatches and no setbacks are reported. Layton was assured by everyone in a position to speak that MacArthur's communiqués are entirely undependable. It is a waste of time to read them.

Campbell asked Layton afterwards whether he knew what was going on in the Pacific, if MacArthur gives an entirely distorted picture. Layton said he could not find out from anyone how the fighting was really going. Evatt, when he was over here, arranged for a British Spitfire wing to be sent out to Australia. On its arrival MacArthur had the wing sent 400 miles out into the bush of northern Australia, where there is no chance of it getting any fighting. The general impression in Australia is that the fighting will take much longer and be much tougher than we have any idea of here.

Curtin, the Australian Prime Minister, made a great impression on the delegation. He was considered a small-town Socialist politician at the time he was appointed, but is now, in their opinion, one of the most outstanding Empire statesmen we have had for years. Layton thinks he and his party will be in office for a long time. Menzies is apparently completely bust.

No one had any suggestion what to do about MacArthur and all that, but Layton suggested that if four or five star war reporters were sent out to New Guinea, the Americans wouldn't dare censor their dispatches. This is just wishful thinking of course. Curtin will be over here in six weeks' time, and something may be hammered out then.

Among the guests at this party were Brendan Bracken and Lord Beaverbrook. After Layton had spoken, Sam Storey got up and said how cut off from us here were the people in the Dominions: they didn't think we adequately studied their point of view. For instance they were very interested in post-war aviation, wanted to work in with us, and did not want to be swamped by the Americans. A prominent Australian politician (name not given) asked Storey who was responsible for civil aviation in this country. Sam Storey told him: 'The Lord Privy Seal, Lord Beaverbrook.' To which the politician replied: 'Oh, that bloody bastard!'

Storey was passing this off as a joke, when Beaverbrook, evidently furious, shouted from the end of the table: 'Oh, shut up: tell us about yourself and Reuters'! Storey was for a time chairman of Reuters, when it was at its lowest ebb. There was a hushed silence. Storey went very white and sat down. Gerald Barry, editor of the *News Chronicle*, shouted that Beaverbrook's was the most insulting remark he had ever heard. Layton got up and dithered; Beaverbrook eventually apologized for his outburst; Storey apologized for his story and the party broke up prematurely.

Campbell had some talk with Layton as he was going away. Layton showed him the transcript of an interview given in November to the Australian military commentators by Mac-Arthur's Chief of Staff. These are regular monthly meetings and the form is always the same. MacArthur's man began with a review of military strategy in general and went on to describe the strategy of the great generals of the past. Hannibal, Napoleon, Lee, and Wellington were mentioned. But, he told his audience, in General MacArthur we have a military leader whose strategy includes yet transcends that of all these great soldiers of the past!

February 9, 1944
Had lunch with Dr Hill, who is to be the new secretary of the British Medical Association. He has rather a good radio voice and is the Radio Doctor. I suppose he is about forty; short and fat with a round face, double chin, grey hair, and spectacles he is usually looking over. He seems a progressive sort of bloke; told me that his mother was left a widow when he was thirteen months old and had never earned more than £3 12s. 6d. per week. However, he got scholarships, and reached his present situation via Trinity Cambridge, the London Hospital, and a job at Oxford as Deputy Medical Officer of Health.

I was mainly concerned to ask him about Churchill's health, as he would know the medical chit-chat on the subject. He says Churchill is overstraining his heart and that this condition appeared as an irregular pulse when he was suffering from the slight lung infection he had. He should drop his brandy, his cigars, and his job, and take things very easy. If he does not, he will not be here for long. In any case he will not be able to lead this country after the war. I asked him if he would insure Churchill's life for two years. He was aghast at the very idea and said he would not insure it at all. He would expect Churchill to have a heart attack from which he would recover, followed by another from which he would not.

February 12, 1944
The editor of the only Socialist paper in New Zealand came to the office the other day. Owing to his Socialist views he is necessarily very close to the New Zealand Prime Minister. He says there are 100,000 to 120,000 Americans in New Zealand, and that they get along very well with the New Zealanders. More than 40,000 of the Yanks are marines, who are much better disciplined and much better soldiers than the ordinary run of American.

He took precisely the same view of MacArthur and of his communiqués as Layton did. To illustrate this, he said a friend of his was in a reconnaissance plane and reported seeing eleven Japanese ships in a convoy sailing on a certain course. American bombers went out and reported sinking nine of them; a further force of bombers was sent out, which reported sinking the remaining two. All this was published officially by MacArthur. Next day this same man saw eight of the ships proceeding on their way obviously undamaged!

On the Italian front, Naples had fallen to the Allies on October 1, 1943, but the expected advance to Rome did not take place. In November the front became deadlocked on a line south of Monte Cassino. In January an attempt to outflank the Germans was made by landing behind their lines at Anzio, just south of Rome. This was almost a disaster. The Allied forces barely managed to avoid being hurled back into the sea and were isolated and besieged until the Cassino front cracked in May, after a long and furious assault which included the bombardment of the famous Benedictine monastery of Monte Cassino. On June 4 the Allies entered Rome.

It was an anticlimax. For, two days later, the long-awaited invasion of northern France took place.

February 14, 1944

On the Cassino front it appears to have been decided to shell the monastery. The Germans are using it as an observation post; we are making no headway and are blaming it on the Germans in the monastery. The destruction of Monte Cassino, which has been the inspiration of all Western monasticism and a centre of devotion since the 6th century, just illustrates one aspect of the appalling blunder we made in invading Italy. 'Slogging up Italy', as Alexander called it, can only mean the destruction of many really priceless historical monuments, for which we shall have to endure the opprobrium for centuries. Everything we ever said about the Turks using the Parthenon as a powder magazine will recoil on our heads. Besides the civilization of Europe depends so much on its architecture, and we are playing a leading part in the obliteration of it.

The papers, including (I regret to say) the *Mirror*, publish leading articles saying that one English soldier's life is worth more than any historical monument. So it is to his wife and parents, but not to the country at large.

It is hard to say what can be done about it now. We are committed to bombing and to our Italian campaign by bad decisions, dating back in some cases for a good few years. The situation is quite out of the hands of the present Government, as it is of everyone else. We shall just have to let the storm blow itself out and hope that there will be some bits left of us at the finish.

A comic little row has developed in the American press. In a leader the *Church of England Newspaper* opined that Roosevelt was not irreplaceable. Whereupon several of the big American papers – the *World Telegram*, as well as the *News* and the *Tribune* – launched a ferocious attack on this 'influential, authoritative, Government-supported organ of the established Church of England'! I wonder why the Americans are so touchy. This is a piffling little paper (one of five Anglican papers) claiming a sale of 30,000. I have never even seen a copy of the thing nor, till today, heard of the existence of its thirty-two-year-old editor Eric Upward: and come to that, what a gorgeous name for a man with such a job! The American papers belabour us constantly – and the really

17

important papers at that – but when Upward lets out a squeak, a whole avalanche descends on us.

February 18, 1944
Professor Southwell took me last night to the dinner of the Royal Society Club, where I sat between him and Bragg. Southwell said one of the headaches of London University over the Beveridge scheme was, if everyone had a £20 funeral, where would the corpses come from for the dissecting rooms of the teaching hospitals?

The strategic bombing offensive against Germany employed the greatest share of Britain's war production. It was indiscriminate, large-scale, and costly. It certainly smashed up German industrial towns. But it does not seem to have seriously affected German war production. Damage was mainly to homes, not factories, yet this did not affect the morale of the civilian population. The offensive went on through 1943 to 1944, first mainly against the Ruhr, then Hamburg, then Berlin. In April it was stopped, and Bomber Command – to the indignation of its commander, 'Bomber' Harris – was put at Eisenhower's disposal for Operation Overlord.

The ineffectiveness of strategic bombing was not generally recognized at the time. But the distinguished scientist Professor Blackett, Scientific Adviser on the naval side of Overlord, had no illusions. The information he gave Cecil King in the following conversation is now known to have been substantially correct.

March 15, 1944
Had lunch with Professor Blackett, big, untidy, in the most extraordinary overcoat – large, light-coloured herringbone pattern with a belt. He is *most* intelligent and has now been made Scientific Adviser to Admiral Ramsay, who is in charge of the naval side of the Second Front. He said he thought the U-boat war was now over. Sinkings had been below the 100,000-ton mark for seven or eight months, and though they might rise above this level he did not think they would again amount to anything serious.

I asked him about rocket guns, pilotless planes, and all that. He said there were about a hundred bases in northern France, on

which the Germans had expended so much labour and concrete
that it was hard to believe that it was pure bluff. We had been
bombing these platforms in a rather desultory way and had
probably put out seventy-five of them. They could, of course, be
repaired, but they would then be bombed again. It was hard to
understand why the Germans attached any great importance to
these things, as they are all above ground and were obviously going
to be bombed. On the other hand, it is strange that they have
made no serious attempt to defend these sites by either A.A.
guns or fighter planes. They exist for some so far undisclosed
purpose.

About the air war, he said he thought 'Bert' Harris a very poor
strategist but a good commander. He managed to keep up the
morale of his men in spite of their cruel losses, and he did it by
convincing them that bombing alone could win the war. Their
losses were about four or five per cent per raid and they had to do
thirty before they were rested. It was clear from this that they
were unlikely to survive their first spell of operations.

Until the bombing of Hamburg last spring our bombing of
Germany had been a complete flop. Blackett thought it had probably raised German munition production, and we had lost a
trained airman for every man, woman, and child we had killed
in Germany by bombs. When the Germans bombed us in 1940–41,
twenty-five per cent of their bombs fell on built-up areas: our own
figure until last spring was about eight or nine per cent. We now
had instruments (I gathered some of them based on radio-
location) which at least showed us when we were over a town,
and that even in thick cloud. In spite of all the heavy bombing of
the last few months, it was officially estimated that German
production was down by no more than nine or ten per cent.
Blackett did not believe in our bombing policy, claiming that
until last spring it had achieved nothing; that opposition by
Bomber Command to the withdrawal of the necessary planes had
held up the defeat of the U-boat for nine months; and that
Bomber Command had been the principal opponents of the
Second Front.

I said it was hard for us newspaper men to get any clear impression, as we were so bombarded by the competing services

and Government departments with propaganda for each one's own pet policy. Blackett said how true this was, and how in the case of the R.A.F. it went so far as downright lying and faking of evidence to support the bombing policy. The R.A.F. had done their best to convince the Americans that night bombing was the only thing, but mercifully had not succeeded. Blackett regarded day bombing by the Americans as militarily more successful than our night bombing. It was more effective against any chosen target, and had the additional advantage of destroying numbers of German fighters. He went on to quote a saying of Churchill's before the war, made to a friend of Blackett's, that 'the day a nation at war no longer aimed at the destruction of the enemy's armed forces, but waged war on the civil population – that day that nation was doomed'!

We then turned to the Pacific war. Blackett said the American fleet was very efficient, in many respects more efficient than ours because quicker at picking up new ideas. He said the claims of their sinkings by submarine were fairly dependable, that their handling of large ships was better than ours, and their high-angle A.A. gunnery at sea anything from eight to ten times as good as ours. Part of the reason for this was that our Navy has traditionally a messing system under which the sailors make their mess their home. This takes up space (I suppose the American sailors, like the German, make their shore barracks their home), with the result that an American battleship carries 800 men more than our corresponding ships. These extra men are all put on to A.A. guns. Apart, however, from the question of size of crew, the American A.A. equipment is better, and we are at present negotiating for a supply of their guns. Admiral 'Ernie' King of the U.S. navy is anti-British, but apparently has some reason on his side when he argues that with their present A.A. equipment our ships are not safe in the Pacific against Japanese air attack. King is apparently like Harris: he thinks he can win his war off his own bat. Conditions in the Pacific must be rather strange – MacArthur, who apparently has dyed hair, is not on speaking terms with Nimitz! Our intelligence people say that the morale of the American marines, navy, and air force in the Pacific is good, but morale of the army is very low even there. This intelligence officer told

Blackett that the Americans were the most mother-dominated race in the world!

April 14, 1944
Everyone is getting bored with the delay over the Second Front. I even hear it called the Second-hand Front. I know this is unfair, but then the Government has done its best to imply that an attack was imminent when they knew (and the Germans knew) it wasn't.

Had some talk with Bill Greig. He says Beaverbrook is as unpopular as ever, and Bevin and Morrison are furious because, while not a member, he turns up at meetings of the War Cabinet and takes part in the discussions. Bevin and Morrison are divided by hatred and contempt of long standing and there is apparently no hope of reconciliation. Bevin does not want to be Prime Minister (though quite determined to keep the job from Morrison): he wants to remain Labour Minister to get back the returning soldiers into their jobs.

Greig says the real 'War Cabinet' meets at about midnight at 10 Downing Street and remains drinking brandy until about 1.30. It consists of the Prime Minister, Harvie Watt, Brendan Bracken, and Cherwell [*Professor Lindemann, Lord Cherwell*]. Beaverbrook is prevented by his asthma from staying up late. Churchill is drinking heavily again and his appearance shows a most marked deterioration. Cherwell is stronger in favour than ever, and both the Minister of Food and the President of the Board of Trade have been very annoyed when forwarding memoranda for the Prime Minister, to get back their papers annotated by Cherwell without reference to the Prime Minister at all. The same thing happened to Ernest Brown at the Ministry of Health, only this time the annotations were by Lord Moran.

April 18, 1944
As more and more people back from the Mediterranean tell their stories, it becomes clearer than ever that American material of all sorts, American transport, and American engineering are of the very highest order, but the value of American troops in action

is almost nil. Their air force has borne very heavy losses and its morale seems reasonably good, but the ordinary infantry is at or below the Italian level. The navy and marines are said to be good, but of course we have not seen them in this theatre of war. Their generals and staff are fully as bad as one would expect, and can hardly be improved except as the result of a lot of hard fighting in which really large numbers of Americans are involved. Americans will never learn from others, only from their own experience.

May 24, 1944

Looking into Hodgson's the book auctioneers at 2.45 this afternoon, I was surprised to see Sir Alan Brooke, the Chief of the Imperial General Staff, looking at some books to be auctioned tomorrow. Outside was his Rolls Royce with Union Jack flying from the radiator cap. On the eve of the invasion one imagined him working feverishly, but evidently not. Perhaps his part of the work is done.

May 27, 1944

The current joke in the War Office is that the battle order for the invasion has now been fixed. First to go in are the Commandos, to be followed by the Guards, then the Tanks, then the infantry, followed by N.A.A.F.I. and E.N.S.A.[1] – then the American suicide squads!

M. spent yesterday in Holloway Prison Hospital and was much impressed by the service and by the matron. The latter told her that some women come in so encrusted with dirt that they have to be bathed three times (in one day) before they can be shown to a doctor. This problem of dirt has become much worse since the outbreak of war. What an appalling reflection this is on social conditions still prevailing in this country.

Visited the [Royal] Academy today with M., largely to see the painting and drawing of Monty by Augustus John. M. thinks, and I agree, that they are portraits of a man who is entirely superficial, though possessed of great vitality. It is interesting if this is really John's evaluation of Monty; on the other hand it may effectively be only *Portrait of a Puritan by a Libertine*!

June 3, 1944

Here is another American story going round. An American was
seen lurching down the street and a pal said: 'Feeling all right?'
The first man said: 'What do you mean?' So the second said:
'Well, you're kind of lurching. I thought you might be ill.' 'No,'
said the first man, 'it's these medals: it's so hard to keep your
balance.'

Another story going round is about a farmer who was asked
how he got on with the Americans. He said he got on very well
with the Americans, but had no time for the white men they had
brought with them! This feeling is fairly common – that the
negroes are nicer and better behaved than the ordinary Yank. So
there is some indignation when negro soldiers are condemned to
death for raping English girls. In the most recent case the evidence
would certainly have resulted in an acquittal in an English court.
In the far more numerous cases of rape or murder by white
American soldiers, the punishment, if any, is of a wholly different
order of severity.

*June 6, 'D-Day': by the evening 156,000 Allied troops were landed in
France. By the end of the next day there were 250,000 of them involved in
the tremendous battle to push inland from sixty miles of Normandy beach.*

*The first onslaught did not produce any spectacular result. Montgomery,
who under the Supreme Commander Eisenhower commanded all the land
forces, proceeded cautiously. It took a month for the British to capture
Caen. But at the end of July, when the Americans broke through in the
west of Normandy, the German defences crumbled. Hitler's counter-attack
towards Avranches ended with the isolation and surrender of 50,000
German troops at Falaise.*

*On August 25 the Allies entered Paris; on September 2, Brussels. On
August 15, Allied forces had landed in the south of France.*

*The Germans were in full retreat no less in eastern Europe, and by
August the Russian armies were in Poland and Rumania. The war was
undoubtedly won – though the fighting was by no means over.*

June 6, 1944

So this is D-Day! The first news of the landing came over the

German wireless at 6.35 a.m., but no mention was made in the seven o'clock [B.B.C.] news, to which I listened in.

What I shall remember of today was the thunder of the planes going over London from 4.30 this morning (hence my listening to the seven o'clock news). From wandering about the London streets you would never guess anything was up: the same proportion of men in uniform as usual, even including parachutists; perhaps rather more naval officers than we normally see. One or two knots of people waiting for evening papers. Otherwise no difference from the average Tuesday. Weather cold, cloudy, and blowy, which one would suppose would be unfavourable – perhaps the forecast is good.

June 7, 1944

There was a conference at the Ministry of Information this morning, at which it was stated that there were no grounds for optimism, nor for pessimism.   This unhelpful remark led up to a complaint that this morning's newspapers were too optimistic. They took their line from Churchill's statements yesterday, which apparently did not please the generals. Churchill – unexpectedly – made no further statements today, which may mean something or nothing.

June 12, 1944

After the Ministry of Information conference last night an American colonel got up and spoke about their Rangers (the equivalent of our Commandos). He said they never took prisoners if they could help it, but if they *did* take prisoners, shot them on the smallest provocation. For instance, if they were being marched along a road and came to a dead American, they would shoot one of their prisoners out of hand. This, of course, is murder of a particularly cowardly kind, but it is difficult to fathom the mentality of an American colonel who will boast of such crimes to a conference of 300 correspondents. Putting it on its lowest level, this sort of thing gives the Germans an excuse for any sort of reprisals they may care to inflict on our men.

Had written some time ago to Father Steuart, the well known

preacher, asking him to suggest the name of someone who would be able to explain to me, intelligently and authoritatively, the Catholic point of view on current problems. He suggested Father John Murray, a Jesuit attached to the Farm Street church, whom I visited today.

In conversation it appeared that he thought Catholics were mildly progressive in home politics, but took a Catholic view on European affairs. This seemed to consist of sympathy for Italian Fascism, but not Nazism, and preoccupation with Poland and Spain, which to non-Catholics are countries of very secondary interest. He spoke of the Russians as 'barbarous Asiatics'.

I asked him why it was that though Catholics were so punctilious in their religious observances, in their daily lives they were no better than their neighbours. He said that in their home life at least, Catholics did behave better. By this he seemed to mean that the sexual morality of Catholics is superior to that of non-Catholics. It certainly is in Ireland, but equally certainly is not in many European countries. Commercial morality, down to theft, he seemed to think of lesser significance, and vices such as greed, sloth, malice, and the rest hardly entered the picture.

From this I asked him whether the Catholic Church really made such a fuss about birth control as appeared from the papers. He said they did. I asked why. He said it was the teaching of the Church. I asked what constituted such teaching. Was it laid down in the equivalent of Acts of Parliament? He said no: that there was a very small body of defined truth, most of which dates from the early Councils of the Church; and that besides this, which would occupy very few quarto pages of print, there was only the teaching of the Church, which consisted of a lot of doctrines which had never been defined but which had never been questioned. I said I had thought that there was a book or books wherein one could look up the established Catholic doctrine on any subject – volumes of decided cases, in fact. He said no, there were no such books.

I asked him about the prospect of union with the Church of England. He said there was a great deal of collaboration, which would continue, but no prospect of union at all. The main obstacle in his opinion was the impossibility of defining what is the teaching of the Church of England on any single subject. I thought this a good point.

I said what would do more for bringing the English people back to Rome than anything else would be the election of a non-Italian pope. He said he thought Italian popes were a good idea, as until recently Italy was a weak and divided country and after this war would certainly not be a great power, so that no serious jealousies are created. He did think, however, that it would be a good idea if the curial cardinals at Rome were not so overwhelmingly Italian. I said that the Italians were a despised race, and after the war would be a laughing stock for quite fifty years. He said it was so wrong to think of them as ice-cream vendors and not recall their magnificent artistic achievement. I said that in this war they had shown themselves cowards, that physical courage is certainly not the only virtue, but it is certainly one universally and in all ages held in high esteem, and that by this standard the Russians had gained very great prestige and the Italians lost what little they had. He said he thought this unfair as their hearts were not in the war and their equipment was no good.

We touched on the confessional. I said, supposing a man comes to confession who says he is a professional burglar, what then? He said no Catholic would come with such a tale. If he did, he would be told to give up his burgling and return when he had done so. This seemed to leave no room in the Catholic world for the criminal classes – the original Salvation Army public, in fact. But he said that in questions involving money, there are often circumstances to be taken into account. In fact, he implied, a good deal of financial dishonesty would be tolerated, but not adultery. Their most difficult problems related to birth control, particularly where one party was a Catholic and the other not. This is indeed a delicate problem I had not thought of!

In general I was surprised that Father Murray put up such a poor performance. I understand Jesuits are trained for about thirteen years: this one had been educated at the universities of Paris, Rome, and Freiburg-im-Breisgau for just this sort of work. In effect he made out quite a good case for the progressiveness of Catholics in home politics, but almost said that in foreign affairs

they are Catholics first and Englishmen second. In his defence of
Catholics in general he did not pretend that they were better than
their neighbours, except in sexual morality. Is even this true? I
feel that with a little thought I could put up a better case for his
Church than he put up himself.

*Shortly after D-Day Hitler's secret weapon revealed itself. It was a stunted,
pilotless aeroplane, travelling between 300 and 400 miles per hour and
emitting a distinctive chugging noise, which abruptly cut off just before it
crashed detonating the ton of high explosive in its nose. Stoically weary
London greeted the V1s, alias 'buzz-bombs', 'flying bombs', 'zoombies',
'robots', 'doodlebugs'. The Press taunted it: 'ridiculous robot', 'Buzz
off!' (the* Mirror). *The V1 was not difficult to destroy. It could be shot
down by either A.A. guns or fighter planes. But enough got through to make
life very disagreeable in southern England. Six thousand Londoners were
killed and 1,500,000 evacuated.*

*By early September the V1s were mastered: the air defences had got
their measure, and the Allied forces were overrunning their launching sites
in France. At that moment the V2s appeared, far more formidable
weapons. They were rockets, they travelled much faster than the V1s, and
there was no effective defence against them. If Hitler had had more of them
and had been able to launch them earlier he could have obliterated London.
As it was, the V2 killed 3,000 people and the complete evacuation of
London reached the planning stage. The V2 menace faded out towards the
end of the year as the Allies captured these launching sites, too.*

July 16, 1944
The great event of the day is the first full-dress pilotless plane
attack on London. We had just turned out our bedside reading
lights at 11.30 when off went the warning, followed almost
immediately by the roar of a plane apparently diving on Lincoln's
Inn. However, it flew over, was then fired at, and eventually came
down with a crash – at Kentish Town. This was rapidly followed
by two others, which were being fired at before they came within
earshot of us. It was obvious that there was something odd about
them, as they were flying very low, apparently very slowly, and
the engine had a peculiar deep throb. They came over London
at intervals of perhaps a quarter of an hour for ten hours; there

was then a short interval and then they started again, finally packing up for the day at lunchtime. As soon as the first plane had gone I realized that this was a renewal of Monday night's attack.

Admiral Thomson, the Chief Censor, told Campbell this afternoon that in all 104 of these planes arrived in this country last night and this morning. They seem to have fallen thickest in south-east London, but there are reports of 'incidents' in Sussex, in Windsor, and in St Albans. The planes are jet-propelled, which gives them an orange flame in the tail. They carry about 2,000 pounds of H.E., have a wingspan of sixteen feet, are about twenty-five feet long, and are said to look like rather fat birds. The Government at the moment is in two minds whether to keep on the present warning system and whether or no to shoot at the planes. In the meanwhile they think the planes are brought to earth by intercepting beams from France and Germany, and that we can exercise our ingenuity bringing them to earth in some place that does not matter. At the moment the Government seems to be worried and not too sanguine of success.

June 17, 1944
The pilotless planes are becoming tedious. We had three hours of them last night and several alerts this afternoon. I went to Kentish Town to see the damage done by one of the first. It is quite considerable. It is now revealed that they carry over a ton of H.E. and I can well believe it. It is curious that they have been saved up until now and have apparently not been used against our invasion ports. The German propaganda machine is working flat out on the subject and speaks of the 'pall of smoke covering south-east England'. This is the merest boloney as the things hardly ever cause fires. However, if they go on for a long time they will do a lot of damage and very considerably add to people's strain and war weariness. I was talking to the door porter at the office this afternoon, who told me that one of our firemen had his house destroyed at Nunhead on Thursday night [June 15]. 'He lost everything, even his chickens,' was the graphic description.

June 18, 1944
What a night we had! The alert went about 11.30 last night, and

from then till eleven o'clock this morning we had a fair plastering. About 1.0 a.m. I went on to the office roof, where one could see the robots coming in from the south-east and travelling west. They could be seen even at that range as glowing sparks, but whether because of their own jet-propulsion unit or because of the glare of the searchlights was quite impossible to say. The guns were shooting at them continuously. Their marksmanship seemed bad, and it was quite impossible to say whether the robots came down because they had run their course or because they were hit. In any case they all seemed to explode on the ground. I was on the roof about twenty minutes and saw five come down. The night was then very clear, but later on clouds came up and the planes came nearer in. One could hear their throb as they came over, the engine would then often cut out, there was a pause while the plane dived to earth and then a roar as the contraption exploded. One fell in Farringdon Street, smashed up some houses, and killed two old people; another got Charing Cross Bridge plonk in the middle – the bridge looks all right except for the rails, which lead down into the water; Wellington Barracks chapel was hit this morning and 150 guardsmen are said to be dead; Woolwich Arsenal was hit; and other robots fell as far apart as Basingstoke and Colchester. The *Daily Sketch* headed their leader yesterday: 'Ridiculous weapon'; today the [*Sunday*] *Graphic* says: 'Pilotless and pointless'. The general opinion seems to be, however, that the Germans have really got something. I don't know how many nights like last night South London will stand up to.

June 19, 1944
The official hand-out statement that the speed of these brutes is only 200 miles per hour is complete nonsense. Several of the staff yesterday saw robots simply walking away from Spitfires, and one saw a Mosquito having the same experience. I get the impression that these robots do not all go at the same speed all the time. When they are going slow it is quite likely a Spit or a Typhoon can overtake them, but this would be less true of night fighters and still less true when, particularly at the end of its run, the robot is going flat out.

June 20, 1944

The main event of the day has been a conference by Morrison on the robot planes. He said that since Thursday evening [June 15] 780 robots had been shot off, of which 570 had arrived in this country and half of these had fallen in the London area. The casualties are about 650 killed in London and twenty-five outside it, with 2,500 seriously injured admitted to hospital. The worst night was Saturday, when 200 were sent; the mildest last night with only sixty-three. The proportion destroyed by our fighters had been rising and the latest figure was twenty-four per cent. The best time to get them was over the Channel and just inland, when they were gaining height and therefore slow. He attached no particular importance to the quiet we have enjoyed today, which might be due to a number of causes. In any case we were to have fewer alerts and no gunfire in London. Their departure platforms had been bombed and would continue to be. This would keep down the menace, but the only way to stop it would be by capturing the rocket coast.

Morrison thought all the robots had been aimed at London, though some turned up as far afield as Cheltenham. About one in seven seemed to have a device for emitting wireless signals which could be picked up in France, and the course of the robot thus plotted. We were arranging to jam this. I think the morale of London would be seriously affected if this sort of thing went on for long. The effect so far has been a certain amount of evacuation and a great rush for the tubes, queues for which were lining up in the early afternoon.

June 23, 1944

Last night was our worst yet: nothing nearer than Russell Square, but a blitz which began about 2.0 and lasted till 7.0. The men on the *Mirror* roof at one point saw sixteen robots come down over London in twelve minutes. Morrison made a speech in the House today rather making light of the little brutes, but I don't think the general public shares this opinion. Not only do we have long alerts at night, but continual ones in the daytime as well. Most of my office people would prefer a straightforward Blitz, even if the casualties are larger.

June 26, 1944
Rather a bad night last night and quite a bad day too – but I *saw* one of the robots at close range. I came out of the office to go to lunch while one of the little devils was thundering overhead, and caught a good view of it between clouds, speeding north: it eventually crashed in York Way near King's Cross. They are very neat little brutes, making a surprising amount of noise for their size.

A feature of today's list of bombed places was the considerable number in Hampshire. Obviously these had been aimed at Portsmouth, Southampton, or the Isle of Wight, and had overshot the mark. Morale is not very high since one landed just outside Waterloo on Friday morning about 9.30, killing many people on their way to work. Victoria was knocked out on Sunday morning with a direct hit between platforms 1 and 2, followed by a fire.

There is a feeling of optimism abroad in official circles, where there seems to be an idea that we can master this problem. In the meanwhile we are building up a vast balloon barrage and are bombing the departure platforms. We have captured twenty-nine of these places near Cherbourg, and two others which look undamageable by bombs of any calibre and are obviously for the discharge of some kind of missile far bigger than the present ones.

The Americans seem to be fighting better in France and are certainly very much more popular in this country than they were earlier.

June 27, 1944
What a night! The blower went at 11.45 and from then till 2.0 these damned robots continued to drop all around us, one crashing into Peabody Buildings in Wild Street and killing a lot of people. This one didn't sound the nearest, though it must actually have been so, as it is only 150 yards from our flat. At the height of the attack the rain was coming down in sheets and, without a moon, everything was pitch dark. M. saw one of the nearby robots flashing past looking like a flaming meteor, with the whole outline of the plane lit up.

Today a few more people have failed to turn up in the office because of the destruction of their homes. Only this morning when I was in the news room, two men were being told that their block of flats near Regent's Park had been hit since they reached the office at 11.0. They went off to see how their belongings had fared.

June 28, 1944

Had a rather quieter, because clearer, night, but made up for it by a very noisy day. We are building up a great balloon barrage by pulling in the balloons from all over England. Yesterday, however, there was a severe thunderstorm and many of the balloons caught fire; today there is a gale blowing and most of the balloons are grounded. Whenever there was a crash of thunder yesterday, the men in the office said: 'One of ours'!

June 30, 1944

A very rough day, with bombs at midday on Aldwych, Warren Street, and the Regent Palace Hotel. I arrived on the scene at Aldwych before the dust had cleared away. The whole area was carpeted with broken glass and bits of lamp standard. The bomb, like all three over us today, cut off its engine some distance away and came in on a silent glide. It fell on the roof of the Air Ministry, then into the road, where it went off, completely wrecking two buses, blasting the Air Ministry and the income tax part of Bush House, killing a horse, causing two fires, and so on. Bill Greig and Castle [Mirror *picture editor*] were on the top deck of a bus coming round from the Strand and saw the whole business. It is marvellous that their bus was quite undamaged. I thought the casualties low, with a few cuts from flying glass and one Waaf [*member of the Women's Auxiliary Air Force*] being carried off on a stretcher. The reporter we sent down, however, said he saw about forty corpses lined up – most of them people killed in the street (it was about 2.15 p.m.), but some of them in the Air Ministry, particularly the ground floor. I ran from Lincoln's Inn, and yet by the time I arrived the fire brigade and ambulances were there, bleeding girls in ragged clothes were being got down from the first floor of Bush House, a trouserless man was taking refuge in the Air Ministry, the Waaf was being pushed into her ambulance, and others with slight cuts were being helped away.

The woman in the greengrocer's made the best comment: 'Hitler'll get hisself disliked if he goes on like this!'

Parliament is thoroughly windy: the House of Commons rose today at 12.45! Yesterday was the only occasion this week it has sat for any time.

We are still allowed to say almost nothing about the pilotless planes, so I shall be interested to learn what is thought on the subject in Aberdeenshire, when I get there next week.

July 1, 1944
Whether I was badly shaken by the bomb in Aldwych or whether there were more bombs near us last night I don't know, but I just couldn't sleep. For the first time in my life I heard every hour strike from 12.0 to 7.0 inclusive. We have had a steady procession all day today, the nearest being Aldersgate Street station. In the composing room three men were made homeless, one last night and two this morning by bombs in different parts of South London. We had a leader for tomorrow about evacuation, but have been asked to change it as the Government has decided today to bring in an evacuation scheme. It is to be secret (!) so as not to encourage the Germans.

The reason for the move to Church House is that the building is more modern, and therefore less likely to collapse on Members if it is hit while the House is in session.

July 8, 1944
Churchill made a statement in the House on Thursday [July 6] on the flying bomb. Bill Greig said he spoke 'like a man drugged', almost inaudible and stumbling over his words. He had little to say and didn't say it well. He revealed that about 2,700 of these bombs had been discharged, which had killed about 2,700 civilians. He announced an evacuation scheme, which in fact only applies to South London; said everything was being done to stop the things, but that in the meanwhile we must just grin and bear it.

In Scotland they could make nothing of the official news, and

18

in the early days were just mystified, but gradually everybody had letters from friends in London and the whole thing began to take shape.

There is now a huge balloon barrage in position and a belt of guns twenty miles deep. These are to be supplied with American radar sets, which are accurate up to twenty-nine miles, and what with this and that better results are expected. I gather that the percentage of bombs dispatched that reach this country is remaining very constant, and that we are not within sight of mastering the damned things. The railway stations – particularly Euston and Paddington – are crammed with refugees, South Wales and Blackpool being the favourite havens of safety (though there is already hardly standing room in Blackpool!).

July 9, 1944
Campbell spent an afternoon in the House of Commons this last week, from which he gathered the following impressions. There will be a General Election within six months – as soon, that is, as victory is obviously assured. The Tories think that in the new House the Labour Party will be the largest with perhaps 280 seats; the Tories should get 250 and the balance will be made up with Liberals, Commonwealth, and Independents. They assume that Labour would not attempt to form a Government, but would approach Churchill to lead another coalition. It is assumed that Attlee would more or less fade out and that the Labour Party leader would be Morrison, if Bevin could be got to acquiesce. This picture is unnaturally simplified as (1) Churchill is said to be in a very bad way indeed, and (2) though Morrison is the obvious leader of the Labour Party, Bevin's hostility is still implacable.

July 18, 1944
Much more doodlebug activity since Saturday. The weather has been favourable and evidently they have got a lot of launching platforms working. More and more people are leaving London and no one can say morale is high. When the internal warning went in the office a couple of weeks ago, most people took no notice, but now there is a general scuttle for shelter.

The fighting in Normandy is fierce and expensive and is resulting in paltry gains, mostly in the American sector. In Italy we have made slight gains too. The Russians continue to sweep on and are getting very near their 1941 frontiers, except for the Baltic states.

July 20, 1944
The buzz-bombs have been very bad. Tuesday night [July 18], which I spent in the train, was the worst night to date, and last night was none too good. Fetter Lane got a direct hit while I was away. There were no casualties but the office is in a frightful mess – not only windows and window-frames blown in or sucked out, but locks torn off internal doors, partitions blown down, and even the wall of my own room blown out at a crazy angle into the passage.

The story going round the House this week – obviously concocted by some wag – is of Duncan Sandys [*Churchill's son-in-law*] at Chequers with the Prime Minister. Churchill's favourite theme is of the great burden resting on him and of the unfairness that any one man should have to bear so great a responsibility. He was groaning away on the usual lines, so Duncan Sandys, to cheer him (according to the story), pointed out that Hitler had an even greater burden to bear – so had Mussolini – because, after all, everything was going wrong for them. To which Churchill replied: 'Ah! but Mussolini has this consolation, that he could shoot his son-in-law!'2

July 23, 1944
Heard in the yard of Geraldine House yesterday as the internal warning went. 'We'd better take cover, mate: here comes Hitler on his motorbike!' Said by the driver of a lorry to his mate as a doodlebug approached.

July 24, 1944
I met Bill Greig in the passage today. He says the Labour people are not as happy as they were. They say there is a swing in the services away from regimentation (very naturally!) and that this will tell in favour of the Tories. Churchill is still staying up all

night drinking brandy, but is much more spry than he was a few weeks back. Greig thinks this is only a flash in the pan, but that he will probably hang on somehow for another eighteen months. He has just recently been on a trip to Normandy, which I imagine to be mainly prestige stuff – in fact electioneering.

I see the Mexicans have just stopped a new rat poison being put on the market under the name 'The Last Supper'. What next?

July 25, 1944

Professor Blackett came to lunch at the flat and produced a few crumbs of information. (1) That we *did* know in advance that the doodlebug had a jet-propulsion engine. This information, however, could not have percolated through to Morrison when he gave the editors his talk [on October 12, 1943]. (2) That he (Blackett) was known in the Admiralty as A.L.D., 'the anti-Lindemann device'. He has a very low opinion of Lindemann: says he fakes his facts to support his case, is the most emotional man he ever met, and that his judgment is more often wrong than anyone's he ever knew. (3) That it is a tragedy that Chequers is so near the headquarters of Bomber Command (which is presumably still at High Wycombe). Blackett regarded Harris as irresponsible and a nuisance, and having far too much influence with the Prime Minister. Harris was openly against the invasion: he thought that it was a silly operation. (4) That now that we had complete air supremacy, daylight bombing was safer than night bombing, though it was difficult to convince Harris of the fact. We had now, however, begun to use our bombers by day, and losses were really very low indeed.

July 26, 1944

M. was at a meeting of the Save the Children Fund and they were telling her about conditions in Battersea, where there has been a lot of damage and the children are very jittery. The local superstition is that Meux's brewery is quite safe, and people herd in there; many children live there. It is in fact neither sanitary nor safe. The upper-class myth is that the Dorchester is the safest building in London. It is no safer than any other modern steel-framed building, but nevertheless it enjoys a special aura. In the slummy areas the favourite shelter is often particularly rickety and unsafe.

I see from the papers that George Bernard Shaw is eighty-eight today and that he has given Ayot St Lawrence, where he has lived since 1908, as a gift to the National Trust. One of the papers – the *Express* I think – even publishes a picture of him in a queer sort of hat with a mica eye-guard, which he said he is accustomed to wear while chopping wood – the said hat being one designed for miners. I cannot feel the smallest interest in this tiresome old man. He wrote some good theatrical criticism fifty years ago and some plays which were good, and may be great, about forty years ago. To people of sixty and upwards he is still a great name, but to me he is that most boring object, an author who should clearly have died about thirty years ago and tries to maintain his position by the most tiresome publicity-seeking antics. It is curious to reflect that both he and Sidney Webb, who did so much to found the Labour Party, are still alive at an advanced age. Their creation shows all the doctrinaire lack of realism you would expect in the child of such parents. I imagine G.B.S. has a position in the political and literary history of this country, but a very much lowlier one than either he or my elders and betters imagine.

August 1, 1944
Was roused from sleep at 11.30 last night by a bomb, which I felt through the floor and which burst open my bedroom door. It was about the only one after a very quiet day. As it was my night fire watching I thought I had better show some signs of activity. Fire engines started rushing past and I really thought it was something near and something bad. So I padded off eastwards in the moonlight, but did not come to my first broken glass until I got to the Old Bailey. Eventually I tracked down the 'incident' to Little Britain, the far side of Bart's [*St Bartholomew's*] Hospital from me. The bomb had landed on some big buildings just across the street from Bart's. There were a lot of N.F.S. [*National Fire Service*] men about and several pumps, a small gas main was burning, but I could see no sign of a real fire. A water tower had arrived and was

being got into position. The ladder was pushed into the attic window of the ruined building just beside the major damage. The top of the long ladder was brilliantly lit with spotlights like young searchlights. Eventually an N.F.S. man came out and started down the ladder, followed by a woman in a rather blood-stained nightdress with a black-out blind wrapped round her middle. She was followed by another N.F.S. man. It was a curious scene, and must have been a very trying ordeal for the woman climbing down a high ladder under dazzling spotlights just after she had been badly shaken up by the bomb.

We are still promised the rocket at almost any minute. Rex North [Pictorial *war correspondent*] was present at a press conference held by Pile of the Anti-Aircraft Command, and afterwards had some chat with people in the Command. They said the installations for V2 are undamageable by bombs and that the only thing to do is to use gas. In any case they thought the war would increase in grimness in the closing six months. I must say I am amazed at the way, once we are on top, we cheerfully discuss ways and means of waging war fully equal to the Germans' at their most brutal. Surely now we have the upper hand it is for us to show that our moral code is better (if it is!), and not, by bullying neutrals and the slaughter of women and children, show the world that our better behaviour in the early stages of the war was due to our impotence and nothing else.

August 4, 1944
The lobby correspondents were given a talk last night, from which the following facts emerged. 1,000 of the German rocket projectiles have been made and are now ready for launching. This can be done from any stretch of road, provided there are thirty feet of concrete beneath it. The range is 300 miles and they are radio-directed for the first fifty seconds, which is too short a period to give us a chance of jamming the direction. The Germans are a bit nervous of the things and don't know how many may come back and hit them. The area in Poland where they were tried out is likely to fall into Russian hands very soon and investigation on the spot should prove helpful. It had been intended to evacuate Parliament and the Government to Stratford-on-Avon,

but this would not now be done. Facilities would be afforded for the evacuation of people from London whether for holidays or anything else; some Government departments may move, but the services and the Government will stay put. Churchill thinks the rocket will not arrive at all, but is prepared to let the Cabinet have its way in all this. The big installations in the Pas de Calais, which were thought to be for launching rockets, are now found to be underground hangars for very large pilotless planes. The General Staff estimates that within six weeks all the 'vital points' in France will be in our hands. Asked what was meant by 'vital points', the Government spokesman would not answer.

At this meeting it was stated that we have captured some of the men who release flying bombs. They were apparently being given a spell in the front line as a rest! It seems it is a hazardous business, and the operator has to be completely clothed in asbestos. Part of the risk must be the blow-back of the rocket that gets the flying bomb into the air and part must be the danger from the number that crash when taking off.

August 7, 1944
The news is taking a more and more sensational turn. In the east the Russians are on the borders of East Prussia, are advancing into the Baltic provinces and into Galicia. In Italy we have taken Florence after some very stiff fighting. But in France things are going best of all. The Americans, after breaking through at Avranches, are now in occupation of most of the centre of Brittany.

The puzzling factor about the military situation is that since the relief of Stalingrad, getting on for two years ago, the Germans have not staged one strategic counter-offensive. They caught the Russians on the wrong foot at one point and recaptured Kharkov, but taking a wide view it is fair to say that for over eighteen months the Germans have been retreating without one attempted comeback.

September 2, 1944
The ease and speed of the advance into France – we claim 200,000 prisoners in the north and 70,000 prisoners in the south – lead one to wonder why the operation was so long delayed. It is certain to

be argued that if we had not landed in North Africa (as Smuts wished) but in France, the war could have been finished a year ago with much greater prestige for us and correspondingly less for the Russians. The Italian campaign, in any case, remains in all its meaninglessness. If it really was known that the German reserves were as low as they appear to be, then the outcry last year for a 'Second Front now' was well founded. Not only could the war have been won then, but the destruction of so much of Europe by our bombs could have been avoided, to the great advantage of our prestige in Europe. Clearly what will trouble our consciences most when the war is well and truly over is all the information which will come out of Germany of the number of women and children we killed with our bombs while having no effect on the course of the war. Already one fact is becoming crystal clear and that is that all our talk of starving Europe has been hooey. All the correspondents say that food in Normandy was more plentiful than in English country districts, and the same thing seems to be true too of the food position in Paris.

September 9, 1944
Yesterday evening I was sitting at an open window in the Royal Institution when there was a loud explosion. It sounded as if one of the Hyde Park guns had gone off. There was no follow-up: most people thought it was a clap of thunder. However, I looked into the office in the evening and learned that it was indeed V2. There had been two explosions caused apparently by rocket shells, one in Epping and one at Chiswick. The former did no damage; the latter destroyed six houses, seriously damaged fifty, and killed four people. There was little blast, but the explosion, unlike those of V1, made a crater fifteen feet deep and fifty feet across. Any mention of the explosion is rigidly censored, and so far we have had no others. The Chief Censor says they are believed to have been fired from Holland.

September 12, 1944
I was awake at 6.15 this morning when there was a tremendous bang, followed by a long rolling echo – another V2, this time on Kew. I thought I heard another at about 9.0, but I was right

indoors and it was hard to be sure. However, this was much further off and seems to have been in Essex. Two fell yesterday morning, one in Essex and one near Swanley; and about four seem to have arrived this morning, two or three in Essex, one in Kent, and the one at Kew. They make an incredible noise and would prove very destructive to a big building. In open ground or among small houses they make too big a crater to cause any very serious trouble. The whole subject is still rigidly censored and in fact most people – certainly up till today – regard the noises as explosions of gas mains or what not. Bart says at least one of yesterday's exploded in mid-air and our reporter saw an R.A.F. man loading the pieces on a lorry.

Bart's son is home on leave after nine weeks in the line. He is in a commando, whose mission on D-Day was to proceed up the Orne from the beaches and reinforce the airborne division which had taken the bridges. Of his original 500, only 120 were alive and unwounded at the end of the nine weeks. He said the work of the airborne troops on D-Day was superb; he also spoke highly of our tanks, but has a poor opinion of our infantry. All the best men go into the R.A.F., the Navy, or the Tanks, and what is left gets into the infantry.

Our attack on Troarn was a failure he attributed to the Guards' tank division. The timing with the R.A.F. was arranged to a split second, but the Guards started half an hour late and completely jammed their only line of communication with unofficial baggage lorries piled high with folding chairs, camp beds, and what not. As a result, the supporting tank division could not get through and was seven hours late; the infantry never got there at all.

The only Americans Peter saw were parties who came up the line to buy souvenirs – £20 to £25 for a German pistol, £5 for a steel helmet, and so on. No doubt the purchasers will go home with a wonderful yarn of the heroism with which they won these trophies in battle! Everywhere, Peter said, the Germans fought well but were desperately short of men.

Cars still have cards in the windscreen bearing the legend 'Doctor' or 'Press', presumably in the hope of getting special treatment from the police in time of need. Yesterday I saw a car with the printed card 'Geologist', which surely constitutes the strangest claim to special treatment in traffic.

September 17, 1944

Cudlipp is here for a week or two on leave from Rome. He was asked to help with the problems of V.D. and of accidents behind the front, and therefore saw all the relevant figures. He said the deaths from accidents – mostly motor accidents and burns from petrol fires – are from two to five times as numerous as the deaths in action. I don't suppose these figures hold good in the thick of a big attack, but they do at other times. V.D. is also very bad. One of our attacks had to be held up for a week while a thousand V.D. cases were removed from Naples hospital. Within four weeks of our landing in Sicily the equivalent of a brigade was down with it. The Americans have much more penicillin than we have and use it for syphilis. It is very effective according to Cudlipp, but has rather a high mortality rate. We only have enough penicillin for wounds.

September 25, 1944

On Wednesday [September 20] had dinner in a private room at the Savoy with Herbert Morrison and Bellenger, the meeting having been arranged by the latter at my instigation. My first sight of Morrison some years ago was when standing beside him in a public lavatory. I was not impressed, but then this is hardly the best setting! I saw him in the *Daily Mirror* debate and once in the street since, but he never made much impression. Closer to, he is a much more convincing personality. He has iron-grey hair, a strong chin, a good head, and is by no means insignificant. He is disconcerting to talk to with his one eye and his spectacles. We talked about this and that. He obviously does not expect a General Election till March at the very earliest.

Eventually I said my piece, which was this. That it is not easy for a very popular paper like the Pic to support a party as such, but easy to support a policy if there seems to be any serious probability of it being carried into effect; still easier to support a political leader if he has the sort of personality you can build up.

The Labour Party has an admirable programme, but does it really mean business? On the face of it, no. It is about to go to the country appealing for votes for Attlee as our next Prime Minister. Such a choice was irresponsible: I wouldn't employ him as a lift attendant. (Morrison and Bellenger: 'He's really not as bad as all that.') The second man in the Party hierarchy was Greenwood, a nice old man with a fine appearance and a grand head, but he is now just a wreck. The only possible leaders of the Party were Bevin and himself. I should regret the selection of Bevin on political grounds, but at least he is not ridiculous. Mistakes over the leadership leave me with the feeling that the Labour Party wants office but not power. This impression is confirmed if one recalls the history of the Labour Governments of 1924 and 1929. Instead of bringing in some obviously sound Socialist legislation and risking being voted down in the House, they snatched at office, footled around, and eventually (in 1924) were thrown out on a silly issue which did them no credit at all.[3]

Morrison agreed on this, and said they should either have ridden for a fall with a view to getting a majority in 1929 or they should have done a deal with the Liberals. They did neither. We went on talking on these lines, Morrison pointing out that the policy of the Party and its leadership were not his sole responsibility. I said I quite saw that, but that unless the bugs could be got out of the mechanism, the Party would not be worth support. And so we parted after three hours or so. I wonder will anything emerge?

September 29, 1944
I met an American colonel the other night who, in between smuggling American clothes and alarm clocks into England for his lady friends, has been over to Paris several times. He was in the Crillon immediately after the occupation of Paris. He was offered a choice of suites; he and his colleagues found a bottle of champagne and a bottle of brandy in each bedroom – and there was no bill to pay. The women were embarrassingly ready to be kissed, slept with, or anything else. He attended a doctor for some slight ailment, but again the Frenchman would not hear of any payment.

October 12, 1944

As a result of the conference at Dumbarton Oaks, a tentative scheme has been put forward for a world security organization [*the United Nations Organization*]. It is very like the old League of Nations and quite clearly won't work. There are to be five permanent members of the Executive Council: Russia, America, and Britain, together with China and France! The first clause of the proposals records the sovereign freedom and independence of every state represented in the new league. This means that we go on record with the statement that Nicaragua and Russia are equally free, independent, sovereign states. This is mischievous rubbish. The fiction that France is one of the world's great powers and that Germany and Japan are not, is another obvious source of trouble. The Russians, moreover, are insisting on the right of veto in any case involving sanctions. If ever there was a stillborn scheme, this is it.

October 26, 1944

Bellenger bustled into the office this afternoon after having had some talk with Churchill at the House. Churchill told a friend of Bellenger's that the war against Germany would not finish for another year, and Japan would take another year beyond that. This is a far more depressing picture than any I have heard of for a long time. However, it may be true, though it rather looks as if the Russians were determined to bring things to a conclusion this winter. It is an appalling thought, as it would mean the reduction of central Europe to a smoking heap of ruins, haunted by starving savages. Such a conclusion to the war could not possibly suit our book. Would it suit anyone's?

October 27, 1944

Sinclair was in trouble last night in the House over the story, which has been going round Fleet Street for many months, of an R.A.F. farm in Regent's Park which, in defiance of the rationing regulations, sent presents of pork to people in high places. One of the recipients whose name was given in the House was Sinclair. We had the story long ago, but were headed off publishing it on the grounds that two courts martial were pending and that the matter was sub judice. The courts martial were never held, but the excuse shut us up. Now it has been raised by Hopkinson in the House. Sinclair tried to make it all sound so innocent, but it was a definite breach of the rationing regulations, the meat went to a number of people in high places – and there were no prosecutions. The offence was not very serious and small fines only would have been inflicted, but the attempt to hush the whole story up was disgusting.

The *Mirror* chairman, Cowley, is dying and there has been some discussion in the office about the whereabouts of his relations. His secretary has been with him for twenty-four years and knows nothing of his history beyond the facts that he was earning £1 a week when he was twenty and that he was assistant cashier of the *Evening News* when the Harmsworth brothers bought it in 1894. I heard that he had a brother who was once a hairdresser in Fleet Street, but no one else seems to know of this rumour. His sons think he has, or had, a brother and believe that he has sisters to whom he pays annuities, but they don't know them, nor even where they live (the three sons are all in their thirties). No one knows where he was born or brought up, though the sons say he seemed to know the Holloway district [of London] very well indeed, and they imagine he may have lived there as a child. It is an astonishing story of secretiveness in a man whom I knew well for eighteen years and who had no real cause to conceal his humble origin – though it may have been because he was a Jew and wished to conceal the fact.[4]

November 9, 1944
Our photographer is just back from Brussels. He was very struck by Monty's insistence on extreme speed in burying our dead, so that reinforcements coming up see no British corpses but a lot of German ones. I see one of the papers this week has a crack about 'God Almonty'!

November 18, 1944
An acquaintance coming up today from Beaconsfield only just caught the train and travelled in the guard's van. The guard told

her that his mother-in-law's house had been bombed and that the only part of her that was recovered was her ear. This was identifiable by the earring she wore. The inquest was held on the ear, all the rest of her having vanished!

M. tells me that when she was at Aylesbury on Monday she saw the actual document giving a woman a three months' remission of her sentence. This is an elaborate document addressed 'To the Governor of my prison at Aylesbury and all others whom it may concern GREETING' and is signed both by the King himself and by the Home Secretary! A reprieve is signed only by the Home Secretary, but any remission, however piffling, by the King.

November 23, 1944

Had lunch today with John North. According to him, the troops in Italy showed a great reluctance to take their mepacrine. It transpired that they believed it was being given them to make them impotent, and so prevent V.D. This story was almost universally believed and so led to some unnecessary malaria. The authorities were unable to discover if the yarn came from an enemy source.

Just before the capture of Tunis our army was almost incapacitated by the sick feeling caused by this stuff. Fortunately the German high command chose the same day as our own to administer it, and both armies were incapacitated together. What luck that they should both choose the same moment for beginning precautions against the summer malaria!

November 24, 1944

Had dinner last night with Wilfrid Roberts to meet Sir William Beveridge and Honor Balfour. We dined at the Gargoyle Club in Dean Street, of which Beveridge is an unexpected member. He is a curious-looking man with a very weather-beaten red face and white hair. But for his vitality, I think you would take him for a small retired farmer, or something of the kind. He has unimpressive fat hands with short fingers. To talk to, he is very quick and intelligent, and most attractive in the boyish way he enjoys being suddenly famous. Honor Balfour, who sees a lot of him, says that one day he was recalling with delight the number of men who had done great things after the age of sixty-five. He has astonishing freshness and vitality: mentioned in casual conversation the most daunting programme of speeches in widely different parts of the country.

He regards his work on social security as finished; he is already getting rather bored with the subject of full employment and was more intrigued with the book he is writing on the preservation of peace. I don't think Beveridge is an original thinker, but he has much administrative experience and a great gift for simple exposition. His great achievement over social security was to present us with a scheme for the future which was generally wanted and was worked out in detail. On full employment he really can only assure us with the conviction carried by his great prestige that unemployment can be cured. This is a propaganda job which is by no means yet complete. On the preservation of peace he appears to be going to dish up the old ideas of the League of Nations with a few new trimmings. Like all other Liberal plans it is based on the assumption that great powers, where their vital interests are at stake, will behave like intelligent Liberals. All history goes to prove the reverse.

November 25, 1944
I was sitting in Campbell's room reading the Sunday Pic proofs when there was a shattering bang and the whole building shook: evidently a rocket and not far off. I rushed up on the roof to see a big cloud of reddish dust drift away on the wind. The rocket had obviously fallen in Holborn, somewhere opposite the end of Chancery Lane. I sped round to Lincoln's Inn. There was much broken glass everywhere, including two broken windows on our staircase – mercifully, however, not in our flat. It appears that the rocket fell on the back of the First Avenue Hotel, destroying parts of the hotel that had not already been burnt, and also knocking down houses on the west side of the passage leading from Holborn into Gray's Inn. The rumour was flying round that the death roll was thirty-six. I should say this was an exaggeration.

By December 1944 the British and American forces were strung out on a long line from northern Belgium down to Switzerland. The last thing they expected was a German counter-attack. On December 16 von Rundstedt struck through the Ardennes with twenty-six divisions, punched a hole in a weakly held sector of the Allied lines, and drove sixty miles towards Antwerp before he was stopped. This was Germany's last gasp, but it gave the Allies an unpleasant shock. During this fighting Montgomery was put in charge of the Allied forces on land. (As had been agreed before D-Day, he had relinquished his command of the Allied forces to Eisenhower after the initial fighting. He continued to command the British forces.) By December 25 the Rundstedt offensive was checked, and then the Germans were quickly pushed back.

They could now offer little effective defence of their homeland. Between January and March the western Allies broke into Germany from many different points. The Russians too were fighting inside Germany, and early in April they joined up with the Americans on the Elbe.

Between February 4 and 11 the Big Three met again, at Yalta. Final strategy, and features of the post-war world including the United Nations, the division of Germany, and Poland, were discussed. On Poland, Stalin – whose troops had overrun that country in January – gave pledges that it would remain independent and democratic. Despite Churchill's justified scepticism these were accepted by Roosevelt, who was now in the last month of his life. After Yalta Stalin cynically disregarded his pledges and set about ensuring Communist control.

Another weak country in the centre of the stage was Greece. In the aftermath of the German withdrawal at the end of 1944, the Greek resistance forces – mainly Communist – made a bid for power. They were defeated by the landing of 60,000 British troops in support of the King of Greece. In this instance Stalin made no move to help his fellow Communists.

Italy had become in the public eye almost a sideshow. In August 1944 the Allies had pressed on from Rome to Florence, and were now in control of most of Italy. But throughout the winter the 'slogging match' continued. In early April Alexander broke through into the Po valley, and on April 29 the German forces in Italy surrendered. The day before this, Mussolini was shot by Italian partisans and hung upside down in an Italian square together with his mistress. Two days later Adolf Hitler committed suicide together with his new wife, Eva Braun.

In April, too, the Americans landed at Okinawa, the island at the tip of the Japanese mainland. On all fronts Japanese resistance was crumbling,

*and from May to August 1945 American bombers tore up Japan's cities in
what has been called the 'greatest air offensive in history'.*

*Britain's bombing offensive against Germany was reopened. Its climax
was the horrific attack on Dresden in February 1945, which caused a fire-
storm in which at least 25,000 lost their lives. The offensive ended soon after.*

December 1, 1944

No one has yet any explanation of the appointment of Alexander
to be Field Marshal as from June 4, while Monty's appointment,
which was not antedated, is only from September 1. It looks, and
probably is, just personal bias, not to say spite, by Grigg, Churchill,
Roosevelt, or who have you.

December 2, 1944

At dinner on Wednesday was Mrs Turner (E. Arnot Robertson),
who has just been doing a round of American hospitals with
Esmond [Rothermere] and Bill Astor. They constituted a sort of
Brains Trust. She said the American wounded were of two kinds,
a very small super-tough group from the backwoods and a large
mollycoddled town-bred group. The latter she said were deeply
shocked that anyone should stand up to them, let alone shoot real
bullets at them. One of their reactions was a sadistic one and the
other was a breakdown in morale. At all the hospitals there was
only one answer to the question of what to do with the Germans:
'Slaughter the lot – men, women, and children!' A doctor told
her that none of the wounded would – or could – be sent back to
fight even if they suffered only the lightest of flesh wounds.
'Junior', as she put it, who had always been listened to and
played up to as the centre of interest for the family, just couldn't
stand his first contact with reality.

George [*Sir George Thomson*] the other day at dinner ex-
patiated on the collapse of morals we have seen in recent years.
That there has been a lamentable deterioration in sexual morals,
that theft is so widespread as to become a serious administrative
problem (for instance at the *Mirror* our typewriters have to be
chained to the desks), that truth telling by prominent public
figures, Cabinet ministers and so forth, is becoming quite rare – all

19

this is obvious, but George's point was rather different. He said that the torturing of prisoners (by the Germans) would have been unthinkable in any war in the last century: that it marked a return to the 17th or even the 16th century. So far as I know – and I have known him for quite twenty years – he is not a religious man, but he attributed the collapse of morals to the collapse of religion and put a lot of the blame for this, in England anyway, on the Church.

December 9, 1944
Bellenger says he is one of a small group – with Garro-Jones and Noel-Baker among them – who are trying to rid themselves of Attlee as the Labour Party leader. They recently had Cripps to dinner, who said he is perfectly willing to serve in a Labour Government under Morrison. However, he warned the party that Attlee will not go quietly, as he is rather pleased with his own record in the last year while Churchill has been away so much. Cripps thought that all the Labour ministers would in fact leave the Government before the election, in spite of Churchill's blandishments. The only doubtful one is Bevin, who, however, appears to have lost considerable political stature of recent months.

December 13, 1944
Had dinner with Hore-Belisha and his wife. Hore-Belisha very clever and amusing, but with no sense of direction. His wife was captured as a member of an ambulance unit and spent four years in occupied territory, mostly Poland and Belgium. She said the Russian army struck her with terror, in much the same way as a swarm of locusts; that the Germans are much more frightened of the Russians than the Russians are of the Germans; that the Germans are really not very concerned about us, but that the Russians hate and despise Britain and everything British.

Hore-Belisha is curious in that a man so egotistical should say, obviously truthfully, that he cannot blow his own trumpet in public and so people are unaware of the good work he did at the War Office. He is admittedly moving into the Tory fold (I told him he was backing a horse just as it was showing unmistakable signs of losing the race), his reason being rather ingenious. He says that our population is aging and therefore is bound to become more Conservative. By 1970 we shall have so many people over sixty that the country is bound to have some kind of a Conservative administration. This will certainly be a factor in the situation, but the rising importance of Communist Russia will, in my opinion, turn us either towards communism or by reaction to some kind of fascism. Mrs Hore-Belisha said how widespread in Europe is fear of Russia, although Russian soldiers are abnormally prone to homesickness.

Hore-Belisha mentioned in passing how he had once asked Lloyd George what he thought of a book about himself by E.T. Raymond. Lloyd George said he never read books about himself!

Esmond [Rothermere] came to lunch today. He was very amusing about the Prime Minister: said his political views are based on personal prejudice. He is in favour of King George of the Hellenes because he has known him for many years – and likes him. He is in favour of Marshal Tito because he has met him and likes him too. Young King Peter of Yugoslavia does not interest him.[5] He disliked de Gaulle intensely and was always making jokes about him, but when he went to Paris he had a marvellous reception from the people. He was much affected by this, tears poured down his cheeks, and when he looked up he saw de Gaulle was weeping too. From that moment they were friends and Anglo-French relations took a decisive turn for the better. So spoke Esmond and there is much in what he says, but I think that quite apart from personalities Churchill has shown a sentimental preference for royalty as such.

1945

VE-DAY!

Daily Mirror

Tuesday, May 8, 1945
No. 12,911 ONE PENNY
Registered at G.P.O. as a Newspaper.

IT'S OVER IN THE WEST

TODAY is VE-Day—the day for which the British people have fought and endured five years, eight months and four days of war.

With unconditional surrender accepted by Germany's last remaining leaders, the war in Europe is over except for the actions of fanatical Nazis in isolated pockets, such as Prague.

The Prime Minister will make an official announcement—in accordance with arrangements between Britain, Russia and the U.S.—at 3 o'clock this afternoon.

ALL TODAY AND TOMORROW ARE PUBLIC HOLIDAYS IN BRITAIN, IN CELEBRATION OF OUR VICTORY.

We also remember and salute with gratitude and pride the men and women who suffered and died to make triumph possible, and the men still battling in the East against another cruel enemy who is still to be defeated.

War winners broadcast today

You will hear the voices of the King, Field-Marshal Montgomery and General Eisenhower when they broadcast over the B.B.C. today and tonight.

After the King's speech at 9 o'clock, and separated from it by the news bulletin comes "Victory Report," a stirring programme which will contain the recorded voices of the war leaders and after famous personalities of the war.

Additional features of the B.B.C. Thanksgiving programme, which will end at 2 a.m. tomorrow, include, at 8 a.m. an address by the Archbishop of Canterbury at a Thanksgiving Service for Victory, and at 9.20 a tribute to the King.

★ VE-SCENE TRAFALGAR SQUARE

It was a high old time in Trafalgar-square last night. Everybody wanted to climb something. This party of Wrens and Allied soldiers celebrated by clambering on one of the famous statues round the Nelson plinth—an unusual feature present—the Nelson of its column—turned a blind eye.

London had joy night

"Daily Mirror" Reporter

PICCADILLY CIRCUS, VE-VE—THIS is 21—and we are all going mad. There are thousands of us in Piccadilly-circus. The police are smacking us on the back.

And so a glorious night of pre-making the most of it, will surely last a long time.

We are dancing the Conga and the Ji and "Knees up, Mother Brown," and we are all for being mad and wholehearted and having tremendous fun.

The sky is so many a colour and so on. Then are we not masters of low-flying jive-gang?

bombers "showing up" the "celebrating Londoners."

We have been waiting for this night in celebrated. We went about as we always go about—a long time we've been up the has been here.

A train of gay glaces down here at Leicester Square, are dressed up dozens of girls and soldiers of all the Allied nations are out and jitterbugging and smiling bang—gaudy and—and yelling their scarf to—and at midnight. We are—

frantic are yelling of Roll out the Barrel.

We sang it when we went to France in 1939 and we sang it as we waited in France last year. "How we sang it" far tonight.

We shall never forget—"Roll"—

About to-night cheers a New Zealand airline climbed up the summit of a lamp post Down below, they sang and joked, and

He stood there pouring down the crowds to the silk of the lamp on his brow, and

Continued on Back Page

★ P.M. BROADCAST
BY THE KING

The King will broadcast at 9 o'clock tonight. There will be a Thanksgiving Service on the B.B.C. at 8.27, at 8.23 pm

Continued on Back Page

Daily Mirror

WED JUN 16 1945

FORWARD WITH THE PEOPLE

No. 12,946 ONE PENNY
Registered at G.P.O. as a Newspaper.

PEACE

JAPAN SURRENDERS— ALLIES CEASE FIRE

Piccadilly quiet— Chinatown crazy

"Daily Mirror" Reporter

FOR five nights to announce the peace crowds thronged London's Piccadilly celebration in advance—and when the news came most of them went home.

Far by midnight nearly had gone home—exhausted—and when the announcement faintly came there was no Piccadilly standing, no dancing.

Throughout the rest of Britain the news was taken quietly and there were no big, wildly jubilant crowds to greet the return of world peace.

Soon after your o'clock more than 1,000 people came in front of Buckingham Palace calling:
"We want the King."

But in midnight they had struggled as usual. They included two U.S. soldiers, a Wraf and four civilians.

When told the news the Americans shouted "Cmon!" and threw their man in the air.

And there was made an effort to cheer for the King but it was too weak and the crowd soon went away.

Not a Song

There were not more than a hundred people crowd in the midnight—the normal number and there wasn't even a song.

Five dead thousands had streamed towards the famous Circus from the side streets. As early as 8.30 there was scarcely a foot of road free. Cars, cleaning at snail's pace, nosed through, tooting and singing with people, came out and women and newspapers.

Mostly, hands and laughter, the put-cuffs—and shouts of forward calculated oriented with horning starts and loud flashes.

Either hope from the peace up and down went and women who were freed that might for hours caused by the 750-odd offshore outings in the Piccadilly.

The local causation in the peace upon has been the only cause.

Missing number 473 Figures were killed and 216 wounded.

200 ships back soon from East

Sending of the Far East "craze fire" means that 200 boats of the British Pacific Fleet will be very quickly under way for home.

Three round of what is known as the "First fighting" engaged in fighting and enjoying the main Fleet.

Fleeing Britain naval forces will move towards Japan and later sent to carry out the sea. Among in strength a fleet of road Iron Clay, draining at snail's pace they'll be back. Around home, moored to receive, on effort to cheer for the King but it was too weak.

Striking Britain naval forces will attack the enemy's Pacific coast under cover of battleships. These forces will be formed up to suit the home moored to receive, in strong demobilisation groups.

M-crackle three in an Admiralty wireless chamber now for weeks—commencing to start up.

It is likely to be at least between six to nine mainly barely stirred intricate intervals can be handed over to the civil ports during the next three weeks, but Admiral V. ARMS, Chief of Staff, said yesterday.

Today and tomorrow V-days "Enjoy yourselves" call by Attlee at midnight

"PEACE HAS ONCE AGAIN COME TO THE WORLD. LET US THANK GOD FOR THIS GREAT DELIVERANCE AND HIS MERCIES." IT WAS THE VOICE OF THE PRIME MINISTER, BROADCASTING FROM NO. 10, DOWNING-STREET AT MIDNIGHT TO TELL BRITAIN THAT JAPAN HAS SURRENDERED.

Japan has accepted the Allied terms without qualification. The Jap Emperor is to order all his forces to lay down their arms and obey all commands of the Allied Forces.

PRESIDENT TRUMAN SAID IN WASHINGTON THAT THE ALLIED ARMED FORCES HAVE ALREADY BEEN ORDERED TO SUSPEND OFFENSIVE OPERATIONS.

In his broadcast Mr. Attlee announced that today and tomorrow will be V-Day holidays.

"Let all who can relax and enjoy themselves in the knowledge of work well done," he said.

Arrangements have been made for the formal signing of the surrender at the earliest moment and President Truman has named General MacArthur as the Allied commander to receive the surrender.

Washington reports last night said that the surrender will probably be signed on a battleship, or on Okinawa, scene of one of the most savage battles of the Pacific war.

Emperor to Broadcast

TWO minutes before the midnight announcement of the surrender of Japan the Japanese Emperor revealed over the Jap surrender via U.S Navy Department, broadcast from Indianapolis. Every man in the forces on board was told.

The cruiser's last moment, said the Navy Department, was within a few minutes' steam from Leyte, in the Philippines.

880 men lost in sunk A-bomb ship

Some otherwards, however, mean so much that President Truman had proclaimed a two-day holiday for the rest of Federal work and announced the U.S. holiday had also delivered an address before the United States.

Mr. Attlee went to the microphone in No. 10 to give the terms of the surrender after a breathless day in which the hopes of the world had been raised and dashed again.

In his White House statement last night President Truman said: "The proclamation of VJ-Day must wait upon the formal signing of the surrender terms by Japan.

Continued on Back Page

Campbell had lunch with Beveridge during the week. Old Bill Bev was in very confident form. He spoke of himself as the future leader – in effect if not in name – of the Liberal Party. He said they had conducted some large-scale tests of political opinion in this country, particularly among troops, and the result was that forty-two per cent would vote Labour, thirty-six per cent Liberal, twenty-one per cent Tory, and one per cent Communist. That there is a strong trend to the Left these days no one will dispute, but Beveridge's figures seem more than optimistic to say the least. But one must remember that he is a professional statistician and should not be too much influenced by wishful thinking.

He said that Churchill is now a querulous old man, no longer of any political importance.

Fred Bellenger returned from Italy today. He is down for a broadcast and so came home. Two of his party of six [M.P.s] were lost in an aeroplane accident. He had interviews with Alexander and Macmillan, and also with Nenni, the Socialist leader, and Togliatti, the Communist. He went to the front, to Florence, to Rome, Naples, and Bari. Italy is in a shocking state: there is no food, no transport, no raw materials, no work. You see the hammer and sickle everywhere with 'Viva Stalin, Viva Roosevelt, Viva Churchill' underneath. Bellenger assumes that when we march into North Italy, the country will temporarily relapse into anarchy.

What the outcome will be, no one knows. Togliatti said he did not want Italy to go Communist; the Pope told members of the parliamentary party that he was very much afraid of communism, not only in Italy.

The six M.P.s had dinner with Macmillan – an unsuitably sumptuous one it sounded. Macmillan afterwards spoke very prosily for an hour or more on Greece. It appears that we now have three divisions there! Bellenger asked point blank what was the Government policy. If the Greeks wanted to shoot each other, surely that was their business, not ours, provided we got the harbours and airfields we wanted for operations against the Germans. Macmillan's very lame answer was that 'saving civilization' was surely worth some sacrifices. Bellenger retorted that if 'saving civilization' in Greece took three divisions, 'saving civilization' in the rest of Europe would take the whole British Army. He got the impression that our foreign policy at the moment is conducted on the basis of Churchill's personal caprice, and that Eden plays the part of a mere errand boy.

January 29, 1945

Walking over Hampstead Heath yesterday (hoping to see some tobogganing and skating as it is very cold), I was discussing with M. the principal effect on the country of five and a half years of war. We agreed that the main change since 1939 has been in the position of women, which, again, was the main domestic long-term effect of the war of 1914–18. Of course their clothes have changed so much. Everywhere one sees women either in slacks or with bare legs. Smoking in the street by women is general, and we are both struck by the way women are determined to claim in every way the same freedom as men. It is all done rather un-intelligently and women are unlikely to gain by the new attitude. But there it is, that is what they want and that is what they mean to have.

M. said she is quite sure that this emancipation in ordinary everyday life is having a big effect on sexual morals and that only a minority of women now have slept only with their husbands: most have a good deal of experience either before or after marriage. At the moment divorce is very prevalent. The numbers of divorces go up year by year, but already a new factor is creeping in. So far divorce has meant the emancipation of adults, but now there are considerable numbers of grown-ups whose parents were divorced and who therefore have strong views on divorce from the point of view of the child. My own view is that divorce should be impossible, but that couples who wish to live together should incur no stigma if they don't marry, provided they have no children. I cannot say, however, that I think sexual morals are at the moment heading in that direction. Anyway, to end up where I started, the general impression left by a London crowd in 1945 is much more like a Moscow crowd of 1932 than I should then have thought possible. There has been, so to speak, a proletarianization of the London public.

George Harris, chairman of Rowntree's, came to see me in the office last week and was full of chat about the chocolate, sweet, and cocoa trade. At present all the cocoa in London is Cadbury's and all the cocoa in the north is Rowntree's. You can buy tins with various makers' names on them, but the stuff inside the tin is identical! He has tried to wage war on Cadbury's cocoa in the south, thinking the time particularly opportune when there was no difference at all in the taste of the three principal brands. He more or less destroyed all the trade of the small manufacturers, bringing their percentage from twenty down to eight, but quite failed to move Cadbury's. I didn't realize cocoa was a profitable product: I thought all the money was in chocolate. But Harris said it was almost the other way round.

He said straight advertising is often quite ineffective, as he found with his clear gums. But as soon as Garland's [the advertising agency] thought of advertising them as something to chew when you can't smoke, the sales soared. It seems odd that a sales angle like this should make all the difference.

February 1, 1945
Campbell had lunch with Bellenger yesterday to pump him still further about his Italian trip. Bellenger was much impressed with Togliatti, the Communist, whom he considered to be head and shoulders superior to any other political figure in Italy. Nenni he

thought was just a Socialist relic of another age. Alexander said nothing about politics, only discussed welfare, but did say he hoped the troops would extract some benefit from the time spent among the great cultural monuments of Italy.

Macmillan made no attempt to justify our foreign policy in the Mediterranean area, and said specifically he couldn't. The Foreign Office people Bellenger's party met were unanimous that Churchill's method of having his own emissaries abroad (resident ministers) was a great source of weakness to this country. Decisions made by Churchill, usually on impulse, were cabled out to Macmillan, while the Foreign Office and our local ambassadors were not even informed of what was going on.

Bellenger learned that the Americans, when they landed in North Africa, were out to buy the goodwill of the populace, and actually gave away a million rations. (They then ran short of food and had to apply to us for rations for their own army – hence a furious row.) Bit by bit they have been receding from this policy as they became more and more clearly aware of what was going on in Italy and their complete inability to deal with the situation. Now they have left the policing of Rome to us (too many of their own military police were racketeers) and are withdrawing from the whole sticky problem as much as they can.

Harry Hopkins has been here on his way to the Big Three meeting and is said to have been instructed to warn Churchill that something very definite must be done very soon if the U.S. is not to slip back into isolationism.

February 17, 1945
The most shattering item was put out tonight by S.H.A.E.F. [*Supreme Headquarters of the Allied Expeditionary Force*], saying that at last the long-expected orders had been given and that to shorten the war we were resorting to terror bombing. Recent attacks on Berlin, Dresden, and Chemnitz had been directed at the refugees swarming into these cities and were part of this policy. This is entirely horrifying. Not only does it make nonsense of all our protestations about our war aims and about our bombing policy: it gives official proof for everything that Goebbels ever said on the subject. It is wicked as well as being typically un-British. I think

part of the reason for this catastrophic announcement must be a desire to please Stalin and partly it must be attributed to the Americans, who are quite irresponsible and desperately anxious to keep down their own casualties by any means however foul. I cannot help feeling that the price, political and moral, we shall have to pay for all this will be a grievous one.

We rang up the Ministry of Information as soon as the news came in, to urge that it be suppressed – a very forlorn hope – and in any case did not print it.

Barbara Ward came to lunch, a most charming and admirable person, assistant editor of the *Economist* and a leading Catholic propagandist. She is about thirty, very feminine, very nice-looking, and exceedingly intelligent. She had been talking to one of the women who went to Yalta. This girl said that each of the three delegations was billeted in a separate town and only saw the others at the Livadia palace when they were actually conferring. The British billet was six miles from the palace. They landed at an airport six hours' drive from their billet and for the whole six hours they met a Russian tommy-gunner (mostly women!) every fifty yards.

The first day, they were told Stalin was coming to call on Churchill and a drove of Ogpu men flowed in, very easy to recognize, she said, by reason of the fact that they all had gold teeth and wore black cloth caps. The British turned out at the appointed hour to do Stalin honour. He didn't turn up, and after two hours they were told he was not coming and everyone relaxed. Then, half an hour later, he arrived surrounded by guards of one kind or another. The delay had all been bluff – part of the security arrangements! His official excuse for not leaving Russia is that he has a weak heart and cannot fly. He does in fact travel about Russia in a train. His arrangements for his personal security were so fantastic that people at the conference felt his position may be less secure than they had thought.

Barbara Ward had also been to a lecture by General Spears this week, this time to the Central Asian Society, where he was even more violently anti-French than he was at Chatham House [*on February 15, when Cecil King had heard him speak on Syria*]. I asked

her why he was so anti-French. After all he had originally sponsored de Gaulle, he spoke French so well, knew France intimately,
and so on. She said he had indeed originally sponsored de Gaulle
and had thought he would remain in his pocket. When de Gaulle
showed a mind of his own, Spears' indignation knew no bounds!

March 9, 1945

The German front west of the Rhine is collapsing, and in a
dramatic sweep some American tanks have taken the bridge at
Remagen and are digging in on the eastern bank. It certainly
looks as if the war were ending. The destruction in Germany is
quite awful, and I am afraid I am far more appalled by the
prospect of rebuilding a prostrate Europe than elated at the idea
of victory.

March 17, 1945

The Russians are attacking in the east, but are up against the thaw
and are making little headway. In the west we are along the
Rhine as far south as Coblenz and are likely to be along the Rhine
for its whole length quite soon. Fighting is very heavy, but those
who should be in the know say this crossing of the Rhine has
shortened the war by two or three months.

In the Far East the Americans have nearly completed the
capture of Iwojima and are still advancing in Luzon.[1] We have
captured most of Mandalay, but are up against stiff opposition.
The Adjutant-General the other day said that Rangoon was
scheduled for capture in April, but that certainly looks highly
unlikely so soon.[2]

March 26, 1945

In the course of our advance we are pulverizing from the air
towns and villages in all parts of Germany in the most irresponsible fashion. We are landing ourselves with the problem of
ruling – for years, as we admit – a population that will be without
houses, without food, without transport, and without work. The
Russians, in the east, restrict their bombing to military objectives
and have captured far more productive capacity intact.

March 30, 1945

Had some talk yesterday evening with Wilfrid Roberts. He told
me something of his experiences in Russia, where he was a member
of the parliamentary delegation that travelled everywhere, even
including Samarkand and Tashkent. Like all the delegation he is
rather reticent, I don't know why. However, this is what he said.

The Russians make no bones about it at all, they won the war
single-handed, and this has given them tremendous self-confidence.
They consider us very inefficient, and any attempt to plead that we
are only a small country with less than fifty million people is met
with the retort that, on the contrary, we are an empire with nearly
600 million people.

The Russians are very critical of our policy in India, and on
entirely materialistic grounds. This vast country in our hands has
no serious military potential; has contributed nothing to the war.
Why do we allow the whole machinery of our administration
there to be clogged by Gandhi and a lot of Hindus with obsolete
ideas? By contrast Tashkent is a thriving industrial city of a
million inhabitants, with plane factories, textile works, and the
most ambitious plans for the future. The delegation saw a repre-
sentation of *Othello* in Uzbek – half of them never having seen the
play in the original!

The Russians are very keen to be friendly with us: they think
us incompetent and effete, but successful, and we also have a sort
of snob value. We are old-timers among world powers while they
are nouveaux riches. The Americans they admire for their
industrial technique, but otherwise regard them as a barbarous
non-European people.

March 31, 1945

The *New Statesman* complains in this week's issue that the Americans are very bad about looting. They did enough of it in France,
but in Germany are quite shameless. I have read this statement
elsewhere, and in the present state of the censorship it could
hardly be published if not true.

Lloyd George is dead and was buried yesterday. His death
received a great deal of attention in the papers, but I thought they

hardly did him justice. His best period must have been before my time but even in 1940–41, when I met him, he was a man head and shoulders over any other politician I have met – including Churchill. His undoing was that he was fundamentally an opportunist, so that there was no underlying principle to make sense of his whole life. However, apart from that he had everything. His understanding of politics today was far greater than that of *my* contemporaries, he was witty, he was eloquent, he had a great sense of the value of men, and he really wanted to help the underdog. I think it was generally regretted that he accepted a title, but I dare say it was thrust on him by his family when he was too old and ill effectively to object.

The First World War had ended suddenly. Between March and May in 1918 the German army won a series of great victories in Ludendorff's spring offensive on the western front; the Allies were on the brink of defeat. Six months later, the German army had collapsed and the war was over.

Nine months before V.E. Day, in fact after the D-Day landings had succeeded, everyone could see that Germany's defeat was inevitable. And when V.E. Day came, on May 8, 1945, there was none of the hysterical exuberance which accompanied the ending of the First World War.

On V.E. Day Philip Zec produced another great cartoon. It showed a wounded British soldier climbing out of a war-shattered landscape, clutching an olive branch labelled 'Victory and peace in Europe'. The caption was: 'Here you are! Don't lose it again!'

But even as the greatest war ever ended, future peace was by no means certain. The post-war world was full of menace: in the closing months of the war hostility and suspicion were poisoning the relationship between the western Allies and Soviet Russia. The Cold War had begun.

'Don't lose it again' had a relevance at home. The Mirror and Pictorial constantly reminded their readers that the British people had won the First World War – but lost their peace. The troops had marched home to loud cheers, but this was followed up by dole instead of a job; their reward was the unemployment and mass poverty of the 1920s and 1930s. This time the British people must not lose the Battle of the Home Front, the battle for a New Britain, which must become truly a 'land fit for heroes'.

On May 23 Churchill dissolved the coalition Government which had lasted since May 1940, and fixed July 5 as the date for a General Election.

Labour offered the public a well presented programme of social recon-struction, based on the principles of the Beveridge Report. Masterminding Labour's campaign was the Mirror's *old foe, Herbert Morrison. Now, he was glad to make use of the* Mirror *staff in preparing his publicity material – even of Philip Zec of the offending petrol cartoon.*

The Conservatives too had their plans for reconstruction, but they succeeded in giving the impression that they were half-hearted about them, and their initial reserve over the Beveridge Report was remembered to their discredit. Their campaign was livened up by the eccentric stunts of Lord Beaverbrook's Express: *'GESTAPO IN BRITAIN IF SOCIALISTS WIN', and so on. The public was intrigued, but not convinced.*

It seemed in fact that Labour were offering something real; the Con-servatives playing at politics. Not even the Conservative Party's greatest electoral asset, Winston Churchill, was effective. The public cheered him loudly wherever he went – and then voted for the party which they thought would give them most homes and jobs.

Just before the election the Mirror *came up with a brilliant slogan, 'VOTE FOR THEM'. 'Them' was not the Labour Party but: 'The man who would fill that chair in your home. The mate you miss at work. The pal you liked to meet in the pub. The boyfriend. These men are still fighting all over the world. . . .' At no time did the* Mirror *suggest which was the party of 'them'. Its readers were in no doubt.*

On July 5, polling day, the Mirror *repeated this slogan, along with a headline 'DON'T LOSE IT AGAIN' and the Zec V.E. Day cartoon.*

This last-minute campaign could have been an election-winner if Labour victory had not already been inevitable. However, it may have changed a substantial Labour victory into a landslide. Labour won 393 seats, against 213 Conservative and allied, 12 Liberal, 22 Independent.

From April to July 1945 Cecil King was out of the country, on a trip to North and South America, and his diary does not record his immediate reactions to these dramas.

September 1, 1945

I got home after the voting in the General Election but before the declaration of the poll.[3] The general impression on both sides was that Labour had done better than had been expected. Tory election tactics, allegedly dictated by Beaverbrook, were pretty generally admitted to have been bad. Attlee himself expected the Tories to have a majority of twenty-five. Bevan was the only prominent politician I know of who said to anyone who would listen that Labour was in with a majority of sixty. The landslide that had in fact taken place came as a surprise to everyone. It was largely contributed to by the service vote, which went about eighty per cent Labour, taking the country as a whole. The *Mirror* and Pic came out very definitely on the Labour–Liberal side and were believed by everyone to have played a large part in the result.

The Liberal Party made a great effort and put 300 candidates in the field, but suffered a crushing defeat. The few Liberals who were returned could have got in as Independents. I think all the Liberals can do now is to retire from the scene.

Churchill should also stage a fade-out but apparently will not do so. The election result came as a particularly heavy blow to him as he has consistently overvalued his popularity. One of the most significant results was in his own constituency at Woodford, where an unknown farmer with a crack-brained policy and no organization polled 10,000 votes against him. These were all anti-Churchill votes and could be interpreted in no other way. There was no 'swing of the pendulum' about them.

Parliament, of course, will be mainly occupied with coal, housing, and jobs, and on that sort of subject Churchill will be quite ineffective. It is generally believed that the Tories have not learnt their lesson and, instead of swinging to the Left and the Tory Reform Group, are if anything moving to the Right. This seems to me crazy, but may easily change if Churchill himself dies.

This present Government has been given a tremendous majority and a lot depends on them. If they make a fair success of the job in the next five years, they are in for a generation. If they fail, then the country is in a very nasty fix, but it would need a revolution to put power into the hands of Bracken, Beaverbrook, Cherwell, Harvie Watt, and so on.

The last act of the war was the most dramatic. On August 6 an atomic bomb was dropped on the Japanese city of Hiroshima, obliterating half of it. Three days later a second atomic bomb was dropped on Nagasaki.

On August 14 the Japanese government capitulated. The Second World War was over.

Another major development of the last month has been the dropping of two atomic bombs. This was obviously a great event in history by (1) marking the achievement of some sort of control over atomic energy, and (2) taking a further big step downwards in the standard of humanity to be expected in wartime.

The moral aspect of dropping bombs that destroyed four square miles of Hiroshima and one square mile of Nagasaki drives home that greatest of modern problems. We have acquired more and more power but have less and less sense of responsibility in using it. The idea of warfare for some centuries has been that the armed forces of the belligerents must be ready for anything, but that civilians should be spared. Our decision to concentrate on night bombers somewhere around 1927 was the first serious breach of this principle. At that time bombing was entirely indiscriminate and could only be aimed at civilians – and civilians in their homes rather than their factories. Neither the Germans nor the Russians took up bombing, not (needless to say) because of its inhumanity but because of its ineffectiveness.

Then along come the Americans with their atomic bomb, burn up about 250,000 civilians, and finish the Jap war. Simultaneously we are bringing to trial as war criminals almost everyone of importance in the Nazi state. Obviously war criminal number one is Harry Truman, who ordered the dropping of the bomb, and these 'trials' of Nazi leaders will merely create a precedent for shooting the political and military leaders of any nation defeated in war in the future.

This war has marked a relapse to the methods of warfare of the 17th or earlier centuries, a moral deterioration which is terrifying. The Germans and the Russians, with many of their atrocities, knew they were fighting more or less for survival; we drifted into our atrocities; but it remains for the Americans, who had already won the war when they dropped the atom bomb, to descend to the lowest depths, and then attempt to justify their action by saying that they ended the war sooner and so spared the lives of their men fighting in the Philippines and about to

20

land in Japan itself. I am so appalled I cannot get it out of my mind. The Americans in so many ways are the most powerful nation in the world – and are so utterly irresponsible. We are not guilty to the degree they are, but Churchill's statement trying to claim as much credit as possible for the atomic bomb was a sickening and shaming episode.

So now the war is over, and after just six years we have peace again. We went into the war – it is hard at this distance of time to recall this – to check Germany's policy of expansion, which looked as if it might soon absorb the whole of Europe. The actual effect has been a radical shift in political power away from western Europe. The capitals of the world are now Moscow and New York. In the future they may be Delhi, Rio, or Chungking, but it is hard to see how London, Paris, Vienna, Rome, or Berlin can ever again play a role comparable with their part in the years between the wars.

Clearly the effect of this war on this country is that of a crushing defeat. The defeat of Germany by the Russians at Stalingrad and subsequently came as a complete surprise to everyone outside Russia. It is from then on that our policy became more and more suicidal. We kept on helping the stronger party (Russia) against the weaker (Germany), and have now created a Frankenstein monster that dominates the European-Asiatic land mass from Vladivostok to Vienna and beyond. It was difficult if not impossible for us to back out, but our agreement to the policy of 'unconditional surrender' was fatal. I did not see an obvious chance for us to take, but clearly from Stalingrad onwards our policy should have been a 'patched-up peace' (as it was called) at the earliest possible moment.

As I see it, in this war, certainly after the collapse of France, we were vitally concerned in not being defeated, but 'victory' was not in our interest, as it could only be achieved by the all-out efforts of Russia and America, who would necessarily reap the rewards of their sacrifices. America's policy was hard to fathom. They believe now that if they had not intervened, Hitler would have beaten the Russians and invaded the U.S. This is obvious nonsense, but it is difficult to see why Roosevelt worked so hard and so adroitly to get his country into the war, to the extent of forcing the Japanese to fight. Did he really think the Japanese any real menace to the U.S.? Was he so crazed with vanity that he wanted to lead the U.S. in a victorious war? Was he determined to bring about America's domination of the Pacific? Or did he, out of sympathy for Britain and Churchill and an ignorance of foreign affairs, drift into a policy which ultimately and unintentionally led to war?

The position as it stands today is that Japan is prostrate; Russia is occupying Manchuria, Mongolia, and part of Korea; the Americans dominate the Pacific and are demanding various islands (including British islands) as bases in permanency. Europe is ruined and starving. What with American and British bombing in the west and Russian deportations in the east, it is difficult to see what of Europe will survive. At present Russia dominates everything east of a line from Stettin to Vienna, and the whole of the Balkans except Greece. The Americans, having contributed largely to the ruin of Europe, are now clearing out; the French are deeply divided between the Gaullists, who are anti-British, and the Communists, who are pro-Russian. No peace treaties have yet been signed, but we are doing nothing to provide western Europe with leadership: and with increasing misery and hunger everywhere there is a natural tendency to look to Russia. I judge that Great Britain is today in the weakest position she has ever been in. Independence seems impossible for a small island; the French so far repudiate any idea of close collaboration with us; and to be a client of either Russia or America is to offer this country as a battlefield in the next war.

September 2, 1945

I have been wondering how I think Churchill will look in retrospect. The papers have been full of tributes to this man who 'through the dark days' and so on 'saved this country', or words to that effect. Most of this seems to me nonsense. Churchill throughout the war (to some extent), and certainly after the collapse of France, was in effect the British Commander-in-Chief. For this position he had experience and immense prestige, particularly with the Navy. It is difficult to see who could have been found who had anything like similar claims. He has great

powers of expression both in speech and writing, and had the
personality to dominate the service chiefs with whom he had to
deal. His shortcomings were that he is old and slow, and above all
that he is a shocking judge of men. He *will* work with friends, and
his friends are people of second- or third-rate capacity. The
consequence of this was that the invasion of Europe took place
in 1944 instead of 1943, when we might have got to Berlin before
the Russians got to Warsaw. The North African landing never
made any sense except on the assumption that Russia would be
defeated; the campaign on the Italian mainland never made sense
anyhow.

But whatever may be said for Churchill the Commander-in-
Chief, very little in my view can be said for Churchill the Prime
Minister, and I think that with the lapse of time this fact will be
more and more apparent. Churchill is a man of the 19th, if not
the 18th, century: he knows little and cares less for the political
currents of the day. To him war is a vast pageant with himself in a
scarlet uniform on a white horse, baton in hand, leading the
British forces forward through the smoke of battle. But war is no
longer a dynastic matter; it is a struggle for power on a national
scale, in which economics are far more important than sentiment
or romance. This war was fought for power, a fact which Churchill
apparently never realized, or anyway forgot very early on. I repeat,
it was fought for power, not for 'victory'. And power is wanted
only as a means to achieve some object of policy. Churchill never
had any policy except 'victory': hence the vacuum in western
Europe today. We have had our way, and Europe looks to us and
the Americans for orders – and we have none to give.

Churchill's Government was weak in personnel and badly
organized. The names that stand out – not very far out – are
probably Bevin as Labour Minister and Anderson as an administrator. Both these men had established reputations long before
Churchill appeared on the scenes. His 'discoveries' were such
trumpery material as Bracken, Cherwell, Harvie Watt, and
Assheton.

Churchill's achievement as Prime Minister is mainly as orator.
In 1940 he made speeches which were the authentic growl of the
British bulldog, and then and later his personality and his pro-

nouncements contributed greatly to maintain our prestige at a high level abroad. He did much to bring America into the war – at the cost of much subservience to Roosevelt – but then I am not at all sure that it was in our long-term interest that America should become one of the belligerents. In any case Churchill, like Lloyd George, whatever he hoped or believed, has in fact presided at an important stage in the dissolution of the British Empire, and future generations are hardly likely, for that reason, to give him the benefit of any doubts. As a statesman I would put Churchill far below Lloyd George, and as a Prime Minister below Campbell-Bannerman.

The more the papers blather about 'historic events' and 'personalities who will live in history' the more certain I feel that history will be little interested in us and our doings. After all, you have only to go back to the last war to see how entirely different it looks in perspective: Lloyd George, Clemenceau, the Battles of the Somme and Passchendaele all fade into insignificance, and the two events that influence us today are the emergence of Soviet Russia and the disappearance of Austria-Hungary. There were other important consequences, such as the growth in stature of the U.S.; the dwindling of France and Turkey; the condition or Germany in 1918, leading straight to Hitler and 1939. None of these things was intended by any of the 'historic figures' of the last war. These are, even at a distance of twenty-five years, seen to have been but puppets in a play whose theme is still obscure and whose climax is still far off.

After the war Cecil King ceased to keep his diary regularly. However, he occasionally recorded his impressions of life in the new Welfare State and of the doings of the Labour Government. He made this entry on Wednesday October 1, 1947.

Yesterday little Attlee startled the political world by the sudden appointment of Cripps to be Minister of State in charge of all economic affairs, while Harold Wilson, aged thirty-one, becomes President of the Board of Trade. This move Attlee apparently discussed with no one. At lunchtime on Monday Wilson knew nothing of his promotion, and it was announced on the wireless at 9.0 in the evening.

In the country at large Wilson is quite unknown and his is a purely Whitehall reputation. But if he can add to his reputation as an administrator the ability to do a spot of political spell-binding, he is then quite a long way on the road to No 10.

Afterword

by CECIL KING

Rereading my diary after many years, one of the first things that strike me is the dissatisfaction which I, and indeed many others, came to feel with Winston Churchill. This was ironical, as the papers whose policy I controlled at that time had urged Churchill's inclusion in the Government before any other newspaper or spokesman, and had later argued that he was the only possible wartime Prime Minister – this at a period in which he had very few friends indeed.

Churchill was a most attractive personality who did a wonderful job for us in 1940. He had a great command of English, both written and spoken, and was after Lloyd George easily the biggest figure in 20th-century British politics. Under all the circumstances he was the best available Commander-in-Chief, and gave our people the leadership they so desperately needed during the war and have so dismally lacked ever since. But his admirers, who were conspicuous by their absence until 1940, have since taken off into wild fantasy. Did not Lord Ismay say Churchill was the greatest human being for 500 years, if not longer? Have Americans not told me that he personally saved this country from surrender in 1940? Of course he did nothing of the kind. Great Britain had no thought of surrender in 1940, but was fortunate in having Churchill to express defiance in appropriate words.

I once asked P.J. Grigg if he had ever known a great man – whatever his criterion of greatness might be. He said no. I said: 'But you were Churchill's Civil Service secretary for five years and Secretary of State for War when he was Prime Minister.' He said: 'I would not call Churchill great.' So I asked what man in his acquaintance attained the nearest to greatness. He said Lloyd George, and that anyone who had served both men – as he had – would put Lloyd George first.

Churchill was no revolutionary or far-seeing statesman. Politics were to him the ideal setting for his ego. He was out of touch with the people of this country and suffered the humiliating defeat of 1945 in consequence.

It also emerges from the diary that I expected the war to lead to a new attitude by new and younger ministers. But the younger men who attained prominence in the Second World War were, like Eden, very ready to play the game according to the old men's rules. Attlee brought some younger men into his administration – Wilson, Gaitskell, Brown, and Robens – but too late for them to acquire adequate experience of office before the Tories came back. And no Prime Minister of recent years has taken any trouble in training his younger men in the skills of administration and politics.

Ministers are selected and promoted almost entirely because of their debating strength or because of their subservience to the Prime Minister. To anyone not a Member of Parliament these qualities are unknown and anyway irrelevant. One looks for competence in administration and a political rapport with the electorate. Hence the general contempt in which politicians are held in Fleet Street and, nowadays, in the country at large. In peacetime it is possible to argue that it does not really matter who is the Minister of Transport (shall we say), as his civil servants will pull him through. But in wartime, incompetence has to be paid for with men's lives, and triumph in debate is more irrelevant than ever. So criticism of failure in Whitehall is not only justified but required.

One failure in Whitehall of which I was particularly conscious was on the propaganda side. In the 1914–18 war my uncle, Northcliffe, was in charge of propaganda to enemy countries, and his efforts were believed by the Germans to have played a large part in undermining their morale. They even struck a medal to denounce him and his propaganda.

In 1939 it was clear that Hitler was far more frightened of our possible propaganda than of our largely non-existent arms, so, naturally, that was the weapon to use while we were building up our military forces. And this was a sphere in which I thought I could be helpful, as I had the same education as the senior civil servants and ministers and had spent my life in advertising and journalism. I supposed in 1939 that I should leave Fleet Street for Government service, possibly permanently, in spite of the success I was having at the *Daily Mirror*. It took me years of war to realize that the powers that be had no intention of organizing a propaganda war against Germany, in spite of the success it had had in the latter part of the 1914–18 war. The reasons for this were not clear, but someone suggested to me that propaganda is the art of propagating some policy, faith, or belief. If you have no policy a propaganda organization would merely make the fact obvious. Towards the end of the Second World War the Ministry of Economic Warfare was doing some propaganda, but not on the scale or with the effect of Northcliffe's efforts twenty-five years earlier.

There were successes as well as failures in the wartime Government. The successes were Anderson and Woolton. Anderson was a superb civil servant and kept the wartime Government administratively on the rails. He was a very dull pompous man, but a great public servant. Woolton got the credit for the successful organization of food rationing: the administration was done by Sir Henry French, another great public servant, but the public relations aspect of the Food Ministry was where Woolton shone. His contribution to the war effort was a great one, in keeping the housewife happy, or as happy as was possible under the circumstances.

An enigmatic figure in the Government was Lindemann, Lord Cherwell. He was not a front-rank scientist and his scientific advice was not really very valuable. But it was put to me at the time that for a scientist, *any* scientist, to have the ear of the Prime Minister as he had was bound to be militarily beneficial. He was a Student (i.e. Fellow) of my college [Christ Church, Oxford], so I met him when I was an undergraduate. Known at the time as 'the Witchdoctor', not yet 'the Prof', he was disliked and distrusted. But though Churchill's assessment of his value was wildly excessive, I got the impression at the time that his contribution was a positive one.

To me the most unattractive member of the wartime Government was Lord Beaverbrook. Looking back over my lifetime I suppose the most dominant figures in the public life of the country were Joe Chamberlain and Max Beaverbrook, both men whose influence has been evil. We are still paying for the Boer War, to mention only one of Joe Chamberlain's crimes, and Beaverbrook's malevolent influence through two Prime Ministers and through his newspapers has still to be assessed. As a minister Beaverbrook was a failure, as were his attempts at political influence through his newspapers. His strength was in backstairs intrigue, where his personality and his money gave him influence over such diverse characters as Bonar Law and Churchill.

The dominant figure on the Labour side of the Churchill Government was Ernest Bevin. I never met him nor even saw him. He kept the country free of strikes during the war and was greatly praised for his part in doing so. Perhaps in retrospect the view of Bevin as a poacher turned gamekeeper was a false one. He bought off trouble at a price which we have been paying ever since – particularly recently when the power and intransigence of the trade unions have become one of the most intractable problems of the day.

In parliamentary terms Attlee and his followers were the Opposition: in real terms Attlee was a subservient and inert member of the Government. Such opposition as there was was provided by Aneurin Bevan, the only man at that stage who could stand up to Churchill in debate and at the same time get across to the man in the street. In so far as there was any opposition during the war it was provided by Bevan in the House and by the *Daily Mirror* and *Sunday Pictorial* outside. I was given an interesting illustration of this. At the end of the fighting, the Government, mindful of the very disorderly demobilization in 1918, asked the generals on what the success of the demobilization scheme would depend. They said it would depend on the attitude of the *Daily Mirror*. If approved by our papers it would be accepted; otherwise it would be dead. Ministers thought this was obvious nonsense and sent Archie Sinclair to get the real answer. He returned from the front with the same opinion. That our general political line was sound was seen in the election result of 1945.

In that year the new Labour Government should have been concerned in building up the strength of the country, politically and commercially, to face a very different new world. But it was more concerned in implementing Socialist doctrine, much of it quite irrelevant to the real problems before us. Cripps and Morrison were never tired of telling me what a colourless non-entity Attlee was – a view with which I could not help agreeing. In our political system it is now difficult, or impossible, for anyone but the Prime Minister of the day to provide the leadership a community needs. Attlee's Government was sustained by Bevin, Cripps, Morrison, and Bevan, three of whom had had experience of office during the war. The result, as I have said, was irrelevant in its major policies, but it made a more distinguished impression than the Wilson administration of 1964 to 1970.

At times in the diary I refer to anti-Americanism. This sprang from two main sources: firstly the American troops were much better paid than ours; and secondly they used their money and their leisure to seduce the wives and daughters of our men, whether they were away fighting or not. All armies in all foreign countries have behaved so, and in Britain the local girls from all accounts were most co-operative, though this merely aggravated the anger of their menfolk. The American tends to be boastful, and his claims of planes shot down were much more exaggerated than our own, which were indeed generously assessed. None of this was unusual nor reflected any particular discredit on the Americans, but Americans want to be loved, and a country that plucks the fruit of victory by coming in late and leaving the casualties to others may be wise but will not be loved.

Perhaps this diary may seem in parts over-critical. But it is an exact record of what I and others felt, thought, and said at the time. We wanted a more vigorous prosecution of the war and a better world after it. We were exasperated by anyone or anything standing in our way. My diary may not have been written in a spirit of charity for all, but there was certainly malice toward none.

June 1970

Notes to Text

1   From then till August 1939 it asserted daily on its front page: 'There will be no war in Europe this year or next.'

2   This Baltic port was up to the end of the First World War part of the German Empire. After the Treaty of Versailles it became a Free City under League of Nations control. Its position in the 'Polish Corridor', the strip of Polish territory separating East Prussia from the rest of Germany, made it a central issue in the diplomatic conflict between Germany and Poland.

3   Eden resigned as Foreign Secretary in February 1938 over what he regarded as Chamberlain's weakness towards Italy. Later in the year Duff Cooper resigned as First Lord of the Admiralty over Munich. At the outbreak of war Eden became Dominions Secretary.

4   An independent magazine of extreme right-wing views.

5   In December 1939 the German pocket-battleship *Graf Spee* was attacked by three British cruisers in the South Atlantic. Slightly damaged, she put into Montevideo, and soon after scuttled herself.

6   In 1915 the British commander on the western front, Sir John French, complained that his failures were due to lack of shells. Northcliffe publicized this, causing a public outcry.

7   The *Mirror* commented: '. . . we salute him in silence and say not one word about or against his record as the nation's leader during the gravest crisis in our history.'

8   Joseph Chamberlain (1836–1914). Imperialist, champion of Tariff Reform, and the man who split the Liberal Party on Irish Home Rule. Colonial Secretary 1895–1900. Neville Chamberlain's father.

9   Sir Austen Chamberlain (1863–1937). Conservative Foreign Secretary, 1924–29. Half-brother of Neville.

10   Weygand succeeded Gamelin as Commander-in-Chief of the Allied forces on May 19, 1940. He was seventy-three.

11   A Liberal M.P., Cecil King's uncle and godfather. He was a member of the Prime Minister's secretariat, 1917–19.

12   On June 16 Churchill had proposed to the French an 'indissoluble' union between Britain and France: one Government, a common citizenship, sharing of resources, etc. The French were not interested.

13   Chamberlain had cancer. He died on November 9, 1940.

14   Cecil King was then living at Culham Court, a Georgian house on the Thames near Henley. There the Kings housed thirty-five poor children who had been evacuated from London. In 1943 the lease ran out and they moved into a flat in Lincoln's Inn, near Cecil King's office.

15   On the evening of September 7 the signal 'Cromwell', meaning 'invasion imminent', was sent out. Part of Britain's preparation to meet the invasion was the calling out of the Home Guard.

16   News stories and factual articles on a number of subjects related to the war effort had to be submitted to the official censor. But there was no censorship of opinions.

17   On the night of November 14, 500 German planes dropped 600 tons of high explosives and thousands of incendiaries on Coventry. 400 people were killed. Churchill wrote: 'On the whole this was the most devastating raid which we sustained.'

1941

1   R.A. Butler became Minister of Education in July 1941.

2   Churchill's suspicions about the *Mirror*'s ownership were not

allayed. A year later, as can be seen in the famous row over the Philip Zec cartoon, Churchill and the Government still suspected that some sinister financial interests were controlling the paper's policies. See page 165.

3 Stuart Campbell was Hugh Cudlipp's successor as editor of the *Sunday Pictorial*. Cudlipp joined the Army at the end of 1940.

4 In September 1942 Cecil King was interested to come across the passage which Churchill had in mind. See page 191.

5 Lord Eustace Percy was President of the Board of Education from 1924 to 1929 in Baldwin's Government. In the same Government Churchill was Chancellor of the Exchequer.

6 The jet engine, developed by (Sir) Frank Whittle. The first flight in which this jet engine was used took place in May 1941. British jet planes came into operation towards the end of the war.

7 In 1940 George Thomson became chairman of the British Committee on Atomic Energy, and was thus very much involved in the development of the atomic bomb, whose destructive potential had by then been realized.

8 American troops did not begin to occupy bases in Northern Ireland until January 1942.

9 In August 1941 Churchill met Roosevelt on board ship at Placentia Bay, Newfoundland. A joint Anglo-American declaration of principle was agreed, based on eight points defining their present and future policies towards the world.

10 Cecil King himself became a director of the Bank of England in 1965.

11 Regulation 18B dealt with the internment of enemy aliens; and of British people who were regarded as security risks, as for example Oswald Mosley and the Fascists.

1942

1 On December 13, Churchill travelled to Washington with his chiefs of staff for the 'Arcadia' conference, in which Britain and America discussed combining their war efforts.

2 Duff Cooper left the Ministry of Information in July 1941 to

become Chancellor of the Duchy of Lancaster, and went to Singapore as Minister of State in the Far East. He was there when the Japanese invaded Malaya.

3   His argument was that just as miners had their liberties restricted in being forced to work in the pits (instead of in factories, which they would have preferred), so should the Press expect some curtailment of its liberties.

4   This refers to the two German battle-cruisers *Scharnhorst* and *Gneisenau* and the cruiser *Prinz Eugen*. On February 11 they left the French port of Brest, sailed right through the English Channel in defiance of the R.A.F. and Royal Navy, and eventually arrived safely in Germany. It was said that this incident cast even more gloom in Britain than the loss of Singapore.

5   Cecil King wrote to Lady Cripps on April 18, 1942:

Dear Lady Cripps,
    I thought you might be interested in the enclosed material about the papers read by men and women under 41. The conclusion is that the Daily Mirror and the Daily Express are by far the most important papers in this age group. The Express group is the creation of Beaverbrook, and though the staff is in many ways more competent and even brilliant than that of any other newspaper, the directing head in every way is Beaverbrook. E. J. Robertson is the executive head of the business in his chief's absence, but the various editors have a lot of independence. Christiansen, the editor of the Daily Express, is not much interested in politics, and, in any case, I expect is kept under a tighter rein than the others because of the greater importance of his paper. Second to Robertson is Plummer, whom I think very capable in a broader way than most newspaper people. John Gordon, the editor of the Sunday Express, is now the ablest of the Sunday paper editors and his weekly article is very popular indeed.
    The policy of the Daily Mail group depends entirely on Esmond Rothermere. He finds it difficult to keep interested in any subject for long, so the papers he manages tend to pursue a rather erratic course.

The Daily Herald is controlled by the T.U.C. – at present its policy is therefore in the hands of Citrine. Cudlipp, the editor, was formerly the editor of the Standard and is very able. His leaders caused the Government more annoyance than anything else in the entire Press.

The News Chronicle and Star are virtually owned by Cadbury. He takes little interest in the papers as long as they pursue a quasi-Liberal policy. Sir Walter Layton used to direct the policy of the paper, but now this seems to be left to a considerable extent to the editor, Gerald Barry.

The Telegraph is owned, as you know, by Lord Camrose who entirely dictates its policy. His eldest son, now MP for Hitchin, has in the past at times had a say in the policy of the paper and it has then taken a less weak and subservient line. Camrose also dominates his younger brother Kemsley and the policy of the Sketch tends to follow that of the Telegraph, though recently they have at times diverged as it is reported that Churchill and Kemsley are not personally on good terms.

Of the Sunday papers, the News of the World has overwhelmingly the largest sale and its policy is determined by Major Davies, the editor, and chairman of the company. The paper never takes a definite line on anything – nor does the People, which has the second largest Sunday sale and whose policy is controlled by Lord Southwood. Of the other Sunday papers, the Sunday Times, Graphic, Chronicle and Empire News are controlled by Lord Kemsley, to whom I have already referred. The Observer has recently ejected Garvin and is said to be largely edited by David Astor, Lord Astor's youngest son. Reynolds sometimes takes a bold and definite line. It is owned, as you know, by the Cooperative movement, but Alfred Barnes, MP is said to control the policy.

The sale of the various papers may not be familiar to you so I will set them down roughly below.

Daily Express	2,700,000
Daily Mirror	1,900,000
Daily Herald	1,600,000

Daily Mail	1,450,000
News Chronicle	1,200,000
Daily Sketch	700,000
Daily Telegraph	650,000
Times	180,000
News of the World	4,500,000
People	3,500,000
Sunday Pictorial	1,900,000
Sunday Express	1,700,000
Empire News	1,400,000
Sunday Dispatch	950,000
Sunday Chronicle	950,000
Sunday Graphic	700,000
Reynolds' News	500,000
Sunday Times	350,000
Observer	200,000

The daily newspaper figures are given before the recent cut of 10% in newsprint rations. Most of the papers cut their sales by 10%; some cut their number of pages, and it would be hard to say what sales are now – roughly 10% below the figures given. Some of the Sunday newspaper figures are approximate, as their exact sales have not been given by the proprietors for a considerable time.

I hope this is the information you want. If it isn't, please let me know.

6 Molotov, the Soviet Foreign Minister, had come to Britain to demand a Second Front.

7 Churchill had decided to fly to Moscow to inform Stalin that there would be no Second Front that year; instead the Allies would invade French North Africa. Churchill's visit lasted for five days, August 12 to 16. Stalin was at first angry and contemptuous about the Allies' inability to open the Second Front, but drew some consolation from the proposed invasion of North Africa and from the British bomber offensive against Germany. The meeting ended amicably.

8 On August 19 Canadian and British forces took part in a hit-and-run raid on Dieppe. It was a costly failure. Over half the Canadians were killed or taken prisoner.

21

9 Sir William Beveridge's marriage, to Mrs Janet Mair. He was then aged sixty-three.

1943

1 The Russians had reached the outskirts of Kiev, which fell to them on November 6.
2 Lebanon and Syria were before the war League of Nations Mandates under French control. In 1941 the Free French proclaimed them republics, but French influence remained strong. In October 1943 the Lebanese government proposed to abolish French influence completely. The Free French countered by ordering in November the arrest of the Lebanese President and most of his ministers. However, British and American pressure forced the French to release the Lebanese government on November 22; and talks were begun between the Free French and Syria and Lebanon for the complete independence of these two countries.
3 The rumour was false. The meeting took place at Teheran.
4 Churchill was in bed with pneumonia from December 11 to 27; he then flew to Marrakesh, in Morocco, to recuperate.

1944

1 N.A.A.F.I. ran the forces' shops and canteens. E.N.S.A. dealt with forces entertainment.
2 Mussolini had his son-in-law, Count Ciano, executed in January 1944. He died a traitor's death, being shot in the back while tied to a chair. Churchill later remarked: 'The end of Ciano was in keeping with all the elements of Renaissance tragedy.'
3 The Labour Government was outvoted over a minor issue: their Attorney General's refusal to prosecute J.R. Campbell, a Communist, for publishing in the *Workers' Weekly* (of which he was acting editor) an appeal to soldiers not to turn their guns on fellow workers in either 'the class war' or a 'military war'.
4 A contrast perhaps to his successor as chairman, Harry Guy

Bartholomew, who though not a Jew occasionally claimed to be one.

5 The Yugoslav Resistance consisted of two rival factions: the royalists (supporting the exiled King Peter II) commanded by Mihailovich, and the Communists under Tito. Churchill switched Britain's support from the former to the latter. In Greece, however, he supported the King. Britain's intervention there was on the King's behalf.

1945

1 In February and March the Americans fought a successful but costly battle for the island of Iwojima. There were 20,000 casualties, but it gave them a base 800 miles from Tokyo. Luzon was the main island of the Philippines, which America had invaded in October 1944.

2 In March 1944 the Japanese invaded Assam but were defeated at Imphal. In midsummer the British began a protracted offensive into Burma. Eventually, in March 1945, Mandalay fell, and on May 3 Rangoon. In this fifteen-month campaign the British destroyed three Japanese armies and the Japanese suffered nearly 350,000 casualties.

3 Although the voting took place on July 5 the result was not announced until July 26. This was to allow time for the collection of the services vote.

(*=new appointment)

Cabinet Post	Jan. 1940 (after resignation of Hore-Belisha)	April 1940	May 1940	August 1940	Oct. 1940	Dec. 194
Prime Minister	Chamberlain	Chamberlain	Churchill*	Churchill	Churchill	Churchill
Minister of Defence			Churchill*	Churchill	Churchill	Churchill
Deputy Prime Minister						
Lord President of the Council			Chamberlain*	Chamberlain	Anderson*	Anderson
Lord Privy Seal	Hoare	Wood*	Attlee*	Attlee	Attlee	Attlee
Chancellor of Exchequer	Simon	Simon			Wood*	Wood
Home Secretary						
Foreign Secretary	Halifax	Halifax	Halifax	Halifax	Halifax	Eden*
Secretary for Dominions						
Secretary for War	Stanley*	Stanley				
Secretary for Air	Wood	Hoare*				
First Lord of the Admiralty	Churchill	Churchill				
Minister of Labour					Bevin*	Bevin
Minister for Co-ordination of Defence	Chatfield					
Minister of Aircraft Production				Beaverbrook*	Beaverbrook	Beaverbrook
Minister of State						
Minister of Supply						
Minister of Production						
Minister of Reconstruction						
Minister without Portfolio	Hankey	Hankey	Greenwood*	Greenwood	Greenwood	Greenwood
Ambassador to U.S.A.						Halifax*

1941	June 1941	Feb. 4, 1942	Feb. 19 and 22, 1942	March 1942	Oct. 1942	Sept. 1943	Nov. 1943 (continued until May '45 except Casey)
rchill	Churchill	Churchill	Churchill	Churchill	Churchill	Churchill	Churchill
rchill	Churchill	Churchill	Churchill	Churchill	Churchill	Churchill	Churchill
			Attlee*	Attlee	Attlee	Attlee	Attlee
erson	Anderson	Anderson	Anderson	Anderson	Anderson	Attlee*	Attlee
e	Attlee	Attlee	Cripps*	Cripps			
d	Wood	Wood				Anderson*	Anderson
					Morrison*	Morrison	Morrison
a	Eden	Eden	Eden	Eden	Eden	Eden	Eden
			Attlee*	Attlee	Attlee		
in	Bevin	Bevin	Bevin	Bevin	Bevin	Bevin	Bevin
ver-ook*	Lyttelton* (Middle East)	Lyttelton (Middle East)	Lyttelton (Middle East)	Casey* (Middle East)	Casey (Middle East)	Casey (Middle East)	Casey (Middle East) [resigned Dec. '43]
	Beaver-brook*						
		Beaver-brook*		Lyttelton*	Lyttelton	Lyttelton	Lyttelton
							Woolton*
en-ood	Green-wood	Green-wood					
ifax	Halifax	Halifax	Halifax	Halifax	Halifax	Halifax	Halifax

Biographical Notes

These notes are confined to the period covered by the book. War Cabinet appointments are dealt with in the chart of Government Changes (page 316).

ABBREVIATIONS

C.-in-C. = Commander-in-Chief
C.I.G.S. = Chief of the Imperial General Staff
Con. = Conservative and Unionist
Dir. = Director
G.O.C. = General Officer Commanding

Ind. = Independent
Lab. = Labour
Lib. = Liberal
Min. = Minister
Parl. = Parliamentary
Pres. = President
Rep. = Representative
Sec. = Secretary

Alanbrooke Field Marshal (1944) Baron (1945) (Sir Alan Brooke). C.-in-C. Home Forces 1940–1; C.I.G.S. 1941–6

Albery Sir Irving. M.P. (Con.)

Alexander A.V. M.P. (Co-operative); First Lord of the Admiralty 1940–5; also Lab. First Lord 1945

Alexander Field Marshal (1945) Hon. Sir (1942) Harold. G.O.C.-in-C. Southern Command 1940–2; G.O.C. Burma 1942; C.-in-C. Middle East 1942–3; Deputy C.-in-C. N. Africa 1943; Deputy C.-in-C. Allied Forces, Combined Operations Mediterranean 1943; G.O.C. Allied Forces in Sicily 1943–4; C.-in-C. Allied Armies in Italy 1944; Supreme Allied Commander Mediterranean Theatre 1944–5

Amery Leopold S. M.P.(Con.); Sec. for India and Burma 1940–5

Anderson Sir John. M.P. (National); Home Sec. and Min. of Home Security 1939–40; Lord Pres. of the Council 1940–3; Chancellor of the Exchequer 1943–5

Asquith C.E. Sec. and Chief Organizer of the National Lab. Organization

Astor 2nd Viscount. Chairman of the *Observer*; chairman, Royal Institute of International Affairs

Astor Colonel Hon. John (Major in the First World War). Chairman of The Times Publishing Co.; M.P. (Con.) 1922–45. Brother of 2nd Viscount Astor

Astor Viscountess (Nancy). M.P. (Con.); first woman M.P. in U.K. Parliament. Wife of 2nd Viscount

Astor Hon. William. M.P. (Con.). Eldest son of 2nd Viscount Astor

Attlee Clement (Major in First World War). M.P. (Lab.); Leader of the Opposition 1935–40; Lord Privy Seal 1940–2; Sec. for Dominions 1942–3; Deputy Prime Min. 1942–5; Lord Pres. of the Council 1943–5; became Labour Prime Min. 1945

Auchinleck General (1941) Sir (1940) Claude. G.O.C.-in-C. Southern Command 1940; C.-in-C. India 1941; G.O.C.-in-C. Middle East 1941–2; C.-in-C. India 1943–7

Back Barbara. Wife of Ivor Back, the distinguished surgeon

Badoglio Marshal Pietro (Duke of Addis Ababa). Commanded Italian forces in invasion of Ethiopia 1935; Chief of Staff 1940: resigned in protest over Italian invasion of Greece; after the fall of Mussolini, Italian premier 1943–4

Baldwin Earl (Stanley Baldwin). Former Prime Min. (1923–4, 1924–9, and 1935–7)

Balfour Honor. Journalist and Lib. candidate

Bartlett Vernon. M.P. (Ind. Progressive); publicist and broadcaster

Beaverbrook Baron (Max Aitken). Proprietor of *Daily Express, Sunday Express, Evening Standard*; Min. of Aircraft Production 1940–1; Min. of State 1941; Min. of Supply 1941–2; Min. of Production 1942; Lord Privy Seal 1943–5

Bellenger Captain Frederick J. M.P. (Lab.); *Sunday Pictorial*'s 'Voice of the Services'; became Lab. Sec. for War 1946

Bevan Aneurin ('Nye'). M.P. (Lab.); became Lab. Min. of Health 1945

Beveridge Sir William. Author of the Beveridge Report on social security; chairman of Inter-departmental Committee on Social Insurance and Allied Services 1941–2; M.P. (Lib.) 1944–5. Former civil servant and academic (Dir., London School of Economics 1919–37)

Bevin Ernest. M.P. (Lab.); General Sec. Transport and General Workers' Union 1921–40; Min. of Labour and National Service 1940–5; became Labour Foreign Sec. 1945

Blackett Professor P.M.S. Professor of Physics, Manchester University; Scientific Adviser on Operation Overlord

Bonham Carter Lady Violet. Governor of the B.B.C. 1941–6; Pres. of Lib. Party Organization 1944–5. Eldest daughter of H. H. Asquith (Lord Oxford), former Prime Min. (1908–15)

Boothby Robert. M.P. (Con.); Parl. Sec., Ministry of Food 1940–1

Bower Commander Robert. M.P. (Con.)

Brabazon of Tara Lieutenant-Colonel Baron (1942) (J. T. C. Moore-Brabazon). M.P. (Con.) 1918–42; Min. of Transport 1940–1; Min. of Aircraft Production 1941–2; pioneer motorist and aviator

Bracken Brendan. M.P. (Con.); Parl. Private Sec. to Prime Min. 1940–1; Min. of Information 1941–5; First Lord of the Admiralty 1945

Bragg Professor Sir Lawrence. Cavendish Professor of Experimental Physics, Cambridge University

Brooke, see Alanbrooke

Brown Ernest. M.P. (Lib. National); Min. for National Service 1939–40; Sec. for Scotland 1940–1; Min. of Health 1941–3; Chancellor of the Duchy of Lancaster 1943–5; Min. of Aircraft Production 1945

Brown W.J. M.P. (Ind.) 1942–5; General Sec., Civil Service Clerical Association 1919–42, Parl. General Sec. from 1942

Butler R.A. M.P. (Con.); Under-Sec. for Foreign Affairs 1938–41; Min. of Education 1941–5; Min. of Labour 1945

Caldecote Viscount (Sir Thomas Inskip). Lord Chancellor 1939–40; Sec. for Dominions 1940; Leader of the House of Lords 1940. Former Min. for the Co-ordination of Defence (1936–9)

Camrose Viscount (1941; Baron, 1929) (Sir William Berry). Principal proprietor and editor-in-chief of *Daily Telegraph*

Carisbrooke Marquess of (Alexander Albert Mountbatten). Grandson of Queen Victoria

Casey R.G. Australian Min. to U.S.A. 1940–2; Min. of State in the Middle East 1942–3; Governor of Bengal 1944–6

Chamberlain Neville. M.P. (Con.); Prime Min. 1937–40; Lord Pres. of the Council 1940. Died November 9, 1940

Channon Henry ('Chips'). M.P. (Con.); Parl. Private Sec. to Under-Sec. for Foreign Affairs 1938–41

Cherwell Baron (1941) (Professor Frederick Lindemann). Student of Christ Church; Professor of Experimental Philosophy, Oxford University; Personal Assistant to Prime Min. 1940; Paymaster General 1942–5

Chiang Kai-shek Generalissimo. Head of Chinese Kuomintang Party; chairman of the Supreme National Defence Council 1939–47; became Pres. of China 1943

Churchill Randolph. M.P. (Con.). Son of Winston Churchill

Churchill Winston Spencer. M.P. (Con.); First Lord of the Admiralty 1939–40; Prime Min. and Min. of Defence 1940–5

Ciano Count Galeazzo. Italian Foreign Min. Mussolini's son-in-law. Shot January 1944

Cooper Duff. M.P. (Con.); Min. of Information 1940–1; Min. of State in the Far East 1941–2; Chancellor of the Duchy of Lancaster 1941–3; U.K. Government rep. with French Committee of National Liberation 1943–4; U.K. Ambassador to France 1944–7

Courtneidge Cicely. Actress

Cripps Sir Stafford. M.P. (Lab.); U.K. Ambassador to U.S.S.R. 1940–2; Lord Privy Seal and Leader of the House of Commons 1942; Min. of Aircraft Production 1942–5; became Lab. Pres. of the Board of Trade 1945

Croft Brigadier Baron (1940) (Sir Henry Croft). Joint Parl. Under-Sec. for War 1940–5

Crowther Geoffrey. Editor of the *Economist*; wartime service in Ministries of Supply, Information, and Production

Cudlipp Hugh. Features editor, *Daily Mirror* 1934–7; editor of the *Sunday Pictorial* 1937–40

Cunningham Admiral of the Fleet (1943) Baron (1945) (Sir Andrew Cunningham). C.-in-C. Mediterranean 1939–42; Naval C.-in-C. Allied Expedi-

tionary Force, N. Africa 1942; C.-in-C. Mediterranean 1943; First Sea Lord
and Chief of Naval Staff 1943–6

Cunningham-Reid Captain A.S. M.P. (Ind.)

Curtin John. Australian Prime Min. 1941–5

Daladier Edouard. French premier 1938–40

Darlan Admiral Jean-François. Vice-Pres. of the French Council of Ministers,
Foreign Sec., and other offices in the Vichy government. Assassinated
December 24, 1942

Davies Clement. M.P. (Lib.); became Leader of the Lib. Parl. Party 1945

Deverell Field Marshal Sir Cyril. Former C.I.G.S. (1936–7)

Dill Field Marshal (1941) Sir John. Commander of the First Army Corps in
France 1939–40; Vice-C.I.G.S. 1940; C.I.G.S. 1940–1

Dowding Air Chief Marshal Baron (1943) (Sir Hugh Dowding). Air Officer
C.-in-C. Fighter Command 1936–40; retired 1942

Driberg Tom. M.P. (1942–5, Ind.; 1945, Lab.); journalist

Duncan Sir Andrew. Dir. of the Bank of England 1929–40; chairman, Executive
Committee of the British Iron and Steel Federation 1935–40 and 1945; Pres.
of the Board of Trade 1940 and 1941; Min. of Supply 1940–41 and 1942–5

Eden Anthony. M.P. (Con.); Sec. for the Dominions 1939–40; Sec. for War
1940; Foreign Sec. 1940–5; Leader of the House of Commons 1942–5

Eisenhower General Dwight D. C.-in-C. Allied Forces in N. Africa 1942–4;
Supreme Commander Allied Expeditionary Force, Western Europe 1944–5

Evatt H.V. Australian rep. in U.K. War Cabinet 1942 and 1943

Foot Dingle. M.P. (Lib.); Parl. Sec., Min. of Economic Warfare 1940–5

Foot Michael. M.P. (Lab.) 1945; former assistant editor of *Tribune* (1937–8);
acting editor of *Evening Standard* 1942

Fraser Air Vice-Marshal Hugh. Dir. of Military Co-operation at the Air
Ministry 1940; Dir.-General of Repair and Maintenance, Ministry of Aircraft Production 1944

French Sir Henry. Sec. to the Ministry of Food 1939–44

Fuller Major-General J. F. C. (retired, 1933). Military scientist and historian,
and author of numerous books on military subjects

Gamelin General Maurice. C.-in-C. Allied land forces until 1940

Garro-Jones G.M. M.P. (Lab.); Parl. Sec., Ministry of Production 1942–5;
deputy chairman of the Radio Board 1942–5

Gaulle General Charles de. French Under-Sec. for War, July 1940; C.-in-C.
Fighting French Forces 1940–3; Pres. of the French Committee for National
Liberation 1943–4; head of the French provisional government and Chief
of the Armed Forces 1944–5; French Pres. 1945–6

Giraud General Henri. C.-in-C. United French Armed Forces 1943–4

Glyn Colonel Sir Ralph. M.P. (Con.)

Goebbels Joseph. German Min. of Propaganda 1933–45

Goodhart A. L. Professor of Jurisprudence, Oxford University

Gort Field Marshal (1943) 6th Viscount. C.-in-C. British Field Force 1939–40;
Inspector-General to the Forces for Training 1940–1, and Inspector-General
Home Guard; C.-in-C. Gibraltar 1941–2; C.-in-C. Malta 1942–4

Grandi Count Dino. Member of the Italian Fascist Grand Council until 1943; Pres., Chamber of Fasci and Corporazioni 1939–43. Former Italian Ambassador in London (1932–9)

Granville Captain Edgar. M.P. (Lib. National, 1931–42; Ind., 1942–5; Lab., 1945)

Greenwood Arthur. M.P. (Lab.); Deputy Leader and acting chairman of the Labour Party; Min. without Portfolio 1940–2; became Lab. Lord Privy Seal 1945

Grigg Sir (Percy) James. Permanent Under-Sec. for War 1939–42; M.P. (National) 1942–5; Sec. for War 1942–5

Halifax Earl of (1944; 3rd Viscount, 1934). Foreign Sec. 1938–40; U.K. Ambassador to U.S.A. 1941–6

Hankey Baron (Sir Maurice Hankey). Min. without Portfolio 1939–40; Chancellor of the Duchy of Lancaster 1940–1; Paymaster General 1941–2. Former Sec. to the War Cabinet (1916) and Imperial War Cabinet (1917); Sec. to the Cabinet (1919–38)

Harmsworth, see Rothermere

Harriman Averell. Pres. Roosevelt's special rep. in Britain and U.S.S.R. 1941

Harris Marshal of the Royal Air Force (1945) Sir Arthur ('Bomber', 'Bert'). Deputy Chief of the Air Staff 1940–1; C.-in-C. Bomber Command 1942–5

Harvie-Watt Sir (1945) George (Harvie Watt). M.P. (Con.); Parl. Private Sec. to Prime Min. 1941–5

Hatry Clarence. Financial speculator

Hearst William Randolph. American newspaper proprietor

Henderson Sir Nevile. Former U.K. Ambassador in Berlin (1937–9)

Herbert Sir (1945) Alan (Patrick). M.P. (Ind.); author and journalist

Hill Dr Charles. Broadcaster: the Radio Doctor; became Sec. of the British Medical Association 1944

Hoare, see Templewood

Hogg Major Hon. Quintin. M.P. (Con.); Joint Parl. Under-Sec. for Air 1945

Hopkins Harry L. Special adviser and assistant to Pres. Roosevelt 1940–5

Hopkinson Austin. M.P. (Ind.)

Horabin T. L. M.P. (Ind. Lib.)

Hore-Belisha Leslie. M.P. (Lib. National to 1942; Ind., 1942–5); Sec. for War 1937–40; Min. of National Insurance 1945. Married Cynthia Elliot 1944

Howard Leslie. Actor

Hudson Robert S. M.P. (Con.); Min. of Shipping 1940; Min. of Agriculture 1940–5

Hulton Edward. Magazine proprietor: owned *Picture Post, Lilliput*, etc.

Inge Very Rev. W.R. Former Dean of St Paul's (1911–34); classicist, theologian, and author

Inskip, see Caldecote

Ironside Field Marshal (1940) Baron (1941) (Sir Edmund Ironside). C.I.G.S. 1939–40; C.-in-C. Home Forces 1940

Ismay General Baron (1945) (Sir Hastings Ismay). Deputy Sec. to the War
  Cabinet 1939–45; Chief of Staff to the Min. of Defence, Winston Churchill,
  1940–5
Iveagh 2nd Earl of (Rupert Guinness). Chairman of Arthur Guinness, Son
  and Co.

Joad C.E.M. Professor of Philosphy in the University of London; author;
  popular philosopher, famous through the B.B.C. Brains Trust

Kemsley Viscount (1945; Baron, 1936) (James Gomer Berry). Newspaper
  proprietor, controlling *The Sunday Times, Daily Sketch, Sunday Graphic*, etc.
Keyes Admiral of the Fleet Baron (1943) (Sir Roger Keyes). M.P. (Con.) to
  1943; led famous attack on Zeebrugge 1918; retired 1935, but replaced on
  active list 1940; Dir. of Combined Operations 1940–1. Died 1945
Keynes Baron (1942) (John Maynard Keynes). Dir. of the Bank of England;
  world-famous economist
King Admiral Ernest J. C.-in-C. U.S. Fleet 1942–5
Knox General Sir Harry. Former Dir. of Military Training, War Office
  (1926–30); Adjutant-General to the Forces (1935–7); retired 1938

Laski Harold J. Left-wing philosopher, politician, author, and academic;
  Professor of Political Science, London School of Economics; became chair-
  man of the Labour Party 1945
Law Richard. M.P. (Con.); Financial Sec. to the War Office 1940–1; Parl.
  Under-Sec. to the Foreign Office 1941–3; Min. of State 1943–5; Min. of
  Education 1945. Son of A. Bonar Law, former Prime Min. (1922–3)
Lawson J. J. M.P. (Lab.); became Lab. Sec. for War 1945
Layton Sir Walter. Chairman of the *News Chronicle*; held important posts in
  Ministries of Supply and Production 1940–3
Leathers Baron (1941). Min. of War Transport 1941–5
Lee Jennie. Wife of Aneurin Bevan; M.P. (Lab.) 1945
Liddell Hart Captain Basil. Military scientist and historian; expert on mecha-
  nized warfare; evolved 'expanding torrent' (Blitzkrieg) method of attack;
  former military correspondent of and defence adviser to *The Times*; former
  personal adviser to the War Min., Leslie Hore-Belisha (1937–8)
Lindemann, see Cherwell
Lloyd George Earl (1945) (David Lloyd George). Former Prime Min. (1916–22)
  and Leader of the Lib. Party (1926–31). Died March 26, 1945
Lloyd George Major Gwilym. M.P. (Lib.); Parl. Sec. to the Ministry of Food
  1939–41; Min. of Fuel and Power 1942–5
Londonderry 7th Marquess of. Former Sec. for Air (1931–5). Described by
  Harold Nicolson as 'Hitler's friend', he claimed that without him Britain
  would not have had the Spitfire
Lothian 11th Marquess of. U.K. Ambassador to U.S.A. 1939–40. Died
  December 12, 1940
Lyttelton Captain Oliver. Pres. of the Board of Trade 1940–1; Min. of State
  1941–2; Min. of Production 1942–5, and Pres. of the Board of Trade 1945;
  managing dir., British Metal Corporation; chairman Associated Electrical
  Industries 1945

MacArthur General Douglas. C.-in-C. Allied Forces, S.-W. Pacific 1942–5

Macdonald Malcolm. M.P. (National); Sec. for the Colonies 1938–40; Min. of Health 1940–1; U.K. High Commissioner in Canada 1941–6. Son of Ramsay MacDonald, Lab. Prime Min. (1924 and 1929–31)

McGovern John. M.P. (Ind. Lab.)

Macmillan Harold. M.P. (Con.); Parl. Sec. to the Ministry of Supply 1940–2; Parl. Under-Sec. for the Colonies 1942; Min. Resident at Allied H.Q. in N.-W. Africa 1942–5; U.K. High Commissioner in Italy 1943–5; Sec. for Air 1945

Maisky Ivan. Soviet Ambassador to U.K. 1932–43

Mander Sir (1945) Geoffrey. M.P. (Lib.)

Margesson Viscount (1942) (Captain David Margesson). M.P. (Con.) to 1942; Government Chief Whip 1931–40; Sec. for War 1940–2

Martin Kingsley. Editor of the *New Statesman*

Maugham Somerset. Novelist and playwright

Maxton James. M.P. (Lab.). Former chairman of the Ind. Lab. Party (1926–31 and 1934–9)

Melchett 2nd Baron (Henry Mond). Deputy chairman, Imperial Chemical Industries

Menzies Robert. Prime Min. of Australia 1939–41

Molotov Vyacheslav. Soviet Commissar for Foreign Affairs

Monckton Sir Walter. Dir.-General of the Press and Censorship Bureau 1939–40; Deputy Dir.-General of the Ministry of Information 1940, Dir.-General 1940–1; Dir.-General of British Propaganda and Information Services, Cairo 1941–2; Solicitor General 1945

Montgomery Field Marshal (1944) Sir (1942) Bernard ('Monty'). Commander of the Eighth Army 1942–3; C.-in-C. Allied Armies, then British Group of Armies, France and Germany 1944–5

Moore-Brabazon, see Brabazon of Tara

Moran Baron (1943) (Sir Charles Wilson). Consultant adviser, Ministry of Health; Winston Churchill's doctor

Morrison Herbert. M.P. (Lab.); Min. of Supply 1940; Home Sec. and Min. of Home Security 1940–5; became Lab. Lord Pres. of the Council 1945

Mortimer Raymond. Writer; literary editor of the *New Statesman*

Mosley Sir Oswald. Founded British Union of Fascists 1932; interned 1940; released 1943

Murphy Robert. Pres. Roosevelt's personal rep. in N. Africa and Italy

Nicolson Hon. Harold. M.P. (National Lab.); author and journalist; Parl. Sec. to the Ministry of Information 1940–1; Governor of the B.B.C. 1941–6

Nimitz Admiral Chester W. C.-in-C. U.S. Pacific Fleet and Pacific Ocean Areas 1941–5

Noel-Baker Philip. M.P. (Lab.); Parl. Sec. to the Ministry of War Transport 1942–5; became Lab. Min. of State 1945

Norman Baron (1944) (Montagu Norman). Governor of the Bank of England 1920–44

North Major John. Author; during the war was on the staff of the War Office

Nuffield Viscount (William Morris). Car manufacturer: chairman of Morris Motors, Wolseley Motors, M.G. Car Co., Riley (Coventry), etc.

O'Casey Sean. Irish playwright

Oliphant Sir Lancelot. U.K. Ambassador to the Belgian government 1939; interned by Germans 1940–1; Ambassador to Belgian government in exile 1941–4

Owen David. Personal assistant to Sir Stafford Cripps 1942; employed in the Ministry of Aircraft Production 1942–3; in 1946 became Sec.-General in charge of the Economic Affairs Dept of U.N.O.

Owen Frank. Editor, *Evening Standard* 1938–41. Former Lib. M.P. (1929–31)

Peake Charles. Chief Press Adviser, Ministry of Information 1939–40; held a number of important diplomatic posts 1941–5

Pearson Sir Neville. Chairman of Arthur Pearson, publishers

Percival Lieutenant-General A.E. G.O.C. Malaya 1941–2

Pétain Marshal Philippe. 'Hero of Verdun' 1916; chief of the Vichy French state 1940–4; Prime Min. 1940–2

Pick Frank. Dir.-General of the Ministry of Information 1940. Former managing dir. of London Underground

Pile General Sir Frederick. G.O.C.-in-C. Anti-Aircraft Command 1939–45

Portal Marshal of the Royal Air Force (1944) Baron (1945) (Sir Charles Portal). Air Officer C.-in-C. Bomber Command 1940; Chief of the Air Staff 1940–5

Pound Admiral of the Fleet Sir Dudley. First Sea Lord and Chief of the Naval Staff 1939–43

Price G. Ward. Journalist and author

Reith Baron (1940). M.P. (National) 1940. Former Dir.-General of the B.B.C. (1927–38); chairman, Imperial Airways 1938–9. Chairman, British Overseas Airways Corporation 1939–40; Min. of Information 1940; Min. of Transport 1940; Min. of Works and Buildings 1940–2; Dir. of Combined Operations, Materials Dept, Admiralty 1943–5

Reynaud Paul. French premier 1940

Rhondda 2nd Viscountess. Chairman and editor of *Time and Tide*

Ribbentrop Joachim von. German Foreign Min. 1938–45. Former German Ambassador to U.K. (1936–8)

Roberts Wilfrid. M.P. (Lib.)

Rommel Marshal Erwin. Commander of the Axis forces in N. Africa 1941–2; commanded German coastal defences in northern France and Holland 1944

Rothermere 2nd Viscount (1940) (Esmond Harmsworth). Chairman, Associated Newspapers (controlling *Daily Mail, Evening News,* etc.); chairman, Newspaper Proprietors' Association

Rothermere Viscount (Harold Harmsworth). See pages 3–4. Died November 26, 1940

Salisbury 4th Marquess of. Former Conservative politician and minister (Leader of the House of Lords 1925–9)

Salter Sir Arthur. M.P. (Ind.). Joint Parl. Sec. to the Ministry of War Transport 1941; head of British Merchant Shipping Mission, Washington 1941–3; Senior Deputy Dir.-General of U.N.R.R.A. 1944; Chancellor of the Duchy of Lancaster 1945

Sandys Duncan. M.P. (Con.); Financial Sec. to the War Office 1941–3; Parl. Sec. to the Ministry of Supply 1943–4; chairman of the Cabinet Committee for Defence against V Weapons 1943–5; Min. of Works 1944–5. Married to Diana, daughter of Winston Churchill

Schacht Dr Hjalmar. Former German Min. of Economics (1934–7) and Pres. of the Reichsbank (1933–9)

Sempill Commander 19th Baron (William Forbes-Sempill). Expert on many aspects of flying, including naval air service; Past President of the Royal Aeronautical Society; employed by Air Ministry as consultant. Married Cecilia Dunbar-Kilburn 1941

Shinwell Emanuel. M.P. (Lab.); became Lab. Min. of Fuel and Power 1945

Sikorski General Wladyslaw. Prime Min. and C.-in-C. in the Polish government in exile

Simon Viscount (1940) (Sir John Simon). M.P. (Lib. National); Chancellor of the Exchequer 1937–40; Lord Chancellor 1940–5. Former Leader of the Lib. National Party

Sinclair Sir Archibald. M.P. (Lib.); Leader of the Parl. Lib. Party 1935–45; Sec. for Air 1940–5

Slessor Air Marshal Sir John. Dir. of Plans, Air Ministry 1937–41; Air Officer Commanding Fifth Bomber Group 1941–2; Assistant Chief of the Air Staff 1942–3; Air Officer C.-in-C. Coastal Command 1943–4; Deputy C.-in-C. Allied Air Forces, Mediterranean 1944–5

Smuts Field Marshal (1941) J.C. Prime Min., Union of S. Africa 1939–48

Southwell Richard. Professor of Engineering Science, Oxford University 1929–42; Rector of the Imperial College of Science and Technology 1942–8

Southwood Baron (J. S. Elias). Newspaper proprietor and publisher; chairman and managing director of Odhams Press, etc.; controlled *Daily Herald*, *The People*, etc.

Spears Major-General Sir (1942) Edward. Prime Min.'s personal rep. with French Prime Min. 1940; head of British Mission to General de Gaulle 1940; head of Spears Mission, Syria and Lebanon 1941; Min. to the Republics of Syria and Lebanon 1942–4

Stanley Oliver. M.P. (Con.); Pres. of the Board of Trade 1937–40; Sec. for War 1940; Sec. for the Colonies 1942–5

Stewart James Henderson. M.P. (Lib. National)

Stokes Richard. M.P. (Lab.)

Storey Samuel. M.P. (Con.); Parl. Private Sec. to the Parl. Sec. to the Ministry of Health 1939–42; former chairman of Reuters

Stuart J.G. M.P. (Con.); Joint Parl. Sec. to the Treasury, and Chief Government Whip 1941–5

Swinton Viscount (Sir Philip Cunliffe-Lister). Cabinet Min. Resident in W. Africa 1942–4; Min. for Civil Aviation 1944–5. Former Sec. for Air (1935–8)

Tedder Marshal of the Royal Air Force (1944) Sir (1942) Arthur. Deputy Air Officer Commanding R.A.F. Middle East 1940–1; Air Officer C.-in-C. R.A.F. Middle East 1941–3; Air Officer C.-in-C. Mediterranean Air Command 1943; Deputy Supreme Commander under General Eisenhower 1943–5

Templewood Viscount (1944) (Sir Samuel Hoare). M.P. (Con.) to 1944; Lord Privy Seal 1939–40; Sec. for Air 1940; U.K. Ambassador to Spain on Special Mission 1940–4

Thompson-McAusland Lucius. Economist at the Bank of England

Thomson Sir (1943) George. Professor of Physics, Imperial College of Science and Technology, London University; chairman, British Committee on Atomic Energy 1940–1; Scientific Adviser to the Air Ministry 1943–4

Tizard Sir Henry. Rector of the Imperial College of Science and Technology 1929–42; Pres. of Magdalen College, Oxford 1942–6; chairman of the Aeronautical Research Committee 1933–43

De Valera Eamon. Irish premier and Foreign Min.

Vansittart Baron (1941) (Sir Robert Vansittart). Chief Diplomatic Adviser to the Foreign Sec. 1938–41. Former Permanent Under-Sec. for Foreign Affairs (1930–8)

Walker David. *Mirror* war correspondent in the Balkans 1941; later became war correspondent with General MacArthur

Ward Barbara. Assistant editor of the *Economist*

Wardlaw-Milne Sir John. M.P. (Con.); chairman, House of Commons Select Committee on National Expenditure 1939–45; chairman, Con. Foreign Affairs Committee 1939–45

Watt, see Harvie-Watt

Wavell Field Marshal (1943) Viscount (1943) (Sir Archibald Wavell). C.-in-C. Middle East 1939–41; C.-in-C. India 1941–3; Supreme Commander, S.-W. Pacific 1942; Viceroy of India 1943–7

Weston Garfield. M.P. (Con.); biscuit and cake manufacturer: controlled companies in Canada and Britain

Weygand General Maxime. C.-in-C. French army, May–June 1940; Vichy Governor-General of Algeria 1941; Gestapo prisoner 1942–5

Williams Sir Herbert. M.P. (Con.)

Wilson Sir Horace. Permanent Sec. of the Treasury and official Head of the Civil Service 1939–42. Was seconded from Treasury in 1935 for special service with Chamberlain

Winn Godfrey. Journalist

Winster Baron (1942) (R. T. H. Fletcher). M.P. (Lab.) to 1941

Winterton 6th Earl of. M.P. (Con.)

Wood Sir Kingsley. M.P. (Con.); Sec. for Air 1938–40; Lord Privy Seal 1940; Chancellor of the Exchequer 1940–3

Woolton Baron (F. J. Marquis). Chairman and managing director, John Lewis group of companies; Min. of Food 1940–3; Min. of Reconstruction 1943–5; Lord Pres. of the Council 1945

Index